For
GRA

POCKET ANNUAL 1999

Bruce Smith

5th Year of Publication

Virgin

Formula 1 Grand Prix Pocket Annual 1999

Copyright © Bruce Smith – Author 1999

ISBN: 0-7535-0326-3

First published in March 1999 by *Virgin Publishing*.

Virgin Publishing Ltd
Thames Wharf Studios
Rainville Road
London
W6 9HT

Typeset by Bruce Smith.

Edited by Mark Webb.

Disclaimer

In a book of this type it is inevitable that some errors will creep in. While every effort has been made to ensure that the details given in this annual are correct at the time of going to press, neither the editor nor the publishers can accept any responsibility for errors within.

Contact: Bruce-Smith@msn.com

CONTENTS

A-Z Formula One Drivers

Team Directory

Circuit Directory

Race Diary '99

WHAT A DIFFERENCE a win makes! Having taken 96 races to produce a rather contrived first victory at the end of the 1997 season, Mika Hakkinen secured a further two more at the start of 1998 and set off at a flying pace on the way to becoming 1998's champion driver. In fact such was the domination of the two McLaren cars in the early part of the season that it seemed the season would be over before it started. The magic of Formula 1 is largely down to the top teams keeping the gap between them as small as possible. It was therefore a great relief that Ferrari got their act together and finally brought pressure to bear. Pressure though is not something that Michael Schumacher seems to handle well. Three times in the past four seasons the German has effectively cracked under the strain in the final race of the season. The World Champion Finn also proved that you can compete at the very top and still maintain both personal discipline and remain a true sportsman. I'd like to believe that is why he got his rewards last season.

Everyone loves an underdog and there can be few true fans that were not delighted to see Jordan take their first winner's place on the rostrum. That it was achieved by Damon Hill will have made it especially sweet for English fans and neither should it be forgotten that Ralf Schumacher ensured that it was not just a win but a one-two to boot!

To my mind though the performance of last season came from Eddie Irvine. He was superb throughout the season and if I could have one F1 wish it would be for Ferrari to allow him to actually race for victory in his Prancing Horse.

The departure of Tyrrell from the World of F1 was to many minds a sad occasion. For me what was more sad was their general demise in recent years without there seeming to be much real chance of them getting to the heights of their previous domination of the sport. The arrival of British American Racing will certainly spice up the calendar both on and off the grid. Their determination to do things their way was never more evident than through their challenge to the FIA in relation to being able to run their two cars with differing liveries. The company's early boasts of winning their first race in Australia had died away by the time of the car launch but in Reynard they have experienced engine developers and with Villeneuve in charge of the lead car, this team could well cause a shock or two in 1999.

Williams have re-grouped and surely will improve on their generally poor showing last year. Confidence will be high and boosted by the knighting of founder Frank Williams in the Queen's New Years Honours List. If there was ever a more inspiring icon of success then it has to be Sir Frank. For the second time in two years he has taken the Champ Car champion into his fold, although this time his new guy Zinardi has had previous, if somewhat limited, experience in Formula 1.

The Prost team must also be looking forward to a better season and the appointment of John Barnard's design company as exclusive technical consultants will be instrumental in this happening.

Stewart now have their most experienced team ever and both Johnny Herbert and the team itself have something to prove in 1999. The arrival of Gary Anderson can only be beneficial but it may not be until the latter stages of the year that they start to show their colours.

Goodyear said farewell to F1 as a tyre supplier, a job which will now be the exclusive domain of Bridgestone. The battle between the tyres proved to be an interesting aspect of The Show in the past two years and it will be missed in the seasons ahead.

Finally, let's hope the five week wait between the penultimate and final GP of the season will never be allowed to happen again. Indeed why not keep even the three week gaps between races to a minimum. The long gap in the calendar schedule took a lot of the gloss off the the final race decider. The excitement that one felt after the race at the Nurburgring, whereby the championship went to the last day of the season, was almost gone by the time the band wagon reached Japan and was not helped by a sleepy early morning rise to view matters. Much better to finish the season a couple of weeks early and keep the momentum going.

Deadlines '99

The cut-off date for completion of this year's annual was 18th January. There were still some questions to be answered at that point, not least in the final calendar of races for the season. However, all the proposed circuits have been included.

Thanks '99

I would like to thank all the Formula One teams for their co-operation in producing this annual. Many thanks also to Mark Webb who wrote the season's review and helped edit and proof read these pages.

If you have any comments or ideas for future editions of this annual you can E-mail me at: Bruce-Smith@msn.com

CAR CHANGES '99

Recent years have seen a number of changes to the specifications laid down by the FIA that govern all factors regarding car safety and design. The 1998 season saw some of the most radical changes yet. During much of the 1998 season we saw teams working and refining these. The 1999 season sees some minor changes – many of which are for safety purposes – and a few of the more important are included here.

Tyres & Wheels

One of the most radical changes in 1998 was the introduction of grooved tyres for standard racing. Tyres consisted of three grooves running around the tyre. For 1999 a fourth groove has been added.

Cables will also be fitted to all wheels to prevent their becoming separated from the car in the event of an accident. This should eradicate the sight of wheels bouncing freely down the track – and even into the crowd – when cars are involved in crashes.

The device for putting a car into neutral will be fitted into the same place in all cars and the driver's seat will be removable from the car with the driver in it.

More Technical

There are several changes which are of a less obvious, more technical nature. They are: The minimum height of the roll hoop above the driver's head has been increased from 50 to 70 mm; The engine oil breather will no longer vent into the atmosphere but into the air intake; A pressure relief valve will be included in the cooling system of each car; The speed of the nose impact test has been increased from 12 m/s to 13 m/s; Sulphur and benzine levels have been significantly reduced for much cleaner regulation fuel.

Grand Prix Review 1998

Pre-Season

There was somewhat less jockeying for seats pre-season as two-year driver contracts were seen out. Damon Hill was the big-name signing for Jordan and the idea of Hill battling on to the podium seemed less ludicrous than in the Arrows. The Ferrari pairing were favourites to fulfil Schumacher's three-year plan to take both Championships, with Irvine doing a subtle act as protegé to the great German. No-one expected the new rules to change the race order very much but more fundamental changes, such as the withdrawal of direct support from Renault, seemed set to cause Williams some problems.

The teams still fell neatly into two groups: Ferrari, McLaren, Williams and Benetton swapping status in the top tier with the smaller teams battling it out in the lower division and seeking promotion. Jordan looked the most likely of these contenders and much was expected of the Prost team too. Although the season looked like it might be a bit of a rerun of the previous year, the prospect loomed of both wealthy new teams and brand new tracks in exotic parts of the world. It was apparent that by the year 2000, Honda and BMW could be back in Formula 1, with the German company perhaps forming what will be a powerhouse alliance with the Williams team. Japanese car maker Honda announced that it planned to return to the sport its engines which dominated in the 1980s, after a seven-year break from the show. But this time it looks as though the Tokyo-based manufacturer will come back with a complete vehicle package – its engine fitted to a chassis of its own with a Honda team managed as a separate division of the company. Honda engines powered the McLaren cars driven to F1 dominance by the late Ayrton Senna and Alain Prost in the 1980s and won six straight Championships in the years to 1991. Even closer was the appearance of British American Racing (BAR), basing itself on the

Tyrrell team, and its Reynard Formula 1 car designed by Australian engineer Malcolm Oastler.

March

The **Australian Grand Prix** was at Albert Park Melbourne and it proved one of the most controversial season openers of all time. During the closing stages of the race the two McLaren drivers found themselves in the lead with Coulthard ahead of Hakkinen. Then, with just a few laps to go, Coulthard conceded his position to the Finn, explaining later that the two had a pact that whoever made it to the first corner in the lead would be allowed to finish ahead of the other at the flag.

Ruling body FIA at first rejected a complaint about the race finish from Australian Grand Prix Corporation chairman Ron Walker. But FIA foreshadowed possible changes by stating that the following week's meeting of the World Motor Sport Council would decide whether to ban the practice of issuing 'team orders' to decide placings of drivers within a team. Walker said he had faxed a protest to the FIA on behalf of the race. Paris-based FIA said in a statement that it had received the complaint but indicated it would take no action against McLaren. 'Team orders specifying the finishing order of drivers within a team have existed in motor sport since the beginning of the century,' the statement said. 'It would therefore not be right to criticise or sanction McLaren-Mercedes for what it did at Sunday's Grand Prix.'

McLaren tried to cool some of the reaction by stating that Coulthard's pact with Hakkinen would be repeated in Brazil but after that they would be allowed to race freely against one another. Chairman Ron Dennis said 'We are not doing anything that is against the spirit of Grand Prix racing.'

The McLaren cars' dominance also highlighted the poor performance of the stragglers. Having seen his cars lapped by the victorious Finn Hakkinen and his British team-mate Coulthard, Williams team chief Frank Williams said 'We've seen it all before, haven't we? One team comes out and starts well and dominates, but it is another matter to keep it going. We will all be doing our utmost now to catch them.' Jackie Stewart, once an ace driver, had to endure an uncompetitive opening round of the Championship with his Stewart-Ford team. 'I'm extremely disappointed,' Stewart said after his poor start to year two. 'We were not as well prepared as we should have been for this race prior to Melbourne. Everyone worked so hard to deliver two cars which should have performed quite well.' Even this early there were question marks over whether Stewart would be given the luxury of his original five-year plan by Ford. Ford has not won a World Championship since 1994, when Michael Schumacher drove a V8-engined Benetton.

For Stewart, the innovative carbon-fibre gearbox was an embarrassment at Albert Park, with Rubens Barrichello unable to engage a gear on the start line. Stewart was uncertain where the carbon-fibre gearbox idea would take his team. 'It's the first one to be unveiled in motor sports ever,' Stewart said. 'So it's a technical breakthrough for us to do this and it's a long shot, but we hope it is going to be helpful.'

The sunny start to the season moved to the **Brazilian Grand Prix** with every expectation that the McLaren dominance of race one would continue. Suddenly they were the ones to beat. The talk in the pit was of their rear-wheel braking system activated by a second brake pedal that assists in pulling the car around corners and also helps traction control under acceleration. Although Ferrari technical director Ross Brawn was considering the system, it didn't make it to Brazil when the team pre-empted any FIA ruling by removing it.

The only thing the same was that the now 'flying' Finn Mika Hakkinen coasted to a third consecutive Formula 1 victory. Completing the sense of déja vu, team-mate David Coulthard was second. Hakkinen was never headed in the 72-lap race after starting from pole position for the third time in his career. The McLarens finished only 1.1 seconds apart but one minute ahead of third-placed Michael Schumacher's Ferrari. Schumacher had the benefit of an updated Ferrari engine and was at least satisfied it went the distance. Alexander Wurz, the 24-year-old Austrian star of the Benetton team, finished a brilliant fourth with a decisive late-race passing move on Heinz-Harald Frentzen (fifth). Italian Giancarlo Fisichella finished sixth in the second Benetton, just ahead of Jacques Villeneuve (Williams), who failed to score in seventh place and was lapped for the second time in the season.

After the dramas of Melbourne, the McLaren drivers said there had been no specific team orders other than to avoid crashing in the dash to the first corner. Hakkinen said it had been very important for him to take the lead at the start. 'My start worked very well for me and it was vital, because it is an uphill start here and very difficult to get away,' he said. 'The worst moment came during the end of the race when I hit something hard – it could have been a bird or something, I don't know.'

While Schumacher promised a closer fight from Ferrari, through upgraded and slightly wider tyres, for the Argentinian Grand Prix, Hakkinen gave his rivals little hope. 'I took it really easy at the end because there was no use pushing it and I could have gone faster than I did,' the 29-year-old Finn said. Hakkinen posted ten fastest laps during the race and finished the race with 20 points in the World Drivers' Championship to Coulthard's 12.

April

Having accepted Mika Hakkinen's challenge, Michael Schumacher pulled off a 28th career victory against the odds in Buenos Aires in the **Argentinian Grand Prix**. Hakkinen had earlier predicted that other teams would 'need a miracle'. But Schumacher's ruthless two-pit-stop drive saw him finish 23 seconds ahead of Hakkinen. Scotsman Coulthard started from pole position and led the opening four laps as both he and Hakkinen used a one-pit-stop race strategy. Schumacher muscled his way past on lap five and after the race Coulthard called Schumacher's driving 'not within the spirit of F1'.

Schumacher said he took advantage of a gap that Coulthard left at the same spot on successive laps. 'David went a bit wide, but when I went for it he left no room for me to go,' said Schumacher. Coulthard said.'I congratulate him for winning, but we should be able to race each other without banging into one another.' Coulthard struggled on to finish sixth after another collision, this time with Villeneuve's Williams FW20, which was unable to continue.

'You just have two guys [Schumacher and Villeneuve] who are prepared to do anything,' Coulthard said as he contemplated the loss of what he thought would be ten points for a Buenos Aires win. 'After what's happened I guess I have to be glad with one point.' Both Schumacher and Eddie Irvine, who stormed home to pass Alexander Wurz's Benetton for third place, 57 seconds behind, raced the new and higher revving Ferrari 047D engine.

Same month, different continent, and Imola kicked off the first European leg of the Championship. David Coulthard put down a marker in the **San Marino Grand Prix** with his flag-to-flag victory, proving that he might push team-mate Hakkinen in the drivers' duel and warding off suggestions that McLaren were interested in signing Schumacher to complete an invincible pairing of man and machine. Championship leader Hakkinen retired in the seventh lap of his 100th Grand Prix due to gearbox problems. After starting from his second consecutive pole position, Coulthard ran a perfect race in his Bridgestone-shod McLaren and won the fourth Grand Prix of his career when easing down to save his engine and brakes as Schumacher cut the margin from 20 to just 4.5 seconds at the finish. 'There was a debris build-up which we couldn't clear on the pit stop and so we were having to drop revs to get the oil temperature down,' said McLaren team boss Ron Dennis.

Although Ferrari couldn't break a 15-year losing streak, since Frenchman Patrick Tambay won in 1983, the Italian team were hardly out of it with Schumacher in second place, and his Irish team-mate Eddie Irvine a strong third. For the first time in a race Schumacher and Irvine used the sidepod mounted 'tower wings'. The Coulthard fan club was in good spirits as the Scot reached 23 points in the Championship to Hakkinen's 26, with Schumacher third on 20, Irvine fourth on 11.

May

The McLaren boys were fastest in the warm-up and nobody expected anything other than a grey streak to cross the finish line first in the **Spanish Grand Prix**. Pedro Diniz stalled on the grid and had to start in the pit lane. Hakkinen made it to the first corner without incident and pulled away. On the high-speed Catalunya circuit there was no prospect of anyone overtaking Hakkinen as long as his car remained reliable. Hakkinen was over eight seconds ahead in as many laps. Schumacher was overtaken at the start so it was Irvine who challenged in the first half of the race. While Hakkinen was setting a fastest lap Irvine and Fisichella pitted together, Fisichella coming out first. The two of them then clashed on the track on lap 28 and they were left having a heated discussion on the walk back to the pits.

Michael Schumacher, in the meantime, was looking comfortable in third until he got a ten-second penalty for speeding in the pit lane – handing third to Wurz. The Ferrari team clawed the place back later when carrying out a better tactical pit stop than Benetton. Meanwhile Herbert, Villeneuve and Barrichello were running seventh, sixth and fifth, with only a few seconds separating them. Hakkinen and Coulthard's only problem was lapping these drivers on their way to a one-two victory! Schumacher kept third, Wurz fourth, Barrichello fifth and two valuable points for Stewart. Villeneuve got a point.

Hakkinen and McLaren proved their superiority once again in the **Monaco Grand Prix** when the Finn ended a six-race losing streak with victory on the streets of Monte Carlo. He joined 1982 World Champion Keke Rosberg as only the second Finnish driver to win at Monaco. In doing so Hakkinen had equalled Rosberg's career total of five Grand

Prix victories. 'I remember Keke once telling me that the most wonderful GP to win was Monte Carlo. He said it was unbelievable.' For 17 laps Coulthard had shadowed Hakkinen before his Mercedes V10 motor expired in a cloud of smoke, a rare technical failure for the dominant McLaren team. 'The pressure here is incredible, it is so difficult to keep your concentration all the way and not make mistakes,' Hakkinen said.

Behind Hakkinen in the points came an unusual mixed bag of Fisichella, Irvine, Salo, Villeneuve and Diniz – a fourth and sixth for Arrows, Salo having driven well right from the start.

June

Schumacher came back again at the **Canadian Grand Prix** and drove a masterful race despite suffering a time penalty. Fisichella grabbed second again, and Irvine clung on to third, with Wurz fourth and the two Stewarts getting points this time, occupying fifth and sixth as Magnussen fought in vain to keep his job. He ran as high as fourth during the race. It was a chaotic contest from the first moments. Ralf Schumacher, stalled on the grid, watched as his brother got past Hakkinen into second and then Wurz cut across the first corner and hit a Sauber. Both Saubers crashed out. A race restart was scheduled and cars repaired in readiness. Start number two saw Hakkinen stall and Ralf Schumacher spin off. Hakkinen limped into the pits and Alesi was out. Coulthard led behind the safety car. Irvine went into the pits for a new tyre. The safety car stayed out until lap five and then released the remaining 17 cars with Coulthard just heading Schumacher.

Barrichello went past Frentzen and Villeneuve into fourth behind Fisichella but dropped back on lap 11 after a mistake. The safety car re-emerged on lap 15 to clean up after Diniz and again on lap 20 when Salo had a shunt and left debris on the track. Lap 20 also saw Schumacher shunt Frentzen into the gravel. Villeneuve had to retire on lap 23, to the disappointment of his home crowd, after trying out the gravel and then getting hit by a stray Minardi. He then surprised everyone by returning a couple of laps later. On lap 35 Michael Schumacher was awarded a ten-second penalty because of his earlier shunt with Frentzen. Frank Williams complained immediately, and the stewards penalised the Ferrari man. Schumacher came out to battle with Hill for second. It was all over for Hill from lap 40 when he went in for his second pit stop having been overtaken by his arch rival. Hill was then in and out of the pits before finally succumbing. After the race Hill called the German a 'bully'.

The start of the **French Grand Prix** was technically aborted when the orange lights came on a split second after the five reds went out. The race didn't get started because of a red flag for Verstappen who stalled on the grid – not such a good restart to his career. The incident gave Schumacher another crack at Hakkinen, who looked to have got away first. Second time around the Ferraris crept through in front of the McLarens and Schumacher had a 1.5 second lead by the end of the second lap. Irvine held off the McLarens and Schumacher held a lead of more than 30 seconds over Hakkinen at one point. Damon Hill went out with throttle problems to continue the Jordan problems. The season thus came impressively alive for Ferrari as Schumacher crossed the line to cut Hakkinen's Championship lead to only six points. Irvine only just made it over in second, Hakkinen in third. Villeneuve came home fourth, Wurz fifth, while Coulthard amazingly came back to snatch sixth place after terrible pit stop problems.

July

In what was a fairly barmy **British Grand Prix**, the bizarre conclusion was the sight of Schumacher claiming his third consecutive win while his car sat stationary in the pit lane. Hakkinen had earlier missed his opportunity after holding a 40-second advantage with 16 laps to go, when the race came under the control of the safety car for five laps. This bunched the field and gave Schumacher the chance to pounce on Hakkinen's previously damaged McLaren. With Hakkinen's car slowing over the final five laps, Schumacher built a lead of 22 seconds, which enabled him to make his final-lap pit stop and still secure victory. The German had pulled into the pits on the final lap to serve a ten second stop-go penalty for passing Alexander Wurz's Benetton during a yellow-flag caution period earlier in the race. The pit lane is considered an extension of the race track and the computer timing system declared Schumacher the winner. Reports indicated that Ferrari wanted Schumi to race for them until the end of the 2002 Grand Prix season with the prospect of earnings in the region of $300 million.

It wasn't the tidiest of starts at the **Austrian Grand Prix**. Hakkinen and Schumacher were well in front of the difficulties but Panis didn't get off the grid and the Arrows shunted each other and Diniz span into Coulthard. The safety car was out on the first lap and got them off to a rolling start two laps later. Coulthard needed a new nose cone and tyres. Schumacher overcooked it and dropped into third but overtook Fisichella a lap later to regain second. Hakkinen hung on defiantly, putting in the odd fastest lap for good measure. Schumacher countered with his own fastest lap but then went out on lap 17, losing the front section of the car. But two laps later Schumi re-emerged from the pits with a new nose but in eighteenth place. Irvine was up to second and Coulthard put on a charge towards third. Alesi and Fisichella knocked each other out. Michael Schumacher climbed and climbed, past Herbert, past Villeneuve, past Trulli to get up behind his brother who was running in fourth. Hakkinen was out in front by nearly 15 seconds. By lap 51 the two Schumachers were duelling and senior nearly hit junior before getting past him on lap 56. Eddie Irvine's job in third was now to lose a second or so a lap so that his team-mate could catch up and get the required points, which duly occurred on lap 68. The spectators' thoughts went back to the team orders dispute of the opening race of the season. Coulthard had pulled off a second place after running last. Ralf Schumacher scored for Jordan in fifth place for the second race running and Villeneuve picked up a point for sixth.

August

World Championship leader Hakkinen and team-mate Coulthard were confirmed as McLaren's drivers for the 1999 Formula 1 season shortly after the pair had taken the first two positions on the grid for engine supplier Mercedes-Benz's home **German Grand Prix** at Hockenheim. Mercedes motorsport boss Norbert Haug admitted that they had spoken to Ferrari's Michael Schumacher about joining the team next year, but said he was happy with the decision to stick with their current line-up. 'I am delighted to have David and Mika as our team pairing for the fourth consecutive year,' he said. 'The team has always supported these guys and today they are stronger drivers than ever.' 'The team spirit and consistency of both David and Mika this season has played a key part in our decisions,' said team boss Ron Dennis. 'We are fortunate to have two top drivers in our team and there is every indication that they are going to get even better.'

As if to confirm Ron Dennis's assertion, Mika Hakkinen scored his sixth victory of the season at the German Grand Prix, increasing his World Drivers' Championship lead over Michael Schumacher (Ferrari) to 16 points with only five races remaining. It was the seventh race win of the year for McLaren, which increased its lead over Ferrari in the Constructors' Championship to 26 points.

Coulthard finished second as the McLaren team recorded its fifth one-two finish of the year. Jacques Villeneuve snatched his first podium finish of the season in third.

Hakkinen, starting from his eighth career pole, came into the pits on lap 26, briefly handing the lead to Coulthard, but only until the Scot pitted himself a lap later. 'We've got a great package – a very good car and very good tyres,' said Hakkinen. 'I thought at one stage I may have been able to get past,' said Coulthard. 'It's very difficultt, though, when you are racing against someone driving the same car as you. It's hard to get past a car with the same performance as you.' Damon Hill finished fourth – his first points for almost 12 months – with Michael Schumacher fifth and brother Ralf sixth.

It was not Ferrari's weekend and after qualifying, Michael Schumacher was left hoping for a substantial improvement in his car's performance, or rain. 'It is definitely the wrong time and the wrong place to have my worst qualifying of the season,' said Schumi. When the race got underway Wurz stalled directly in front of Schumacher on the grid but the German dived brilliantly across to the other side of the track to avoid hitting Wurz, with Heinz-Harald Frentzen in the Williams fortunate not to have his nose cone removed in the process. From that point on, however, there was little for the 130,000 German crowd to cheer.

Electronic signals were used for the first time during qualifying for the German race. The screen at the first bend behind the gravel trap had three modes: permanent yellow (danger, slow down), flashing yellow (immediate danger, slow down), red (stop the race). The new signals were on trial as a means of alerting drivers to dangerous situations instead of, or in addition to, the traditional flags.

Michael Schumacher turned the tables and actually lapped Mika Hakkinen when going through to win the **Hungarian Grand Prix**. Damon Hill held on for fourth at one of his favourite tracks (where he had previously never finished outside the top two).

The day had started well for Hakkinen, who made it to the first corner with Coulthard behind, followed by Schumacher and Irvine. Coulthard successfully held off Schumacher despite a mistake and Hakkinen maintained a few seconds' lead through the first set of pit-stops. Coulthard fended off the German until a second set of pit stops saw Schumi dive out ahead of the Scot and with clear track to the back of Hakkinen. When Hakkinen pitted a lap later, he too gave away his place to the German. Hill, meanwhile, was striving to stay ahead of Villeneuve, but in vain.

Schumacher pulled away and survived a detour off the track while Hakkinen slowed down enough for Coulthard to overtake him. Schumacher pulled out a big enough lead to pit again and return to the track ahead of Coulthard. Hakkinen slowed and was reeled in by Villeneuve, Hill and then Frentzen. Alesi was in seventh but a lap down, so Hakkinen was just safe for sixth place and one vital point. As Schumacher took the plaudits, spectators got on to the track before the race was over.

It was party time for Jordan in Spa as Damon Hill and Ralf Schumacher came home first and second in the **Belgian Grand Prix**. What happened? It was an exceptional race but in fact it was part of the Jordan revival which saw them all the way to the last race. Alesi was third, Frentzen fourth – all four cars on Goodyear tyres.

The rain at Spa falls mainly on the track. It stopped five minutes before the start, leaving some drivers on wets, some on intermediates. The conditions may have contributed to what was a massive first corner smash-up. Tyres, bodywork and wings were flying everywhere with Coulthard's car coming off worst. Irvine limped away from the carnage but there were no casualties and Irvine was OK to restart with the spare car. Hakkinen, Villeneuve, Schumacher and Hill seemed to make it through or beyond the problem. Ten minutes later saw the remaining drivers back on the grid with 44 laps left to go. Some drivers, notably Damon Hill, took the opportunity to get rid of their wet tyres and move to intermediates. Lap one wasn't much better the second time around. Hakkinen span off at La Source and was written off by an impact from Herbert. Coulthard span but got back on the track in last place. The safety car withdrew at the end of this calamitous start and Hill led Schumacher away with Villeneuve taking Alesi for fourth place. The rain started again on lap 5 as Villeneuve recovered from a slight spin. Fisichella span on lap 7 as a dog-fight broke out between Hill and Schumacher. The German got past on lap 8 and moved quickly ahead. Drivers pitted to change to wet tyres with Schumacher gaining further seconds. Hill and Ralf Schumacher established themselves in second and third as Villeneuve went off. Lap 23 saw Michael Schumacher nearly collide with Diniz and two laps later he smashed into the back of Coulthard (running one off the back) and lost a wheel. The car limped back to the pits but only for Schumacher to jump out and storm over to the McLaren pit!

The race still needed winning and Hill caused a few missed heartbeats when he missed the Bus Stop Chicane but kept running. Fisichella and Nakano went out in tandem and the safety car came on again on lap 28. Hill, Alesi and Frentzen pitted to take advantage of this situation as the remaining drivers bunched again. Only six cars were left running on lap 30, stacked behind the safety car – Hill, Ralf Schumacher, Alesi, Frentzen, Diniz, Trulli. With the safety car still in effect, Coulthard reappeared because, with only seven cars on the track, he had a chance of points if someone else were to retire. After the restart on lap 32, Hill briefly saw Schumacher in his mirrors but he lapped faster than his team-mate and pulled away to nearly three seconds ahead, holding a static two-second lead in the closing stages. Coulthard, five laps down, still overtook Alesi on lap 42.

September

It was announced that the flotation of Formula 1 Holdings on the London Stock Exchange would not now take place for two or three years. The principle reason for the delay was a perceived lack of understanding of the sport from potential city investors. As an introduction to the City, Formula 1 will issue bonds backed by future pay-per-view television revenues. Bernie Ecclestone was rumoured to have a hand in many sport-business ventures during the year, including buying TV rights to football and launching a new tennis circuit with Boris Becker.

In front of the *tifosi* Schumacher and Irvine did the one-two in the **Italian Grand Prix** to show McLaren that it wasn't going to be a walkover, especially with Hakkinen back in fourth. The Finn was flying in pursuit of the Ferrari number one until he span on lap 45. He then had to cling on as the others ran him down one by one. Ralf Schumacher continued Jordan's improvement in third with Damon Hill in sixth.

The two McLarens established a big lead with Schumacher recovering from a terrible start. Coulthard unexpectedly passed Hakkinen to carve out a lead of his own. The McLaren luck turned, however, on lap 17 when Coulthard's engine blew up and Schumacher passed Hakkinen and began to pull out a considerable lead which brought him level on points with the Finn.

It was announced that IndyCar champion Alex Zanardi would return to Formula 1 to lead Williams' challenge. He has recorded 14 victories and 25 podium finishes in 48 CART races. Driving for the Target/Chip

Ganassi team, Zanardi won the Rookie of the Year title in 1996 and followed that up by winning consecutive Drivers' Championships, sealing the 1998 crown in Vancouver on 6 September.

Jordan confirmed that Damon Hill would remain with the team for 1999 and would be partnered by 32-year-old Heinz-Harald Frentzen. 'Obviously I'm delighted Damon will be with us for what we both believe will be a realistic opportunity for him to add a second world title to his 22 Grand Prix victories,' said team owner Eddie Jordan.

The Nurburgring was likely to favour the McLaren cars if their drivers could hold their nerve against the Schumacher comeback during the **Luxembourg Grand Prix**. The two Ferraris led the way from the start, followed by two McLarens. Schumacher took over early from Irvine, who would employ the obvious tactic of holding back the Mercedes cars. Schumacher put in a fastest lap on lap 4 but Hakkinen held the gap and put in a fastest circuit on lap 10. Hakkinen got up to Irvine and pressurised the Ulsterman into a mistake on lap 13, passing him and eating into Schumacher's 8.5 second advantage. All six Benetton, Jordan and Williams drivers were in the top ten behind the leaders. A series of fastest laps by Hakkinen preceded Schumacher pitting (8.6 seconds) and the German rejoined but all in all fell over 17 seconds behind. On lap 27 Hakkinen pitted (8.7 seconds) and judged it perfectly to re-enter the track ahead of Schumacher, but only just. Hakkinen held off Schumacher for ten laps until the German pitted again (7.4 seconds). One lap later the Finn was in the pits (6.9 seconds) and again back on the track in front. The pit-line sparring over, Hakkinen pulled away to a five second lead and towards the end of the race Schumacher hit traffic and could make no further impression. The final margin was 2.2 seconds, worth four points in the Championship with one race to go and a long testing period in between as the teams readied themselves for Japan.

October

Brazilian racing driver Pedro Diniz was signed by Swiss-based Sauber Petronas for the 1999 season. 'We are delighted that we could sign Pedro Diniz who has the necessary experience with four years in Formula 1 and 65 Grands Prix under his belt,' said Peter Sauber.

After a five-week lay-off before the **Japanese Grand Prix**, Michael Schumacher imposed himself on free practice at Suzuka with one storming lap that proved his determination. The German emerged in the second session to score an important psychological victory over title rival Mika Hakkinen (fifth fastest). Takagi, in his home GP, put up a spirited drive for twelfth.

In the Saturday practice Michael Schumacher held on to pole position after a blistering performance in which he needed only two flying laps. Hakkinen improved to grab a position alongside him. Behind them, David Coulthard would line up alongside Eddie Irvine. Ferrari's tactics were predictable: Schumacher to get away cleanly and Irvine to put himself about amongst the McLarens. Back on the grid the drivers lined up in pairs of Williams, Jordans and Benettons.

Another Suzuka showdown had millions of fans in Europe staying up after their Halloween parties to see which of the year's outstanding drivers would clinch it. Shock, disappointment, joy – the usual mixed feelings were produced when Michael Schumacher stalled his car on the grid in pole position and was relegated to the back of the field. It was the second restart, after Jarno Trulli had done the same. Mika Hakkinen's Finnish army of travelling fans began to wave the flags in anticipation of what was eventually an easy victory, having made the first corner in front of Eddie Irvine. Schumacher was not in the mood for giving up. He passed four back markers by the time he crossed the start line and scythed through the field until on lap 32 the left rear tyre couldn't keep up. The McLaren had a smoother ride and wasn't about to spoil those Finns' big day out. At the end Hakkinen galloped along the pit lane to salute his supporters. Damon Hill outbraked Frentzen to get fourth place and let the German know who is boss in the Jordan team.

Looking back over the season, McLaren looked as though they might be giving it away at the mid point. On the other hand, Ferrari had got their act together too. Was Schumacher favoured by race officials at certain points, as has been suggested by no less an observer than John Watson, in order to help Ferrari claw back the McLaren lead and ensure further entertainment for the watching millions? Does it matter? Hakkinen suffered bad head injuries in a crash at the Australian Grand Prix three seasons ago. His recovery as a driver over that period has been remarkable. His manager and compatriot Keke Rosberg said 'I am pleased for everyone involved.'

RACE PROCEDURES

There is a strict timetable laid down by the FIA for the build-up and start of each Grand Prix race. This set of procedures ensures that no team is favoured when it comes to circuit time, qualifying, warm-up and the actual race. Details of these are given below – all times are local. Note that what follows is a general guide only and liable to change.

Circuit Practice

There are four sessions of free practice. These take place on the Friday and Saturday, except for the Monaco Grand Prix when the Friday practice is held on the Thursday. The two sessions on the Friday last for one hour each and are held from 11.00 to 12.00 and 13.00 to 14.00. The two sessions on the Saturday last for 45 minutes each and are held from 9.00 to 9.45 and 10.15 to 11.00. A change from the 1998 season is that there is no limitation on the number of laps permitted. Prior to this, there had been a limit of 30 laps across the two sessions.

Qualifying Session

A single one-hour session is held for qualifying (prior to 1996 there used to be two sessions). This takes place on the Saturday from 13.00 to 14.00. Since 1997, each driver has been limited to a maximum of 12 qualifying laps, and a lap will count towards the qualifying laps provided the driver has started it before the expiry of the 60-minute clock. The 12 laps are normally performed by teams as three- or four-lap sessions. This is at the discretion of teams and drivers – the usual scenario is an 'out' warm-up lap, where the tyres are brought up to race temperature, two flat-out laps, where drivers go all out for a fast time, and a final 'in lap' as drivers come back into the pits.

The fastest lap out of those registered will count as the qualifying time. To qualify for a race, all drivers must establish a lap time that is within 107% of the time set by the fastest driver in the qualifying session. Drivers with times outside this limit will not automatically qualify for the race – the FIA have the right to admit a driver to the race. The driver's grid position is determined by his time. Thus the fastest qualifying time earns the driver the first or pole position on the starting grid. A spare car may be used in the qualifying session in case of accident or mechanical problems. Indeed, some teams even use a special qualifying engine.

From the 1998 season, any car that is given assistance, after stopping, to get back to the pits, will have its fastest lap time of the session deleted.

Warm-up Session

A 30-minute warm-up session is held on the Sunday of the race, and this normally starts four and a half hours before the start of the race. If, after this, rain occurs, then an extra 15-minute session may be sanctioned to allow teams to make wet-weather changes.

The Start

The race follows a set countdown to the start. Thirty minutes prior to the race the pit lane is opened for just 15 minutes. During this window all cars must leave their paddocks and make their way to the starting grid. A horn is sounded two minutes prior to the pit lane closure and 15 minutes prior to the start of the race, the pit lane is closed. Any cars not out of the paddocks must now start from the pit lane – this effectively places the car at the back of the grid.

Once all cars are formed on the grid, a series of time boards is used to display the amount of time remaining to the start of the race. These are carried through the grid and personnel must adhere to their significance.

Ten minutes before the start of the race, all personnel, except drivers, team members and officials, must leave the starting grid. Boards are shown at five minutes, three minutes, one minute and 30 seconds before the start of the race. At the one-minute board, engines are started and all technicians and team staff are required to leave the grid. During this period a series of lights is used to signal stages of the start countdown. There are five banks of lights, each with five lights. Ten minutes prior to the race, the bottom two sets of red lights (ten in all) flash on and off twice. Five minutes prior to the start, the first two (vertical) red lights are extinguished. At this point, all cars must have their wheels fitted – if not, they must start from either the pit lane or the back of the grid. The next two go out with three minutes to go and another two with one minute to go. The penultimate set of red lights is turned off with 30 seconds to go.

When the count reaches zero, a green flag is displayed and the final set of red lights goes out, to be replaced by a set of five green lights across the top of the board – this signals that the cars on the starting grid can advance on their single formation lap. Cars must adhere strictly to their grid position and no overtaking is allowed (cars can be disqualified for doing so). The green lights go out 20 seconds after the cars start the formation lap; should the start need to be aborted, they are replaced by a set of five flashing orange lights. Cars return to their grid position and wait for the start.

When all cars are stationary on the grid, a series of red lights (two vertical at a time) comes on, one light after the other, until they are all switched on – there is approximately a one-second delay between each set of red lights being turned on. There is then a pre-set delay of up to three seconds, at which point all the red lights are extinguished together and the race can commence.

If rain should come after the five-minute mark then the race director has it within his power to allow teams to change their tyres if they wish. In this case abort lights are shown and the race start countdown begins again from the 15-minute mark.

Stopping the Race

The race may be stopped as a result of accidents or adverse weather conditions. If at any time during the final red-light sequence the race needs to be aborted, the lights freeze in their current state and the race is aborted.

If the race has to be stopped once underway it is done by the waving of a red flag. If the race is stopped before two laps are completed, cars return to their original grid positions and the race is restarted. A new time will be given for the race start and this is normally as soon as feasibly possible after the original race was stopped. Cars that might have had to start from the pit lane now have an opportunity to join the starting grid. In the case of an accident, drivers have the opportunity to use their spare car. If this cannot be made ready in time to join the grid, the car will start from the pit lane.

If more than two laps but less than 75 per cent of the race is completed, the race restarts on a dummy grid, according to positions at the time the race was stopped. The distance of the restarted race is that required to make up the full race distance, less three laps (thus, the overall race is shortened by three complete laps).

If the race is stopped with more than 75 per cent completed, the race is deemed to have been run and positions at the point of the race being stopped are the finishing positions.

Race Distance

A Grand Prix race must not be shorter than 160 miles. The number of laps that a race comprises is the smallest number of laps that will exceed this distance. There is also a two-hour time limit on a race. Should this time limit be exceeded (perhaps due to bad weather conditions), the chequered flag will be shown to the leader at the end of the lap in which the two-hour mark is passed – even if the scheduled race distance has not been completed.

Pit Lane

There is a maximum speed assigned to all pit lanes that must not be exceeded. The maximum speed varies from circuit to circuit and is between 50 and 75 mph (80 and 120 kph).

Cars starting from the pit-lane can only join the race after the cars on the starting grid have all passed the exit from the pit lane. Cars in the pit lane are not able to take part in the formation lap.

Penalties

Minor violations of rules – such as pit lane speeding, 'jump' starts and dangerous driving (to name three) – may be penalised by a Stop-Go penalty. The driver is required to return to his paddock and wait for a ten-second count.

Drivers and teams who do not adhere to the rules face other penalties. For example, a driver who drives an extra lap, say in a practice session, is likely to get a fine. This is typically US$5-10,000. A driver who is found to have driven recklessly or created a crash that was avoidable might receive a suspended race ban that would be invoked if he repeated the feat in the time frame specified.

Over and Understeer

Two terms are often used regularly by drivers and commentators: oversteer and understeer. In a perfect world the car will be setup perfectly to ensure it takes the correct racing line around a curve or through a corner. If, when trying to drive the racing line, a driver finds himself going towards the corner and therefore having to compensate, the car is suffering from oversteer. If, on the other hand, the car goes towards the outside edge of the corner and again the driver has to compensate to maintain the racing line, the car is suffering from understeer.

Oversteer is when there is a lack of grip at the rear of the car. This can result in the driver losing the back of the car and spinning off. Tyre wear also increases. It is normally cured by increasing the amount of rear wing on the car, i.e. making it more perpendicular to create drag and therefore downforce. Oversteer can also be corrected by making the suspension softer and reducing the ride height of the car.

understeer !

Oversteer is a lack of grip at the front of the car which means that it turns two slowly and out towards the outside edge of the corner. It is caused when there is too little front wing or the front suspension is too stiff, or a combination of both. It can therefore be cured by increasing the front wing and softening the suspension.

too

Cars can suffer understeer during a race even if they are set up correctly. This happens when they are following behind a car 'on its gearbox'. The lead car has airflow over its front and rear wings to maintain downforce. However, the front of the following car is in a 'hole' because the front car is deflecting the air over it – therefore the front of the following car has reduced stability. Unless a car intends to brake late and try an overtaking manoeuvre at a corner, it will normally 'backoff' to ensure stability through the corner. ■

ANNUAL KEY

The Formula 1 Grand Prix Pocket Annual is divided into several clear sections that arrange information, statistics and reviews in relevant sections which are clearly defined in the Contents list on pages 3 and 4.

At the start of each section you may find a small guide or key to specific information and abbreviations used.

Country abbreviations are used and the key to these is listed below.

Arg	Argentina	Fra	France	Pac	Pacific
Aus	Australia	GB	Great Britain	Pes	Pescara
Aut	Austria	Ger	Germany	Por	Portugal
Bel	Belgium	Hol	Holland	SA	South Africa
Bra	Brazil	Hun	Hungary	San	San Marino
Can	Canada	Ita	Italy	Swi	Switzerland
Dal	Dallas	Jap	Japan	USA	United States
Esp	Spain	Mex	Mexico		of America
Eur	Europe	Mon	Monaco	USAE	USA (East)
Fin	Finland	NZ	New Zealand	USAW	USA (West)

Flags and Signals

There are ten flags that can be shown and these are illustrated on the inside back cover of this annual. A flag's significance may be changed depending on whether it is held stationary or waved.

Red Flag: This is only shown at the start/finish line and is used to indicate that the race has been stopped.

White Flag: When held stationary it indicates the presence of a slower vehicle on the track. When waved it indicates that the driver may be seriously obstructed by a slower vehicle ahead of him on the track.

Black Flag: Shown with white number to indicate the driver to whom it applies. The driver indicated must stop at the pit within one lap and report to the clerk of the course. (This will normally be at the driver's pit paddock where a Stop-Go penalty might be indicated or disqualification.)

Black and White (Diagonal) Flag: Used only once per driver as a warning for unsportsmanlike behaviour.

Black with Red Spot Flag: Shown with white number to indicate the driver to whom it applies. The driver indicated has a mechanical failure and must stop at his pit.

Blue Flag: This flag is used to indicate that a faster car is following. When held stationary the driver concerned must give way, when waved the driver must give way urgently. During a race, failure to give way when the blue flag is waved may result in a penalty. A blue flag is also used at the exit from the pit lane to indicate to the driver exiting that traffic is approaching on the track.

Yellow and Red Striped Flag: When held stationary it indicates that there is oil or water on the track, when waved there is a slippery surface immediately ahead.

Yellow Flag: This flag indicates a hazard ahead and there should be no overtaking. When held stationary it indicates that there is a hazard on the track and drivers should drive well within their limits. When waved, cars must slow down and be prepared to change direction or follow an unusual line. When double waved, cars must slow down and be prepared to stop as the track is partially or wholly blocked.

Green Flag: This is used to signify the end of a danger area that will have been marked by a yellow flag. Effectively it is an all-clear. Also used to signify the start of the warm-up lap.

Chequered Flag: Signifies the end of the race.

GP Results '98

At a Glance

GP	Winner	Pole
Australian	M.Hakkinen (McLaren)	M.Hakkinen (McLaren)
Brazilian	M.Hakkinen (McLaren)	M.Hakkinen (McLaren)
Argentinian	M.Schumacher (Ferrari)	D.Coulthard (McLaren)
San Marino	D.Coulthard (McLaren)	D.Coulthard (McLaren)
Spanish	M.Hakkinen (McLaren)	M.Hakkinen (McLaren)
Monaco	M.Hakkinen (McLaren)	M.Hakkinen (McLaren)
Canadian	M.Schumacher (Ferrari)	D.Coulthard (McLaren)
French	M.Schumacher (Ferrari)	M.Hakkinen (McLaren)
British	M.Schumacher (Ferrari)	M.Hakkinen (McLaren)
Austrian	M.Hakkinen (McLaren)	G.Fisichella (Benetton)
German	M.Hakkinen (McLaren)	M.Hakkinen (McLaren)
Hungarian	M.Schumacher (Ferrari)	M.Hakkinen (McLaren)
Belgian	D.Hill (Jordan)	M.Hakkinen (McLaren)
Italian	M.Schumacher (Ferrari)	M.Schumacher (Ferrari)
Luxembourg	M.Hakkinen (McLaren)	M.Schumacher (Ferrari)
Japanese	M.Hakkinen (McLaren)	M.Schumacher (Ferrari)

Summary

M.Hakkinen (Fin)	McLaren	8 wins	9 poles
M.Schumacher (Ger)	Ferrari	6 wins	3 poles
D.Coulthard (GB)	McLaren	1 win	3 poles
D.Hill (GB)	Jordan	1 win	
G.Fisichella (Ita)	Benetton		1 pole

Key to Results and Tables

r = retired, dq = disqualified, dnq = did not qualify, dnf = did not finish
dns = did not start, fl = fastest lap. † (in results) = fastest lap.

Round 1: Australia – Melbourne

Date: 8 March 1998
Track: 3.280 miles Distance: 58 laps, 190.240 miles
Conditions: Sunny throughout Fastest Lap: Mika Hakkinen – 1:31.649
Lap Record: H-H.Frentzen – 1:30.585, Lap 36 at 130.935 mph, 9 Mar 1997

Pos	Driver	Car	Laps	Time/Reason	Fastest	mph
1	Hakkinen	McLaren	58	1:31.45.996	†1:31.649	124.964
2	Coulthard	McLaren	58	1:31.46.698	1:32.356	124.947
3	Frentzen	Williams	57	+ 1 lap down	1:33.554	122.616
4	Irvine	Ferrari	57	1:31.47.075	1:33.790	122.592
5	Villeneuve	Williams	57	1:32.20.799	1:35.661	121.824
6	Herbert	Sauber	57	1:31.46.420	1:35.624	121.815
7	Wurz	Benetton	57	1:31.48.637	1:34.738	121.757
8	Hill	Jordan	57	1:31.47.279	1:34.196	121.728
9	Panis	Prost	57	1:32.03.548	1:34.319	121.345
r	Fisichella	Benetton	43	R-wing damage	1:34.319	121.469
r	Alesi	Sauber	41	Engine	1:34.878	120.940
r	Trulli	Prost	26	Gearbox	1:34.885	121.916
r	Rosset	Tyrrell	25	Gear selection	1:38.116	107.982
r	Salo	Arrows	23	Transmission	1:36.032	120.038
r	Tuero	Minardi	22	Engine	1:36.475	115.973
r	Nakano	Minardi	8	Transmission	1:39.676	103.797
r	Schumacher, M.	Ferrari	5	Engine	1:35.774	120.717
r	Diniz	Arrows	2	Hydraulics	1:39.916	109.749
r	Schumacher, R.	Jordan	1	Accident	1:50.966	106.906
r	Magnussen	Stewart	1	Accident	1:52.363	105.586
r	Takagi	Tyrrell	1	Spin	1:53.124	104.867
r	Barrichello	Stewart	0	Gearbox	–	–

Starting Grid and Qualifying Times

1	Hakkinen (Fin)	1:30.010	2	Coulthard (GB)	1:30.053
3	Schumacher, M. (Ger)	1:30.767	4	Villeneuve (Can)	1:30.919
5	Herbert (GB)	1:31.384	6	Frentzen (Ger)	1:31.397
7	Fisichella (Ita)	1:31.733	8	Irvine (GB)	1:31.767
9	Schumacher, R. (Ger)	1:32.392	10	Hill (GB)	1:32.399
11	Wurz (Aut)	1:32.726	12	Alesi (Fra)	1:33.240
13	Takagi (Jap)	1:33.291	14	Barrichello (Bra)	1:33.383
15	Trulli (Ita)	1:33.739	16	Salo (Fin)	1:33.927
17	Tuero (Arg)	1:34.646	18	Magnussen (Den)	1:34.906
19	Rosset (Bra)	1:35.119	20	Diniz (Bra)	1:35.140
21	Panis (Fra)	1:35.215	22	Nakano (Jap)	1:35.301

Drivers outside 107% rule:
None

Round 2: Brazil – Interlagos

Date: 29 March 1998
Track: 2.660 miles   Distance: 72 laps, 191.520 miles
Conditions: Sunny to cloudy   Fastest Lap: Mika Hakkinen – 1:19.337
Lap Record: J.Villeneuve – 1:18.397, Lap 28 at 122.471 mph, 30 Mar 1997

Pos	Driver	Car	Laps	Time/Reason	Fastest	mph
1	Hakkinen	McLaren	72	1:37:11.747	†1:19.337	118.464
2	Coulthard	McLaren	72	1:37:12.849	1:19.646	118.445
3	Schumacher, M.	Ferrari	72	1:38:12.297	1:19.627	117.247
4	Wurz	Benetton	72	1:38:19.200	1:19.863	117.109
5	Frentzen	Williams	71	1:37:14.445	1:20.271	116.765
6	Fisichella	Benetton	71	1:37:19.574	1:20.010	116.662
7	Villeneuve	Williams	71	1:37:23.653	1:20.129	116.581
8	Irvine	Ferrari	71	1:37:28.184	1:20.378	116.490
9	Alesi	Sauber	71	1:37.42.228	1:20.623	116.211
dq	Hill	Jordan	70	1:37:29.652	1:21.035	114.821
10	Magnussen	Stewart	70	1:37:41.719	1:20.991	114.584
r	Herbert	Sauber	67	Neck injury	1:21.456	114.518
r	Panis	Prost	63	Gearbox	1:20.449	115.928
r	Barrichello	Stewart	56	Gearbox	1:21.758	112.931
r	Rosset	Tyrrell	52	Gearbox	1:23.342	111.318
r	Tuero	Minardi	44	Electrics	1:23.293	112.236
r	Diniz	Arrows	26	Gearbox	1:22.969	112.950
r	Takagi	Tyrrell	19	Engine	1:23.226	113.424
r	Salo	Arrows	18	Engine	1:23.565	112.876
r	Trulli	Prost	17	Fuel pressure	1:22.933	112.301
r	Nakano	Minardi	3	Spin	1:24.475	107.814
r	Schumacher, R.	Jordan	0	Spin	–	–

Starting Grid and Qualifying Times

1	Hakkinen (Fin)	1:17.092	2	Coulthard (GB)	1:17.757
3	Frentzen (Ger)	1:18.109	4	Schumacher, M.(Ger)	1:18.250
5	Wurz (Aut)	1:18.261	6	Irvine (GB)	1:18.449
7	Fisichella (Ita)	1:18.652	8	Schumacher, R.(Ger)	1:18.735
9	Panis (Fra)	1:18.753	10	Villeneuve (Can)	1:18.761
11	Hill (GB)	1:18.955	12	Trulli (Ita)	1:19.069
13	Barrichello (Bra)	1:19.344	14	Herbert (GB)	1:19.375
15	Alesi (Fra)	1:19.449	16	Magnussen (Den)	1:19.644
17	Takagi (Jap)	1:20.203	18	Nakano (Jap)	1:20.390
19	Tuero (Arg)	1:20.459	20	Salo (Fin)	1:20.481
21	Rosset (Bra)	1:20.748	22	Diniz (Bra)	1:20.847

Drivers outside 107% rule:
None

Round 3: Argentina – Buenos Aires

Date: 12 April 1998
Track: 2.646 miles
Conditions: Cloudy
Lap Record: G.Berger – 1:27.981, Lap 63 at 108.290 mph, 13 April 1997

Distance: 72 laps, 190.080 miles
Fastest Lap: Alexander Wurz – 1:28.178

Pos	Driver	Car	Laps	Time/Reason	Fastest	mph
1	Schumacher, M.	Ferrari	72	1:48:36.175	1:28.272	105.206
2	Hakkinen	McLaren	72	1:48:59.173	1:28.281	104.837
3	Irvine	Ferrari	72	1:49:33.920	1:28.933	104.281
4	Wurz	Benetton	72	1:49:44.309	†1:28.178	104.117
5	Alesi	Sauber	72	1:49:54.461	1:29.000	103.956
6	Coulthard	McLaren	72	1:49:55.826	1:28.468	103.933
7	Fisichella	Benetton	72	1:50:04.612	1:28.507	103.796
8	Hill	Jordan	71	1:49:17.781	1:29.310	103.085
9	Frentzen	Williams	71	1:49:43.772	1:29.592	102.678
10	Barrichello	Stewart	70	1:49:03.354	1:30.408	101.856
11	Trulli	Prost	70	1:49:18.377	1:30.876	101.623
12	Takagi	Tyrrell	70	1:50:15.941	1:31.057	100.739
13	Nakano	Minardi	69	1:49:18.217	1:31.168	100.173
14	Rosset	Tyrrell	68	1:48:49.538	1:33.091	99.154
15	Panis	Prost	65	Engine	1:29.201	103.488
r	Tuero	Minardi	63	Accident	1:30.992	100.567
r	Villeneuve	Williams	52	Accident	1:29.694	104.004
r	Herbert	Sauber	46	Accident dam.	1:29.857	103.429
r	Schumacher, R.	Jordan	22	Suspension/spin	1:31.541	105.349
r	Salo	Arrows	18	Gearbox	1:32.519	100.226
r	Magnussen	Stewart	17	Transmission	1:32.808	99.181
r	Diniz	Arrows	13	Gearbox	1:33.350	99.684

Starting Grid and Qualifying Times

1	Coulthard (GB)	1:25.852	2	Schumacher, M. (Ger)	1:26.251
3	Hakkinen (Fin)	1:26.632	4	Irvine (GB)	1:26.780
5	Schumacher, R. (Ger)	1:26.827	6	Frentzen (Ger)	1:26.876
7	Villeneuve (Can)	1:29.941	8	Wurz (Aut)	1:27.198
9	Hill (GB)	1:27.483	10	Fisichella (Ita)	1:27.836
11	Alesi (Fra)	1:27.839	12	Herbert (GB)	1:28.016
13	Takagi (Jap)	1:28.811	14	Barrichello (Bra)	1:29.249
15	Panis (Fra)	1:29.320	16	Trulli (Ita)	1:29.352
17	Salo (Fin)	1:29.617	18	Diniz (Bra)	1:30.022
19	Nakano (Jap)	1:30.054	20	Tuero (Arg)	1:30.158
21	Rosset (Bra)	1:30.437	22	Magnussen (Den)	1:31.178

Drivers outside 107% rule:
  None

Date: 26 April 1998
Track: 2.646 miles   Distance: 62 laps, 189.906 miles
Conditions: Hot and sunny   Fastest Lap: M.Schumacher – 1:29.345
Lap Record: H-H.Frentzen – 1:25.531 at 128.942 mph, 27 April 1997

Pos	Driver	Car	Laps	Time/Reason	Fastest	mph
1	Coulthard	McLaren	62	1:34:24.593	1:29.497	120.618
2	Schumacher, M.	Ferrari	62	1:34:29.147	†1:29.345	120.521
3	Irvine	Ferrari	62	1:35:16.368	1:30.206	119.525
4	Villeneuve	Williams	62	1:35:19.183	1:29.726	119.467
5	Frentzen	Williams	62	1:35:42.069	1:30.283	118.990
6	Alesi	Sauber	61	1:34.30.693	1:30.391	118.543
7	Schumacher, R.	Jordan	60	1:34:34.790	1:31.837	116.514
8	Tuero	Minardi	60	1:35:48.285	1:33.443	115.024
9	Salo	Arrows	60	1:35:55.865	1:31.267	114.873
r	Hill	Jordan	57	Engine	1:30.859	116.968
r	Panis	Prost	56	Engine	1:30.481	118.139
r	Rosset	Tyrrell	48	Engine	1:34.491	113.327
r	Takagi	Tyrrell	40	Engine	1:32.430	116.047
r	Trulli	Prost	34	Throttle	1:32.361	116.363
r	Nakano	Minardi	27	Engine	1:33.889	113.726
r	Diniz	Arrows	18	Engine	1:32.988	114.532
r	Hakkinen	McLaren	17	Gearbox	1:30.115	118.948
r	Fisichella	Benetton	17	Accident	1:31.969	118.263
r	Wurz	Benetton	17	Gearbox	1:31.562	111.680
r	Herbert	Sauber	12	Puncture	1:32.215	115.838
r	Magnussen	Stewart	8	Gearbox	1:35.069	106.364
r	Barrichello	Stewart	0	Accident	–	–

Starting Grid and Qualifying Times

1	Coulthard (GB)	1:25.973	2	Hakkinen (Fin)	1:26.075
3	Schumacher, M. (Ger)	1:26.437	4	Irvine (GB)	1:27.169
5	Wurz (Aut)	1:27.273	6	Villeneuve (Can)	1:27.390
7	Hill (GB)	1:27.592	8	Frentzen (Ger)	1:27.645
9	Schumacher, R. (Ger)	1:27.866	10	Fisichella (Ita)	1:27.937
11	Herbert (GB)	1:28.111	12	Alesi (Fra)	1:28.191
13	Panis (Fra)	1:28.270	14	Salo (Fin)	1:28.798
15	Takagi (Jap)	1:29.073	16	Trulli (Ita)	1:29.584
17	Barrichello (Bra)	1:29.641	18	Diniz (Bra)	1:29.932
19	Tuero (Arg)	1:30.649	20	Magnussen (Den)	1:31.017
21	Nakano (Jap)	1:31.255	22	Rosset (Bra)	1:31.482

Drivers outside 107% rule:
None

Round 5: Spain – Catalunya, Barcelona

Date: 10 May 1998
Track: 2.938 miles
Conditions: Hot and sunny
Lap Record: G.Fisichella – 1:22.242 at 128.604 mph, 24 May 1997

Distance: 65 laps, 190.97 miles
Fastest Lap: Mika Hakkinen – 1:24.275

Pos	Driver	Car	Laps	Time/Reason	Fastest	mph
1	Hakkinen	McLaren	65	1:33:37.621	†1:24.275	122.325
2	Coulthard	McLaren	65	1:33:47.060	1:24.778	122.120
3	Schumacher, M.	Ferrari	65	1:34:24.715	1:24.625	121.308
4	Wurz	Benetton	65	1:34:40.159	1:25.343	120.978
5	Barrichello	Stewart	64	1:33:54.435	1:26.532	120.083
6	Villeneuve	Williams	64	1:33:55.147	1:26.407	120.067
7	Herbert	Sauber	64	1:33:58.147	1:26.354	120.004
8	Frentzen	Williams	63	1:33:42.553	1:26.011	118.455
9	Trulli	Prost	63	1:33:46.888	1:26.394	118.364
10	Alesi	Sauber	63	1:33:47.986	1:25.668	118.341
11	Schumacher, R.	Jordan	63	1:33:49.657	1:26.533	118.306
12	Magnussen	Stewart	63	1:34:01.002	1:27.203	118.068
13	Takagi	Tyrrell	63	1:34:37.820	1:28.066	117.307
14	Nakano	Minardi	63	1:34:11.328	1:27.767	117.230
15	Tuero	Minardi	63	1:34:42.163	1:27.601	117.213
16	Panis	Prost	60	Engine	1:26.502	119.471
r	Hill	Jordan	46	Engine	1:26.501	119.109
r	Irvine	Ferrari	28	Accident	1:25.778	120.938
r	Fisichella	Benetton	28	Accident	1:25.851	120.924
r	Salo	Arrows	21	Engine	1:27.767	118.756
r	Diniz	Arrows	20	Engine	1:27.638	113.012
dnq	Rosset	Tyrrell	–	–	–	–

Starting Grid and Qualifying Times

1	Hakkinen (Fin)	1:20.262	2	Coulthard (GB)	1:20.996
3	Schumacher, M. (Ger)	1:21.785	4	Fisichella (Ita)	1:21.894
5	Wurz (Aut)	1:21.965	6	Irvine (GB)	1:22.350
7	Herbert (GB)	1:22.794	8	Hill (GB)	1:22.835
9	Barrichello (Bra)	1:22.860	10	Villeneuve (Can)	1:22.885
11	Schumacher, R. (Ger)	1:22.927	12	Panis (Fra)	1:22.963
13	Frentzen (Ger)	1:23.197	14	Alesi (Fra)	1:23.327
15	Diniz (Bra)	1:23.704	16	Trulli (Ita)	1:23.748
17	Salo (Fin)	1:23.887	18	Magnussen (Den)	1:24.112
19	Tuero (Arg)	1:24.265	20	Nakano (Jap)	1:24.538
21	Takagi (Jap)	1:24.722			

Drivers outside 107% rule:
Rosset (Bra)   1:25.946

Round 6: Monaco – Monte Carlo

Date: 24 May 1998
Track: 2.092 miles   Distance: 78 laps, 163.176 miles
Conditions: Hot and sunny   Fastest Lap: Mika Hakkinen – 1:22.948
Lap Record: M.Schumacher – 1:21.076 at 91.821 mph, 15 May 1994

Pos	Driver	Car	Laps	Time/Reason	Fastest	mph
1	Hakkinen	McLaren	78	1:51:23.595	†1:22.948	87.902
2	Fisichella	Benetton	78	1:51:35.070	1:23.594	87.751
3	Irvine	Ferrari	78	1:52:04.973	1:24.457	87.361
4	Salo	Arrows	78	1:52:23.958	1:24.582	87.115
5	Villeneuve	Williams	77	1:51:58.811	1:24.381	86.320
6	Diniz	Arrows	77	1:52:06.752	1:24.456	86.219
7	Herbert	Sauber	77	1:52:36.186	1:25.053	85.843
8	Hill	Jordan	76	1:51:47.513	1:26.091	85.343
9	Nakano	Minardi	76	1:51:48.485	1:25.054	85.330
10	Schumacher, M.	Ferrari	76	1:52:16.789	1:23.189	84.972
11	Takagi	Tyrrell	76	1:52:31.704	1:26.506	84.784
12	Alesi	Sauber	72	Engine	1:24.539	86.660
r	Trulli	Prost	56	Gearbox	1:26.501	84.813
r	Panis	Prost	49	Loose wheel	1:24.874	84.433
r	Schumacher, R.	Jordan	44	Accident dam.	1:26.228	84.471
r	Wurz	Benetton	42	Accident	1:23.970	87.376
r	Magnussen	Stewart	30	Suspension	1:26.637	85.356
r	Coulthard	McLaren	17	Accident	1:22.955	88.771
r	Barrichello	Stewart	11	Suspension	1:27.719	83.949
r	Frentzen	Williams	9	Accident	1:26.777	85.487
r	Tuero	Minardi	0	Accident	no time	no time
dnq	Rosset	Tyrrell	–	–	–	

Starting Grid and Qualifying Times

1	Hakkinen (Fin)	1:19.798	2	Coulthard (GB)	1:20.137
3	Fisichella (Ita)	1:20.388	4	Schumacher, M. (Ger)	1:20.702
5	Frentzen (Ger)	1:20.729	6	Wurz (Aut)	1:20.855
7	Irvine (GB)	1:21.712	8	Salo (Fin)	1:22.144
9	Herbert (GB)	1:22.157	10	Trulli (Ita)	1:22.238
11	Alesi (Fra)	1:22.257	12	Diniz (Bra)	1:22.355
13	Villeneuve (Can)	1:22.488	14	Barrichello (Bra)	1:22.540
15	Hill (GB)	1:23.151	16	Schumacher, R. (Ger)	1:23.283
17	Magnussen (Den)	1:23.411	18	Panis (Fra)	1:23.536
19	Nakano (Jap)	1:23.957	20	Takagi (Jap)	1:24.024
21	Tuero (Arg)	1:24.024			

Drivers outside 107% rule:
Rosset (Bra)   1:25.737

Date: 7 June 1998
Track: 2.747 miles   Distance: 69 laps, 189.543 miles
Conditions: Cool and blustery   Fastest Lap: M.Schumacher – 1:19.379
Lap Record: M.Schumacher – 1:19.379 at 124.591 mph, 7 June 1998

Pos	Driver	Car	Laps	Time/Reason	Fastest	mph
1	Schumacher, M.	Ferrari	69	1:40:57.355	†1:19.379	112.657
2	Fisichella	Benetton	69	1:41:14.071	1:20.942	112.348
3	Irvine	Ferrari	69	1:41:57.414	1:21.327	111.551
4	Wurz	Benetton	69	1:42:00.587	1:21.694	111.493
5	Barrichello	Stewart	69	1:42:18.868	1:22.239	111.162
6	Magnussen	Stewart	68	1:42:26.707	1:22.867	110.489
7	Nakano	Minardi	68	1:42:27:937	1:22.907	110.467
8	Rosset	Tyrrell	68	1:43:17.371	1:23.418	109.577
9	Diniz	Arrows	68	1:43:19.361	1:21.814	109.542
10	Villeneuve	Williams	63	1:42:14.604	1:21.233	102.569
r	Tuero	Minardi	53	Electrics	1:22.939	107.302
r	Hill	Jordan	42	Electrics	1:21.933	99.802
r	Panis	Prost	39	Engine	1:21.669	106.617
r	Frentzen	Williams	20	Accident	1:22.430	100.841
r	Coulthard	McLaren	18	Throttle linkage	1:20.852	99.973
r	Herbert	Sauber	18	Spin	1:23.466	99.418
r	Salo	Arrows	18	Steering	1:24.451	99.336
r	Hakkinen	McLaren	0	Gearbox	–	–
r	Schumacher, R.	Jordan	0	Loss of drive	–	–
r	Alesi	Sauber	0	Accident	–	–
r	Trulli	Prost	0	Accident	–	–
r	Takagi	Tyrrell	0	Loss of drive	–	–

Starting Grid and Qualifying Times

1	Coulthard (GB)	1:18.213	2	Hakkinen (Fin)	1:18.282
3	Schumacher, M. (Ger)	1:18.497	4	Fisichella (Ita)	1:18.826
5	Schumacher, R. (Ger)	1:19.242	6	Villeneuve (Can)	1:19.588
7	Frentzen (Ger)	1:19.614	8	Irvine (GB)	1:19.616
9	Alesi (Fra)	1:19.693	10	Hill (GB)	1:19.717
11	Wurz (Aut)	1:19.765	12	Herbert (GB)	1:19.845
13	Barrichello (Bra)	1:19.953	14	Trulli (Ita)	1:20.188
15	Panis (Fra)	1:20.303	16	Takagi (Jap)	1:20.328
17	Salo (Fin)	1:20.536	18	Nakano (Jap)	1:21.230
19	Diniz (Bra)	1:21.301	20	Magnussen (Den)	1:21.629
21	Tuero (Arg)	1:21.822	22	Rosset (Bra)	1:21.824

Drivers outside 107% rule:
None

Date: 28 June 1998
Track: 2.641 miles   Distance: 71 laps, 187.511 miles
Conditions: Warm and sunny   Fastest Lap: D.Coulthard – 1:17.523
Lap Record: N.Mansell – 1:17.070 at 123.355 mph, 5 July 1992

Pos	Driver	Car	Laps	Time/Reason	Fastest	mph
1	Schumacher, M.	Ferrari	71	1:34:45.026	1:17.770	118.664
2	Irvine	Ferrari	71	1:35:04.601	1:18.956	118.257
3	Hakkinen	McLaren	71	1:35:04.773	1:18.493	118.256
4	Villeneuve	Williams	71	1:35:51.991	1:18.913	117.282
5	Wurz	Benetton	70	1:34:47.515	1:19.320	116.941
6	Coulthard	McLaren	70	1:34:52.416	†1:17.523	116.840
7	Alesi	Sauber	70	1:34:54.330	1:19.660	116.801
8	Herbert	Sauber	70	1:35:37.415	1:19.771	115.923
9	Fisichella	Benetton	70	1:35:53.089	1:19.307	115.608
10	Barrichello	Stewart	69	1:34:46.884	1:20.651	115.282
11	Panis	Prost	69	1:35:02.913	1:19.953	114.958
12	Verstappen	Stewart	69	1:35:21.800	1:20.849	114.578
13	Salo	Arrows	69	1:35:43.315	1:21.502	114.150
14	Diniz	Arrows	69	1:36:03.194	1:21.765	113.755
15	Frentzen	Williams	68	Accident dam.	1:19.229	116.480
16	Schumacher, R.	Jordan	68	1:35:42.686	1:19.052	112.506
17	Nakano	Minardi	65	Engine	1:21.883	113.290
r	Takagi	Tyrrell	60	Engine	1:20.299	114.042
r	Trulli	Prost	55	Spin	1:19.869	113.444
r	Tuero	Minardi	41	Gearbox	1:22.761	111.733
r	Hill	Jordan	19	Hydraulics	1:19.490	113.714
r	Rosset	Tyrrell	16	Engine	1:22.435	113.197

Starting Grid and Qualifying Times

1	Hakkinen (Fin)	1:14.929	2	Schumacher, M. (Ger)	1:15.159
3	Coulthard (GB)	1:15.333	4	Irvine (GB)	1:15.527
5	Villeneuve (Can)	1:15.630	6	Schumacher, R. (Ger)	1:15.926
7	Hill (GB)	1:16.245	8	Frentzen (Ger)	1:16.319
9	Fisichella (Ita)	1:16.375	10	Wurz (Aut)	1:16.460
11	Alesi (Fra)	1:16.827	12	Trulli (Ita)	1:16.892
13	Herbert (GB)	1:16.977	14	Barrichello (Bra)	1:17.024
15	Verstappen (Hol)	1:17.604	16	Panis (Fra)	1:17.671
17	Diniz (Bra)	1:17.880	18	Rosset (Bra)	1:17.908
19	Salo (Fin)	1:17.970	20	Takagi (Jap)	1:18.221
21	Nakano (Jap)	1:18.273	22	Tuero (Arg)	1:19.146

Drivers outside 107% rule:
None

Date: 12 July 1998
Track: 3.194 miles   Distance: 60 laps, 191.640 miles
Conditions: Cool and wet   Fastest Lap: M.Schumacher – 1:35.704
Lap Record: M.Schumacher – 1:24.475 at 136.115 mph, 13 July 1997

Pos	Driver	Car	Laps	Time/Reason	Fastest	mph
1	Schumacher, M.	Ferrari	60	1:47:12.450	†1:35.704	107.217
2	Hakkinen	McLaren	60	1:47:24.915	1:35.961	107.009
3	Irvine	Ferrari	60	1:47:31.649	1:36.530	106.898
4	Wurz	Benetton	59	1:47:29.402	1:37.982	105.153
5	Fisichella	Benetton	59	1:47:30.546	1:38.424	105.134
6	Schumacher, R.	Jordan	59	1:47:54.075	1:37.389	104.751
7	Villeneuve	Williams	59	1:48:20.879	1:37.199	104.320
8	Nakano	Minardi	58	1:48:26.357	1:43.755	102.465
9	Takagi	Tyrrell	56	1:47:37.746	1:41.629	99.675
r	Alesi	Sauber	53	Electrics	1:37.202	105.768
r	Diniz	Arrows	45	Spin	1:37.887	100.647
r	Panis	Prost	40	Spin	1:42.346	108.588
r	Barrichello	Stewart	39	Spin	1:40.097	107.844
r	Verstappen	Stewart	38	Engine	1:41.114	108.290
r	Coulthard	McLaren	37	Spin	1:36.120	115.274
r	Trulli	Prost	37	Spin	1:44.083	106.206
r	Rosset	Tyrrell	29	Spin	1:40.948	105.993
r	Tuero	Minardi	29	Spin	1:44.700	105.980
r	Herbert	Sauber	27	Spin	1:37.343	111.868
r	Salo	Arrows	27	Spin	1:38.160	111.173
r	Frentzen	Williams	15	Spin	1:36.884	115.979
r	Hill	Jordan	13	Spin	1:37.223	115.698

Starting Grid and Qualifying Times

1	Hakkinen (Fin)	1:23.271	2	Schumacher, M. (Ger)	1:23.720
3	Villeneuve (Can)	1:24.102	4	Coulthard (GB)	1:24.310
5	Irvine (GB)	1:24.436	6	Frentzen (Ger)	1:24.442
7	Hill (GB)	1:24.542	8	Alesi (Fra)	1:25.081
9	Herbert (GB)	1:25.084	10	Fisichella (Ita)	1:25.654
11	Wurz (Aut)	1:25.760	12	Diniz (Bra)	1:26.376
13	Salo (Fin)	1:26.487	14	Trulli (Ita)	1:26.808
15	Verstappen (Hol)	1:26.948	16	Barrichello (Bra)	1:26.990
17	Takagi (Jap)	1:27.061	18	Tuero (Arg)	1:28.051
19	Nakano (Jap)	1:28.123	20	Rosset (Bra)	1:28.608
21	Schumacher, R. (Ger)	PI	22	Panis (Fra)	PI

Drivers outside 107% rule:
    None   PI=Penalty for Infringement

Date: 26 July 1998
Track: 2.684 miles   Distance: 71 laps, 190.564 miles
Conditions: Hot and sunny   Fastest Lap: D.Coulthard – 1:12.878
Lap Record: J.Villeneuve – 1:11.814 at 134.657 mph, 21 September 1997

Pos	Driver	Car	Laps	Time/Reason	Fastest	mph
1	Hakkinen	McLaren	71	1:30:44.086	1:13.412	126.006
2	Coulthard	McLaren	71	1:30:49.375	†1:12.878	125.883
3	Schumacher, M.	Ferrari	71	1:31:23.178	1:13.029	125.107
4	Irvine	Ferrari	71	1:31:28.062	1:14.066	124.996
5	Schumacher, R.	Jordan	71	1:31:34.740	1:13.972	124.844
6	Villeneuve	Williams	71	1:31:37.288	1:13.730	124.786
7	Hill	Jordan	71	1:31:57.710	1:14.135	124.324
8	Herbert	Sauber	70	1:30:56.888	1:14.639	123.939
9	Wurz	Benetton	70	1:30:58.611	1:14.040	123.900
10	Trulli	Prost	70	1:31:33.536	1:15.709	123.112
11	Nakano	Minardi	70	1:31:44.313	1:15.575	122.871
12	Rosset	Tyrrell	69	1:33:28.193	1:16.100	118.872
r	Verstappen	Stewart	51	Engine	1:15.610	121.425
r	Tuero	Minardi	30	Spin	1:15.769	118.355
r	Fisichella	Benetton	21	Accident	1:14.044	120.698
r	Alesi	Sauber	21	Accident	1:14.791	119.195
r	Frentzen	Williams	16	Engine	1:15.446	116.665
r	Barrichello	Stewart	8	Brakes	1:16.822	107.466
r	Diniz	Arrows	3	Accident dam.	2.02.090	85.897
r	Salo	Arrows	1	Accident dam.	no time	82.303
r	Panis	Prost	0	Clutch	no time	
r	Takagi	Tyrrell	0	Spin	no time	

Starting Grid and Qualifying Times

1	Fisichella (Ita)	1:29.598	2	Alesi (Fra)	1:30.317
3	Hakkinen (Fin)	1:30.517	4	Schumacher, M. (Ger)	1:30.551
5	Barrichello (Bra)	1:31.005	6	Salo (Fin)	1:31.028
7	Frentzen (Ger)	1:31.515	8	Irvine (GB)	1:31.651
9	Schumacher, R. (Ger)	1:31.917	10	Panis (Fra)	1:32.081
11	Villeneuve (Can)	1:32.083	12	Verstappen (Hol)	1:32.099
13	Diniz (Bra)	1:32.206	14	Coulthard (GB)	1:32.399
15	Hill (GB)	1:32.718	16	Trulli (Ita)	1:32.906
17	Wurz (Aut)	1:33.185	18	Herbert (GB)	1:33.205
19	Tuero (Arg)	1:33.399	20	Takagi (Jap)	1:34.090
21	Nakano (Jap)	1:34.536	22	Rosset (Bra)	1:34.910

Drivers outside 107% rule:
None

Round 11: Germany – Hockenheim

Date: 2 August 1998
Track: 4.240 miles   Distance: 45 laps, 190.755 miles
Conditions: Dry but cloudy   Fastest Lap: D.Coulthard – 1:46.116
Lap Record: G.Berger – 1:45.747 at 144.337 mph, 27 July 1997

Pos	Driver	Car	Laps	Time/Reason	Fastest	mph
1	Hakkinen	McLaren	45	1:20:47.984	1:46.252	141.677
2	Coulthard	McLaren	45	1:20:48.410	†1:46.116	141.664
3	Villeneuve	Williams	45	1:20:50.561	1:46.274	141.602
4	Hill	Jordan	45	1:20:55.169	1:46.317	141.467
5	Schumacher, M.	Ferrari	45	1:21:00.597	1:46.381	141.309
6	Schumacher, R.	Jordan	45	1:21:17.722	1:46.350	140.814
7	Fisichella	Benetton	45	1:21:19.010	1:46.831	140.776
8	Irvine	Ferrari	45	1:21:19.633	1:46.459	140.758
9	Frentzen	Williams	45	1:21:20.768	1:46.890	140.725
10	Alesi	Sauber	45	1:21:36.355	1:46.964	140.277
11	Wurz	Benetton	45	1:21:45.978	1:46.880	140.002
12	Trulli	Prost	44	1:20:53.714	1:48.446	138.365
13	Takagi	Tyrrell	44	1:21:07.369	1:48.608	137.977
14	Salo	Arrows	44	1:21:13.440	1:48.899	137.805
15	Panis	Prost	44	1:21:52.283	1:47.775	136.715
16	Tuero	Minardi	43	1:22:35.459	1:50.314	132.443
r	Herbert	Sauber	37	Gearbox	1:47.345	139.861
r	Nakano	Minardi	36	Gearbox	1:49.424	137.251
r	Barrichello	Stewart	27	Gearbox	1:47.544	139.218
r	Verstappen	Stewart	24	Transmission	1:49.147	137.380
r	Diniz	Arrows	2	Throttle	1:51.259	130.270
dnq	Rosset	Tyrrell	–	Practice accident	–	–

Starting Grid and Qualifying Times

1	Hakkinen (Fin)	1:41.838	2	Coulthard (GB)	1:42.347
3	Villeneuve (Can)	1:42.365	4	Schumacher, R. (Ger)	1:42.994
5	Hill (GB)	1:43.183	6	Irvine (GB)	1:43.270
7	Wurz (Aut)	1:43.341	8	Fisichella (Ita)	1:43.396
9	Schumacher, M. (Ger)	1:43.459	10	Frentzen (Ger)	1:43.467
11	Alesi (Fra)	1:43.663	12	Herbert (GB)	1:44.599
13	Barrichello (Bra)	1:44.776	14	Trulli (Ita)	1:44.844
15	Takagi (Jap)	1:44.961	16	Panis (Fra)	1:45.197
17	Salo (Fin)	1:45.276	18	Diniz (Bra)	1:45.588
19	Verstappen (Hol)	1:45.623	20	Nakano (Jap)	1:46.713
21	Tuero (Arg)	1:47.265			

Drivers outside 107% rule:
Rosset (Bra) Did not take part in qualifying session on medical grounds.

Round 12: Hungary – Hungaroring

Date: 16 August 1998
Track: 2.466 miles   Distance: 77 laps, 189.805 miles
Conditions: Hot with cloud   Fastest Lap: M.Schumacher – 1:19.286
Lap Record: N.Mansell – 1:18.308 at 113.349 mph, 16 August 1992

Pos	Driver	Car	Laps	Time/Reason	Fastest	mph
1	Schumacher, M.	Ferrari	77	1:45:25.550	†1:19.286	108.162
2	Coulthard	McLaren	77	1:45:34.983	1:20.546	108.001
3	Villeneuve	Williams	77	1:46:09.994	1:20.078	107.407
4	Hill	Jordan	77	1:46:20.626	1:20.680	107.228
5	Frentzen	Williams	77	1:46:22.060	1:20.356	107.204
6	Hakkinen	McLaren	76	1:45:29.932	1:20.545	106.683
7	Alesi	Sauber	76	1:45:41.961	1:21.439	106.481
8	Fisichella	Benetton	76	1:45:56.357	1:21.060	106.240
9	Schumacher, R.	Jordan	76	1:46:15.311	1:20.875	105.924
10	Herbert	Sauber	76	1:46:20.059	1:21.329	105.845
11	Diniz	Arrows	74	1:45:27.272	1:23.429	103.919
12	Panis	Prost	74	1:45:29.999	1:22.538	103.868
13	Verstappen	Stewart	74	1:45:53.909	1:23.644	103.484
14	Takagi	Tyrrell	74	1:46:08.141	1:22.495	103.252
15	Nakano	Minardi	74	1:47:45.727	1:23.573	101.694
16	Wurz	Benetton	69	dnf/Gearbox	1:21.479	106.387
r	Barrichello	Stewart	54	Gearbox	1:23.294	103.221
r	Trulli	Prost	28	Engine	1:23.318	103.613
r	Salo	Arrows	18	Gearbox	1:23.716	103.187
r	Irvine	Ferrari	13	Gearbox	1:20.984	106.891
r	Tuero	Minardi	13	Engine	1:25.450	101.466
dnq	Rosset	Tyrrell				

Starting Grid and Qualifying Times

1	Hakkinen (Fin)	1:16.973	2	Coulthard (GB)	1:17.131
3	Schumacher, M. (Ger)	1:17.366	4	Hill (GB)	1:18.214
5	Irvine (GB)	1:18.325	6	Villeneuve (Can)	1:18.337
7	Frentzen (Ger)	1:19.029	8	Fisichella (Ita)	1:19.050
9	Wurz (Aut)	1:19.063	10	Schumacher, R. (Ger)	1:19.171
11	Alesi (Fra)	1:19.210	12	Diniz (Bra)	1:19.706
13	Salo (Fin)	1:19.712	14	Barrichello (Bra)	1:19.876
15	Herbert (GB)	1:19.878	16	Trulli (Ita)	1:20.042
17	Verstappen (Hol)	1:20.918	18	Takagi (Jap)	1:20.354
19	Nakano (Jap)	1:20.635	20	Panis (Fra)	1:20.663
21	Tuero (Arg)	1:21.725			

Drivers outside 107% rule:
Rosset (Bra)   1:23.140

Date: 30 August 1998
Track: 4.330 miles   Distance: 44 laps, 190.520 miles
Conditions: Wet   Fastest Lap: M.Schumacher – 2:03.766
Lap Record: J.Villeneuve – 1:52.692 at 138.321 mph, 24 August 1997

Pos	Driver	Car	Laps	Time/Reason	Fastest	mph
1	Hill	Jordan	44	1:43:47.407	2:05.630	110.130
2	Schumacher, R.	Jordan	44	1:43:48.339	2:08.399	110.113
3	Alesi	Sauber	44	1:43:54.647	2:07.597	110.002
4	Frentzen	Williams	44	1:44:19.650	2:06.284	109.563
5	Diniz	Arrows	44	1:44:39.089	2:11.331	109.223
6	Trulli	Prost	42	1:44:42.230	2:11.701	104.207
7	Coulthard	McLaren	39	1:43:51.512	2:10.950	97.544
8	Nakano	Minardi	39	1:46:01.069	2:13.230	95.563
r	Fisichella	Benetton	26	Accident	2:09.528	113.471
r	Schumacher, M.	Ferrari	25	Accident	†2:03.766	115.558
r	Irvine	Ferrari	25	Spin	2:06.561	113.407
r	Tuero	Minardi	17	Electrics	2:19.996	104.546
r	Villeneuve	Williams	16	Accident	2:07.825	114.598
r	Takagi	Tyrrell	10	Spin	–	110.336
r	Verstappen	Stewart	8	Engine	–	108.834
r	Hakkinen	McLaren	0	Accident	–	–
r	Wurz	Benetton	0	Accident	–	–
r	Herbert	Sauber	0	Accident	–	–
dns	Panis	Prost	–	–	–	–
dns	Barrichello	Stewart	–	–	–	–
dns	Salo	Arrows	–	–	–	–
dns	Rosset	Tyrrell	–	–	–	–

Starting Grid and Qualifying Times

1	Hakkinen (Fin)	1:48.682	2	Coulthard (GB)	1:48.845
3	Hill (GB)	1:49.728	4	Schumacher, M. (Ger)	1:50.027
5	Irvine (GB)	1:50.189	6	Villeneuve (Can)	1:50.204
7	Fisichella (Ita)	1:50.462	8	Schumacher, R. (Ger)	1:50.501
9	Frentzen (Ger)	1:50.686	10	Alesi (Fra)	1:51.189
11	Wurz (Aut)	1:51.648	12	Herbert (GB)	1:51.851
13	Trulli (Ita)	1:52.572	14	Barrichello (Bra)	1:52.670
15	Panis (Fra)	1:52.784	16	Diniz (Bra)	1:53.037
17	Verstappen (Hol)	1:53.149	18	Salo (Fin)	1:53.207
19	Takagi (Jap)	1:53.237	20	Rosset (Bra)	1:54.850
21	Nakano (Jap)	1:55.084	22	Tuero (Arg)	1:55.520

Drivers outside 107% rule:
    None

Date: 13 September 1998
Track: 2.466 miles   Distance: 53 laps, 190.005 miles
Conditions: Sunny and dry   Fastest Lap: Mika Hakkinen – 1:25.139
Lap Record: N.Mansell – 1:18.308 at 113.349 mph, 13 Sept 1997

Pos	Driver	Car	Laps	Time/Reason	Fastest	mph
1	Schumacher, M.	Ferrari	53	1:17:09.672	1:25.483	147.632
2	Irvine	Ferrari	53	1:17:47.649	1:26.359	146.431
3	Schumacher, R.	Jordan	53	1:17:50.824	1:26.194	146.331
4	Hakkinen	McLaren	53	1:18:05.343	†1:25.139	145.878
5	Alesi	Sauber	53	1:18:11.544	1:26.840	145.685
6	Hill	Jordan	53	1:18:16.360	1:26.730	145.536
7	Frentzen	Williams	52	1:17:11.164	1:26.656	144.798
8	Fisichella	Benetton	52	1:17:11.752	1:26.659	144.779
9	Takagi	Tyrrell	52	1:18:15.640	1:27.726	142.809
10	Barrichello	Stewart	52	1:18:22.050	1:27.770	142.615
11	Tuero	Minardi	51	1:17:59.838	1:29.093	140.533
12	Rosset	Tyrrell	51	1:18:12.566	1:29.393	140.152
13	Trulli	Prost	50	1:17:27.397	1:26.285	138.737
r	Verstappen	Stewart	39	Gearbox	1:28.583	141.864
r	Villeneuve	Williams	37	Spin	1:26.479	145.816
r	Salo	Arrows	32	Throttle	1:27.866	143.041
r	Wurz	Benetton	24	Gearbox	1:27.620	144.596
r	Coulthard	McLaren	16	Engine	1:25.959	147.715
r	Panis	Prost	15	Vibrations	1:28.395	107.471
r	Nakano	Minardi	13	Engine	1:29.853	140.233
r	Herbert	Sauber	12	Spin	1:29.092	141.711
r	Diniz	Arrows	10	Spin	1:29.124	140.428

Starting Grid and Qualifying Times

1	Schumacher, M. (Ger)	1:25.298	2	Villeneuve (Can)	1:25.965
3	Hakkinen (Fin)	1:25.679	4	Coulthard (GB)	1:25.987
5	Irvine (GB)	1:26.159	6	Schumacher, R. (Ger)	1:26.309
7	Wurz (Aut)	1:26.567	8	Alesi (Fra)	1:26.637
9	Panis (Fra)	1:26.681	10	Trulli (Ita)	1:26.794
11	Fisichella (Ita)	1:26.817	12	Frentzen (Ger)	1:26.836
13	Barrichello (Bra)	1:27.247	14	Hill (GB)	1:27.362
15	Herbert (GB)	1:27.510	16	Salo (Fin)	1:27.744
17	Verstappen (Hol)	1:28.212	18	Rosset (Bra)	1:28.286
19	Takagi (Jap)	1:28.346	20	Diniz (Bra)	1:28.387
21	Nakano (Jap)	1:29.101	22	Tuero (Arg)	1:29.417

Drivers outside 107% rule:
None

Date: 27 September 1998
Track: 2.831 miles
Conditions: Cool and dry
Lap Record: H-H.Frentzen – 1:18.805 at 129.309 mph, 28 Sept 1997

Distance: 67 laps, 189.074 miles
Fastest Lap: H.Hakkinen – 1:20.450

Pos	Driver	Car	Laps	Time/Reason	Fastest	mph
1	Hakkinen	McLaren	67	1:32:14.789	†1:20.450	123.369
2	Schumacher, M.	Ferrari	67	1:32:17.000	1:21.001	123.319
3	Coulthard	McLaren	67	1:32:48.952	1:20.715	122.612
4	Irvine	Ferrari	67	1:33.12.971	1:21.667	122.086
5	Frentzen	Williams	67	1:33:15.036	1:21.394	122.040
6	Fisichella	Benetton	67	1:33:16.148	1:21.506	122.016
7	Wurz	Benetton	67	1:33:19.578	1:21.778	121.942
8	Villeneuve	Williams	66	1:32:20.762	1:21.701	121.397
9	Hill	Jordan	66	1:32:22.990	1:21.741	121.335
10	Alesi	Sauber	66	1:32:29.424	1:21.979	121.207
11	Barrichello	Stewart	65	1:32:28.610	1:23.412	119.388
12	Panis	Prost	65	1:32:29.872	1:22.931	119.361
13	Verstappen	Stewart	65	1:32:52.806	1:23.944	118.869
14	Salo	Arrows	65	1:32:53.413	1:23.552	118.856
15	Nakano	Minardi	65	1:32:56.589	1:24.210	118.788
16	Takagi	Tyrrell	65	1:32:57.269	1:23.392	118.774
r	Tuero	Minardi	56	not classified	1:24.024	102.443
r	Schumacher, R.	Jordan	53	Brakes	1:21.881	118.477
r	Herbert	Sauber	37	Engine	1:22.712	120.764
r	Rosset	Tyrrell	36	Engine	1:24.161	117.218
r	Trulli	Prost	6	Transmission	1:25.328	116.418
r	Diniz	Arrows	6	Hydraulics	1:25.285	116.313

Starting Grid and Qualifying Times

1	Schumacher, M. (Ger)	1:18.561	2	Irvine (GB)	1:18.907
3	Hakkinen (Fin)	1:18.940	4	Fisichella (Ita)	1:19.048
5	Coulthard (GB)	1:19.169	6	Schumacher, R. (Ger)	1:19.455
7	Frentzen (Ger)	1:19.522	8	Wurz (Aut)	1:19.569
9	Villeneuve (Can)	1:19.631	10	Hill (GB)	1:19.807
11	Alesi (Fra)	1:20.493	12	Barrichello (Bra)	1:20.530
13	Herbert (GB)	1:20.650	14	Trulli (Ita)	1:20.709
15	Panis (Fra)	1:21.048	16	Salo (Fin)	1:21.120
17	Diniz (Bra)	1:21.258	18	Verstappen (Hol)	1:21.501
19	Takagi (Jap)	1:21.525	20	Nakano (Jap)	1:22.078
21	Tuero (Arg)	1:22.146	22	Rosset (Bra)	1:22.822

Drivers outside 107% rule:
  None

Round 16: Japan – Suzuka

Date: 1 November 1998
Track: 3.644 miles   Distance: 51 laps, 185.844 miles
Conditions: Warm and dry   Fastest Lap: M.Schumacher – 1:40.190
Lap Record: H-H.Frentzen – 1:38.942 at 130.662 mph, 12 Oct 1997

Pos	Driver	Car	Laps	Time/Reason	Fastest	mph
1	Hakkinen	McLaren	51	1:27:22.535	1:40.426	127.529
2	Irvine	Ferrari	51	1:27:29.026	1:40.870	127.372
3	Coulthard	McLaren	51	1:27:50.197	1:40.905	126.866
4	Hill	Jordan	51	1:28:36.026	1:42.275	125.766
5	Frentzen	Williams	51	1:28:36.392	1:42.331	125.756
6	Villeneuve	Williams	51	1:28:38.402	1:42.273	125.710
7	Alesi	Sauber	51	1:28:58.588	1:42.357	125.235
8	Fisichella	Benetton	51	1:29:03.837	1:42.335	125.112
9	Wurz	Benetton	50	1:27:37.673	1:43.447	124.667
10	Herbert	Sauber	50	1:27:43.035	1:42.858	124.540
11	Panis	Prost	50	1:28:20.327	1:43.073	123.664
12	Trulli	Prost	48	dnf	1:43.164	123.071
r	Nakano	Minardi	40	Electrics	1:44.158	121.918
r	Schumacher, M.	Ferrari	31	Puncture	†1:40.190	127.033
r	Takagi	Tyrrell	28	Accident	1:45.673	121.226
r	Tuero	Minardi	28	Accident	1:45.792	120.394
r	Barrichello	Stewart	25	Hydraulics	1:44.947	121.238
r	Verstappen	Stewart	21	Gearbox	1:45.890	120.525
r	Salo	Arrows	14	Hydraulics	1:45.305	122.991
r	Schumacher, R.	Jordan	13	Engine	1:42.965	125.489
r	Diniz	Arrows	2	Spin	1:46.099	115.685
dnq	Rosset	Tyrrell			–	–

Starting Grid and Qualifying Times

1	Schumacher, M. (Ger)	1:36.293	2 Hakkinen (Fin)	1:36.471
3	Coulthard (GB)	1:37.496	4 Irvine (GB)	1:38.197
5	Frentzen (Ger)	1:38.272	6 Villeneuve (Can)	1:38.448
7	Schumacher, R. (Ger)	1:38.461	8 Hill (GB)	1:38.603
9	Wurz (Aut)	1:38.959	10 Fisichella (Ita)	1:39.080
11	Herbert (GB)	1:39.234	12 Alesi (Fra)	1:39.448
13	Panis (Fra)	1:40.037	14 Trulli (Ita)	1:40.111
15	Salo (Fin)	1:40.387	16 Barrichello (Bra)	1:40.502
17	Takagi (Jap)	1:40.619	18 Diniz (Bra)	1:40.687
19	Verstappen (Hol)	1:40.943	20 Nakano (Jap)	1:41.315
21	Tuero (Arg)	1:42.358		

Drivers outside 107% rule:
Rosset (Bra)   1:43.259

FIA DRIVERS' CHAMPIONSHIP 1998

Pos	Driver	Team	Points
1	Mika Hakkinen (Fin)	McLaren Mercedes	100
2	Michael Schumacher (Ger)	Ferrari	86
3	David Coulthard (GB)	McLaren Mercedes	56
4	Eddie Irvine (GB)	Ferrari	47
5	Jacques Villeneuve (Can)	Williams Mecachrome	21
6	Damon Hill (GB)	Jordan Mugen Honda	20
7	Heinz-Harald Frentzen (Ger)	Williams Mecachrome	17
=	Alexander Wurz (Aut)	Benetton Playlife	17
9	Giancarlo Fisichella (Ita)	Benetton Playlife	16
10	Ralf Schumacher (Ger)	Jordan Mugen Honda	14
11	Jean Alesi (Fra)	Sauber Petronas	9
12	Rubens Barrichello (Bra)	Stewart Ford	4
13	Pedro Diniz (Bra)	Arrows	3
=	Mika Salo (Fin)	Arrows	3
15	Johnny Herbert (GB)	Sauber Petronas	1
=	Jan Magnussen (Den)	Stewart Ford	1
=	Jarno Trulli (Ita)	Prost Peugeot	1

Drivers who failed to score a point:
Shinji Nakano (Jap) – Minardi Ford; Olivier Panis (Fra) – Prost Peugeot; Ricardo Rosset (Bra) – Tyrrell Ford; Toranosuke Takagi (Jap) – Tyrrell Ford; Esterban Tuero (Arg) – Minardi Ford; Jos Verstappen (Hol) – Stewart Ford.

CONSTRUCTORS' CHAMPIONSHIP

Pos	Team	Tyres	Drivers	Points
1	McLaren Mercedes	B	Hakkinen, Coulthard	156
2	Ferrari	G	M.Schumacher, Irvine	133
3	Williams Mecachrome	G	Villeneuve, Frentzen	38
4	Jordan Mugen Honda	B	Hill, R.Schumacher	34
5	Benetton Playlife	B	Fisichella, Wurz	33
6	Sauber Petronas	G	Alesi, Herbert	10
7	Arrows	B	Salo, Diniz	6
8	Stewart Ford	B	Barrichello, Magnussen, Verstappen	5
9	Prost Peugeot	B	Panis, Trulli	1
10	Minardi	B	Nakano, Tuero	0
=	Tyrrell	G	Takagi, Rosset	0

DRIVERS – FINISHING POSITIONS – RACE BY RACE '98

		As	Br	Ar	SM	Sp	Mo	Ca	Fr	Br	At	Ge	Hu	Be	Ita	Lx	Jp	Pts
Alesi	Sauber	r	9	5	6	10	12	r	7	r	r	10	7	3	5	10	7	9
Barrichello	Stewart	r	2	10	r	5	r	5	10	r	r	2	2	ds	10	11	r	4
Coulthard	McLaren	2	2	6	1	2	r	6f	14	r	2f	2	r	7	r	3	3	56
Diniz	Arrows	r	r	r	r	r	6	r	9	r	r	11	r	5	r	r	r	3
Fisichella	Benetton	6	6	7	r	r	2	2	5	r	r	8	8	5	8	6	8	16
Frentzen	Williams	3	5	9	5	8	r	r	15	r	2	7	9	4	7	5	5	17
Hakkinen	McLaren	1f	1f	2	1f	1f	1f	r	3	2	1	5	6	4	4f	1f	5	100
Herbert	Sauber	6	r	7	7	8	r	8	r	8	7	r	10	1	r	r	10	1
Hill	Jordan	8	dq	8	8	r	8	r	7	8	4	4	4	1	6	9	4	20
Irvine	Ferrari	4	8	3	3	r	3	2	r	4	8	4	8	r	2	4	2	47
Magnussen	Stewart	r	10	r	12	6	r	17	8	11	r	–	–	–	–	15	–	1
Nakano	Minardi	r	13	r	14	9	7	11	r	r	15	15	12	ds	r	12	11	0
Panis	Prost	9	15	16	16	r	dq	r	r	12	r	12	dq	ds	r	r	ds	0
Rosset	Tyrrell	r	14	r	dq	dq	8	13	r	r	r	14	r	ds	12	14	r	0
Salo	Arrows	r	9	r	2f	3	10	1f	r	r	r	14	r	r	1	2	rf	3
Schumacher, M.	Ferrari	r	3	1	2f	3	10	1f	1	1	3	5	1f	r	1	2	rf	86
Schumacher, R.	Jordan	r	r	16	6	5	6	9	r	10	12	6	5	2	3	r	r	14
Takagi	Tyrrell	r	r	r	13	11	r	16	r	9	11	13	r	11	9	16	r	0
Trulli	Prost	r	12	r	9	r	11	r	r	7	6	r	r	6	13	r	12	1
Tuero	Minardi	–	–	–	–	–	12	r	11	r	10	r	13	r	11	r	r	0
Verstappen	Stewart	–	–	–	–	–	–	–	12	r	7	6	5	r	13	r	r	0
Villeneuve	Williams	5	7	r	4	6	5	10	4	7	6	3	3	r	8	6	9	21
Wurz	Benetton	7	4	4f	r	4	4	4	5	4	9	11	16	r	7	7	9	17

DRIVERS – GRID POSITIONS – RACE BY RACE '98

Driver	Team	As	Br	Ar	SM	Sp	Mo	Ca	Fr	Br	At	Ge	Hu	Be	Ita	Lx	Jp	Pts
Alesi	Sauber	12	15	13	11	12	14	13	11	8	2	11	11	10	8	11	12	9
Barrichello	Stewart	14	13	14	12	17	11	13	14	16	5	13	14	14	13	12	16	4
Coulthard	McLaren	2	2	1	1	2	2	1	3	4	14	2	2	2	4	5	3	56
Diniz	Arrows	20	22	18	18	15	12	19	17	12	13	18	12	16	20	17	18	3
Fisichella	Benetton	7	7	10	10	4	3	4	9	10	1	8	8	7	11	4	10	16
Frentzen	Williams	6	3	6	8	13	5	5	7	8	6	7	9	9	12	7	5	17
Hakkinen	McLaren	1	1	3	2	1	1	2	1	1	3	1	1	1	3	3	2	100
Herbert	Sauber	5	14	12	11	7	9	12	13	9	18	12	15	12	15	13	11	1
Hill	Jordan	10	11	9	7	8	15	10	7	7	15	5	4	3	14	10	8	20
Irvine	Ferrari	8	6	4	4	6	7	8	4	5	8	6	5	5	5	2	4	47
Magnussen	Stewart	18	16	22	20	18	17	18	–	–	–	–	–	–	–	–	–	0
Nakano	Minardi	22	18	19	21	20	19	18	16	22	10	16	20	15	21	15	20	0
Panis	Prost	21	9	15	13	12	18	15	19	13	6	fq	20	20	18	22	13	0
Rosset	Tyrrell	19	21	21	22	fq	8	22	16	18	22	19	fq	16	16	15	15	0
Salo	Arrows	16	20	17	14	17	8	17	19	9	6	13	13	20	16	16	16	3
Schumacher, M.	Ferrari	3	4	2	3	3	4	3	2	2	4	3	3	4	1	1	1	86
Schumacher, R.	Jordan	9	8	5	9	11	16	5	6	21	9	4	10	8	19	6	7	14
Takagi	Tyrrell	13	17	13	15	21	20	16	20	14	20	18	16	19	10	17	17	0
Trulli	Prost	15	12	16	16	16	14	10	22	12	16	16	13	13	14	14	21	1
Tuero	Minardi	17	19	20	19	19	21	21	18	15	19	21	21	22	17	18	19	0
Verstappen	Stewart	–	–	–	–	–	–	–	21	19	21	20	19	21	–	20	–	0
Villeneuve	Williams	4	10	7	6	10	13	6	5	11	16	3	6	6	2	9	6	21
Wurz	Benetton	11	5	8	5	5	6	11	10	17	17	7	9	11	7	8	9	17

DRIVERS – POINTS TALLY – RACE BY RACE '98

		As	Br	Ar	SM	Sp	Mo	Ca	Fr	Br	At	Ge	Hu	Be	Ita	Lx	Jp	Total
Alesi	Sauber	0	0	2	1	0	0	0	0	0	0	0	0	4	2	0	0	9
Barrichello	Stewart	0	0	1	0	0	0	3	0	0	0	0	0	0	0	0	0	4
Coulthard	McLaren	6	6	0	10	6	0	0	2	0	6	6	6	0	0	4	4	56
Diniz	Arrows	0	0	0	0	0	1	0	0	0	0	0	0	2	0	0	0	3
Fisichella	Benetton	0	1	0	0	2	6	6	1	0	0	0	0	0	0	0	0	16
Frentzen	Williams	4	2	0	0	0	0	0	3	1	1	1	2	0	0	2	1	17
Hakkinen	McLaren	10	10	6	3	10	10	0	4	6	10	10	1	0	0	10	10	100
Herbert	Sauber	1	0	0	0	0	0	0	0	0	0	0	0	0	0	0	0	1
Hill	Jordan	0	0	0	0	0	0	0	0	0	0	3	0	10	3	1	3	20
Irvine	Ferrari	3	0	4	4	3	4	4	6	4	2	0	3	0	6	0	4	47
Magnussen	Stewart	0	0	0	0	0	0	1	0	0	0	0	0	0	0	0	0	1
Nakano	Minardi	0	0	0	0	0	0	0	0	0	0	0	0	0	0	0	0	0
Panis	Prost	0	0	0	0	0	0	0	0	0	0	0	0	0	0	0	0	0
Rosset	Tyrrell	0	0	0	0	0	0	0	0	0	0	0	0	0	0	0	0	0
Salo	Arrows	0	0	0	0	0	3	0	0	0	0	0	0	0	0	0	0	3
Schumacher, M.	Ferrari	0	4	10	6	4	0	10	10	10	4	2	10	0	10	6	0	86
Schumacher, R.	Jordan	0	0	0	0	0	0	0	0	0	0	0	0	6	4	0	4	14
Takagi	Tyrrell	0	0	0	0	0	0	0	0	0	0	0	0	0	0	0	0	0
Trulli	Prost	0	0	0	0	0	0	0	0	0	0	0	0	1	0	0	0	1
Tuero	Minardi	0	0	0	0	0	0	0	0	0	0	0	0	0	0	0	0	0
Verstappen	Stewart	0	0	0	0	0	0	0	0	0	0	0	0	0	0	0	0	0
Villeneuve	Williams	0	0	0	0	0	2	2	0	2	3	4	4	0	1	3	0	21
Wurz	Benetton	2	3	3	2	1	0	0	0	3	0	0	0	3	0	0	0	17

DRIVERS – LAPS COMPLETED – RACE BY RACE '98

		As	Br	Ar	SM	Sp	Mo	Ca	Fr	Br	At	Ge	Hu	Be	Ita	Lx	Jp	Total
Alesi	Sauber	41	71	72	61	63	72	0	70	53	21	45	76	44	53	66	51	859
Barrichello	Stewart	0	56	70	0	64	11	69	69	39	8	27	54	0	52	65	25	609
Coulthard	McLaren	58	72	72	62	65	18	68	70	37	71	45	77	39	16	67	51	837
Diniz	Arrows	2	26	13	18	20	77	68	69	45	3	2	74	44	10	6	2	479
Fisichella	Benetton	43	71	72	17	28	78	69	68	59	21	45	76	26	52	67	51	845
Frentzen	Williams	57	71	71	62	63	9	20	71	15	16	45	77	44	52	67	51	788
Hakkinen	McLaren	58	72	72	17	65	78	0	70	60	71	45	76	0	53	67	51	856
Herbert	Sauber	57	67	46	12	64	77	18	70	27	70	37	76	0	12	37	50	720
Hill	Jordan	57	70	71	57	46	76	42	19	13	71	45	76	44	53	66	51	858
Irvine	Ferrari	57	71	72	62	28	78	69	71	60	71	45	13	25	53	67	51	893
Magnussen	Stewart	1	70	17	8	63	30	68	–	–	–	–	–	–	–	–	–	257
Nakano	Minardi	57	3	69	27	63	76	68	65	58	70	36	74	39	15	65	50	774
Panis	Prost	57	63	65	56	60	49	39	69	40	0	44	74	0	15	36	0	746
Rosset	Tyrrell	25	52	68	48	0	18	68	16	29	69	0	0	0	51	18	0	462
Salo	Arrows	23	18	18	60	21	78	18	69	27	1	44	18	0	32	65	14	506
Schumacher, M.	Ferrari	5	72	72	62	65	76	69	71	60	71	45	77	25	53	67	31	921
Schumacher, R.	Jordan	1	0	22	60	63	44	0	68	59	71	45	76	44	53	53	13	672
Takagi	Tyrrell	1	19	70	40	63	76	0	60	56	60	44	14	10	52	65	28	658
Trulli	Prost	26	17	70	34	63	56	0	55	37	70	44	28	42	50	6	48	646
Tuero	Minardi	22	44	63	60	63	0	53	41	29	30	43	13	17	51	56	28	613
Verstappen	Stewart	–	–	–	–	–	–	–	69	38	51	24	74	8	39	65	21	389
Villeneuve	Williams	57	71	52	62	64	77	63	71	59	71	45	77	16	37	66	51	939
Wurz	Benetton	57	72	72	17	65	42	69	70	59	70	45	69	0	24	67	50	848

CONSTRUCTORS POINTS WON – RACE BY RACE '98

	As	Br	Ar	SM	Sp	Mo	Ca	Fr	Br	At	Ge	Hu	Be	It	Lx	Jp	Tot	Tyres
Arrows	0	0	3	0	0	4	0	0	0	0	0	0	2	0	0	0	6	Bridgestone
Benetton	0	4	3	0	3	6	9	2	5	0	2	0	0	0	1	0	33	Bridgestone
Ferrari	3	4	14	10	4	4	14	16	14	7	2	10	0	16	9	6	133	Goodyear
Jordan	0	0	0	0	0	0	0	0	1	2	4	3	16	5	0	3	34	Goodyear
McLaren	16	16	7	10	16	10	0	5	6	16	16	7	0	3	14	14	156	Bridgestone
Minardi	0	0	0	0	0	0	0	0	0	0	0	0	1	0	0	0	0	Bridgestone
Prost	0	0	0	0	0	0	0	0	0	0	0	0	0	0	0	0	1	Bridgestone
Sauber	1	0	2	1	0	0	3	0	0	0	0	0	4	2	0	0	10	Goodyear
Stewart	0	0	0	0	0	0	0	0	0	0	0	0	0	0	0	0	5	Bridgestone
Tyrrell	0	0	0	0	0	0	0	0	0	0	0	0	0	0	0	0	0	Goodyear
Williams	6	2	0	5	1	2	0	3	0	1	4	6	3	0	2	3	38	Goodyear

49

CONSTRUCTORS TOTAL LAPS – RACE BY RACE '98

	As	Br	Ar	SM	Sp	Mo	Ca	Fr	Br	At	Ge	Hu	Be	It	Lx	Jp	Tot	%
Arrows	25	44	31	78	41	155	86	138	72	4	46	92	44	42	71	16	985	48.52
Benetton	100	143	144	34	93	120	138	140	118	91	90	145	26	76	134	101	1693	83.40
Ferrari	62	143	144	124	93	154	138	142	120	142	90	90	50	106	134	82	1814	89.36
Jordan	58	70	93	117	109	120	42	87	72	142	90	153	88	106	119	64	1530	75.37
McLaren	116	144	144	79	130	95	18	141	97	142	90	153	39	69	134	102	1693	83.40
Minardi	30	47	132	87	126	76	121	106	87	100	79	87	56	64	121	68	1387	68.33
Prost	83	80	135	90	123	105	39	124	77	70	88	102	42	65	71	98	1392	68.57
Sauber	98	138	118	73	127	149	18	77	80	128	82	152	44	91	103	101	1579	77.78
Stewart	1	126	87	8	127	41	137	138	77	59	51	128	8	91	130	46	1255	61.82
Tyrrell	26	71	138	88	63	76	68	76	85	69	44	74	10	103	101	28	1120	55.17
Williams	114	142	123	124	127	86	83	139	74	87	90	154	60	89	133	102	1727	85.07

Winning Margins

Biggest win margin: 27.977 seconds – Italian Grand Prix
Narrowest win margin: 0.426 seconds – German Grand Prix

GP	Ist Place	2nd Place	Margin
Australian	M.Hakkinen (McLaren)	D.Coulthard (McLaren)	0.702
Brazilian	M.Hakkinen (McLaren)	D.Coulthard (McLaren)	1.102
Argentinian	M.Schumacher (Ferrari)	M.Hakkinen (Ferrari)	22.998
San Marino	D.Coulthard (McLaren)	M.Schumacher (Ferrari)	4.554
Spanish	M.Hakkinen (McLaren)	D.Coulthard (McLaren)	9.439
Monaco	M.Hakkinen (McLaren)	G.Fisichella (Benetton)	11.475
Canadian	M.Schumacher (Ferrari)	G.Fisichella (Benetton)	16.716
French	M.Schumacher (Ferrari)	E.Irvine (Ferrari)	19.575
British	M.Schumacher (Ferrari)	M.Hakkinen (McLaren)	12.465
Austrian	M.Hakkinen (McLaren)	D.Coulthard (McLaren)	5.289
German	M.Hakkinen (McLaren)	D.Coulthard (McLaren)	0.426
Hungarian	M.Schumacher (Ferrari)	D.Coulthard (McLaren)	9.433
Belgian	D.Hill (Jordan)	R.Schumacher (Jordan)	0.932
Italian	M.Schumacher (Ferrari)	E.Irvine (Ferrari)	37.977
Luxembourg	M.Hakkinen (McLaren)	M.Schumacher (Ferrari)	2.211
Japanese	M.Hakkinen (McLaren)	E.Irvine (Ferrari)	6.491

Team Match-ups

Team	Driver	Driver	Race		Qualify	
Arrows	Salo	Diniz	5	3	11	5
Benetton	Fisichella	Wurz	7	7	10	6
Ferrari	M.Schumacher	Irvine	11	4	15	1
Jordan	Hill	R.Schumacher	9	6	6	10
McLaren	Hakkinen	Coulthard	12	3	13	3
Minardi	Nakano	Tuero	10	3	11	5
Prost	Panis	Trulli	5	6	7	9
Sauber	Alesi	Herbert	10	4	10	6
Stewart	Barrichello	Magnussen	3	1	7	0
	Barrichello	Verstappen	3	1	8	1
Tyrrell	Takagi	Rosset	9	2	14	2
Williams	Villeneuve	Frentzen	9	7	9	7

FASTEST LAPS BY RACE 1998

Grand Prix	Fin	Driver	Team	Laps	Time	G	T
1 Australian	1	M.Hakkinen	McLaren	58	1:31.649	1	B
2 Brazilian	1	M.Hakkinen	McLaren	72	1:19.337	1	B
3 Argentinian	4	A.Wurz	Benetton	72	1:28.178	8	B
4 San Marino	2	M.Schumacher	Ferrari	62	1:29.345	3	G
5 Spanish	1	M.Hakkinen	McLaren	65	1:24.275	1	B
6 Monaco	1	M.Hakkinen	McLaren	78	1:22.948	1	B
7 Canadian	1	M.Schumacher	Ferrari	69	1:19.379	3	G
8 French	6	D.Coulthard	McLaren	70	1:17.523	3	B
9 British	1	M.Schumacher	Ferrari	60	1:35.704	2	G
10 Austrian	2	D.Coulthard	McLaren	71	1:12.878	14	B
11 German	2	D.Coulthard	McLaren	45	1:46.116	2	B
12 Hungarian	1	M.Schumacher	Ferrari	77	1:19.286	3	G
13 Belgian	r	M.Schumacher	Ferrari	25	2:03.766	4	G
14 Italian	4	M.Hakkinen	McLaren	53	1:25.139	3	B
15 Luxembourg	1	M.Hakkinen	McLaren	67	1:20.450	3	B
16 Japanese	r	M.Schumacher	Ferrari	31	1:40.190	1	G

G=Grid, T=Tyres (B for Bridgestone, G for Goodyear)

DRIVER LAP LEADERS 1998

	Driver	Team	Miles Led	Laps Led
1	M.Hakkinen	McLaren	1,693.210	576
2	M.Schumacher	Ferrari	782.708	268
3	D.Coulthard	McLaren	373.317	120
4	D.Hill	Jordan	113.230	26
5	G.Fisichella	Benetton	66.315	24
6	E.Irvine	Ferrari	2.656	1

TEAM LAP LEADERS 1998

	Team	Driver(s)	Miles Led	Laps Led
1	McLaren	Hakkinen, Coulthard	2066.527	696
2	Ferrari	Schumacher, Irvine	785.364	269
3	Jordan	Hill	113.230	26
4	Benetton	Fisichella	66.315	24

1998 DRIVERS' ALL-TIME RECORDS

Driver	No	WC	1	2	3	4	5	6	P	F	TP	B
Alesi, J.	151	0	1	16	15	11	14	7	2	4	234	1
Barrichello, R.	97	0	0	1	1	8	4	4	1	1	54	2
Coulthard, D.	74	0	4	14	6	4	3	6	8	8	173	1
Diniz, P.	66	0	0	0	0	0	2	3	0	0	7	5
Fisichella, G.	41	0	0	3	1	3	1	3	1	0	36	2
Frentzen, H-H.	81	0	1	2	6	6	8	8	1	6	88	1
Hakkinen, M.	112	1	9	5	12	8	8	6	10	7	217	1
Herbert, J.	129	0	2	1	3	10	5	5	0	1	83	1
Hill, D.	100	1	22	15	5	6	1	3	20	19	353	1
Irvine, E.	81	0	0	3	11	7	5	3	0	0	99	2
Magnussen, J.	25	0	0	0	0	0	0	1	0	0	1	6
Nakano, S.	31	0	0	0	0	0	2	0	0	0	2	6
Panis, O.	75	0	1	3	1	3	4	5	0	0	54	1
Rosset, R.	28	0	0	0	0	0	0	0	0	0	0	8
Salo, M.	68	0	0	0	0	1	5	2	0	0	12	4
Schumacher, M.	118	2	33	19	13	6	4	4	20	35	526	1
Schumacher, R.	33	0	0	1	2	0	5	3	0	0	27	2
Trulli, J.	30	0	0	0	0	1	0	1	0	0	4	4
Tuero, E.	18	0	0	0	0	0	0	0	0	0	0	8
Verstappen, J.	57	0	0	0	2	0	1	1	0	0	11	3
Villeneuve, J.	49	1	11	5	5	3	4	3	13	9	180	1
Wurz, A.	19	0	0	0	1	5	1	0	0	1	21	3

*No=Number of Grands Prix; WC=Number of World Championship
titles; 1, 2, etc.=Number of times finished in this position; P=Number of
Poles; F=Number of Fastest Laps; TP=Total number of World
Championship Points won to date; B=Best position achieved – this is
included primarily for those drivers who have not had a top six finish.*

1998 DRIVERS BY COMPLETION %

Driver	St	Cm	Rt	Fq	Hp	Pts	Psn	Comp%
Hakkinen, M.	16	13	3	0	1	100	1/22	81.25
Schumacher, M.	16	13	3	0	1	86	2/22	81.25
Irvine, E.	16	13	3	0	2	47	4/22	81.25
Villeneuve, J.	16	13	3	0	3	21	5/22	81.25
Coulthard, D.	16	12	4	0	1	56	3/22	75.00
Frentzen, H-H.	16	12	4	0	3	17	7/22	75.00
Wurz, A.	16	12	4	0	4	17	7/22	75.00
Alesi, J.	16	12	4	0	3	9	11/22	75.00
Hill, D.	16	11	5	0	1	20	6/22	68.75
Fisichella, G.	16	11	5	0	2	16	9/22	68.75
Nakano, S.	16	10	6	0	8	0	–	62.50
Schumacher, R.	16	9	7	0	2	14	10/22	56.25
Panis, O.	16	8	8	0	9	0	16/22	50.00
Takagi, T.	16	8	8	0	9	0	–	50.00
Herbert, J.	16	7	9	0	6	1	15/22	43.75
Trulli, J.	16	7	9	0	6	1	15/22	43.75
Magnussen, J.	7	3	4	0	6	1	15/22	42.86
Barrichello, R.	16	6	10	0	5	4	12/22	37.50
Rosset, R.	12	4	8	4	12	0	–	33.33
Verstappen, J.	9	3	6	0	12	0	–	33.33
Diniz, P.	16	5	11	0	4	3	13/22	31.25
Salo, M.	16	5	11	0	4	3	13/22	31.25
Tuero, E.	16	5	11	0	8	0	–	31.25

St=Number of starts; Cm=Races completed; Rt=Races retired in; Fq=Races failed to qualify for (ie, outside 107% rule); Hp=Highest position achieved in a race; Pts=Drivers' World Championship points; Psn=Position in DWC table; Comp%=Race completion percentage.

1998 TEAMS BY COMPLETION %

Team	St	Cm	Rt	Fq	Hp	Pts	Psn	Comp%
Ferrari	32	26	6	0	1	133	2/11	81.25
McLaren Mercedes	32	25	7	0	1	156	1/11	78.13
Williams Mecachrome	32	25	7	0	3	38	3/11	78.13
Benetton Playlife	32	23	9	0	2	33	5/11	71.88
Jordan Mugen Honda	32	20	12	0	1	34	4/11	62.50

Team	St	Cm	Rt	fq	Hp	Pts	Psn	Comp%
Minardi Ford	32	20	8	0	8	0	–	62.50
Sauber Petronas	32	19	13	0	3	10	6/11	59.38
Prost Peugeot	32	15	17	0	6	1	9/11	46.88
Tyrrell Ford	28	12	16	4	9	0	–	41.67
Stewart Ford	32	12	20	0	5	5	6/11	37.90
Arrows	32	10	22	0	4	6	7/11	31.25

St=Number of starts; Cm=Races completed; Rt=Races retired in; Fq=Races failed to qualify for (ie, outside 107% rule); Hp=Highest position achieved in a race; Pts=Constructors' World Championship points; Psn=Position in CWC table; Comp%=Race completion percentage.

5-YEAR DRIVER POINTS RECORDS

Driver	1994	1995	1996	1997	1998
Alesi, J.	24	42	47	36	9
Barrichello, R.	19	11	14	6	4
Coulthard, D.	14	49	18	36	56
Diniz, P.	–	0	0	2	3
Fisichella, G.	–	–	0	20	16
Frentzen, H-H.	7	15	0	42	17
Hakkinen, M.	26	17	31	27	100
Herbert, J.	–	45	0	15	1
Hill, D.	91	69	97	7	20
Irvine, E.	6	10	11	24	47
Magnussen, J.	–	0	–	0	1
Nakano, S.	–	–	–	2	0
Panis, O.	9	16	13	16	0
Rosset, R.	–	–	0	0	0
Salo, M.	–	5	0	2	3
Schumacher, M.	92	102	59	78	86
Schumacher, R.	–	–	–	13	14
Takagi, T.	–	–	–	–	0
Trulli, J.	–	–	–	3	1
Tuero, E.	–	–	–	–	0
Verstappen, J.	10	–	1	0	0
Villeneuve, J.	–	–	78	81	21
Wurz, A.	–	–	–	4	17

– indicates driver did not participate.

DRIVERS' WORLD CHAMPIONSHIP
WINNERS 1950-1998

R=Races; W=Wins; P=Poles; F=Fastest laps

Year	Driver	Age	Ctry	Car	R	W	P	F
1950	Giuseppe Farina	44	Ita	Alfa Romeo	7	3	2	3
1951	Juan-Manuel Fangio	40	Arg	Alfa Romeo	8	3	4	5
1952	Alberto Ascari	34	Ita	Ferrari	8	6	5	5
1953	Alberto Ascari	35	Italy	Ferrari	9	5	6	4
1954	Juan-Manuel Fangio	43	Arg	Merc/Maserati	9	6	5	3
1955	Juan-Manuel Fangio	44	Arg	Mercedes	7	4	3	3
1956	Juan-Manuel Fangio	45	Arg	Lancia/Ferrari	8	3	5	3
1957	Juan-Manuel Fangio	46	Arg	Maserati	8	4	4	2
1958	Mike Hawthorn	29	GB	Ferrari	11	1	4	5
1959	Jack Brabham	33	Aus	Cooper	9	2	1	1
1960	Jack Brabham	34	Aus	Cooper	10	5	3	3
1961	Phil Hill	34	USA	Ferrari	8	2	5	2
1962	Graham Hill	33	GB	BRM	9	4	1	3
1963	Jim Clark	27	GB	Lotus	10	7	7	6
1964	John Surtees	30	GB	Ferrari	10	2	2	2
1965	Jim Clark	29	GB	Lotus	10	6	6	6
1966	Jack Brabham	40	Aus	Brabham	9	4	3	1
1967	Denis Hulme	31	NZ	Brabham	11	2	0	2
1968	Graham Hill	39	GB	Lotus	12	3	2	0
✦ 1969	Jackie Stewart	30	GB	Matra	11	6	2	5
1970	Jochen Rindt	28	Aut	Lotus	13	5	3	1
✦ 1971	Jackie Stewart	32	GB	Tyrrell	11	6	6	3
1972	Emerson Fittipaldi	26	Bra	Lotus	12	5	3	1
✦ 1973	Jackie Stewart	34	Bra	Tyrrell	15	5	3	1
1974	Emerson Fittipaldi	28	Bra	McLaren	15	3	2	0
1975	Niki Lauda	26	Aut	Ferrari	14	5	9	2
1976	James Hunt	29	GB	McLaren	16	6	8	2
1977	Niki Lauda	28	Aut	Ferrari	17	3	2	3
1978	Mario Andretti	38	USA	Lotus	16	6	8	3
1979	Jody Scheckter	29	USA	Ferrari	15	3	1	1
1980	Alan Jones	34	Aus	Williams	14	5	3	5
1981	Nelson Piquet	29	Bra	Brabham	15	3	4	1
1982	Keke Rosberg	34	Fin	Williams	16	1	1	0
1983	Nelson Piquet	31	Bra	Brabham	15	3	1	4
1984	Niki Lauda	35	Aut	McLaren	16	5	0	5
1985	Alain Prost	30	Fra	McLaren	16	5	2	5

Year	Driver	Age	Ctry	Car	R	W	P	F
1986	Alain Prost	31	Fra	McLaren	16	4	1	2
1987	Nelson Piquet	35	Bra	Williams	16	3	4	4
1988	Ayrton Senna	28	Bra	McLaren	16	8	13	3
1989	Alain Prost	34	Fra	McLaren	16	4	2	5
1990	Ayrton Senna	30	Bra	McLaren	16	6	10	2
1991	Ayrton Senna	31	Bra	McLaren	16	7	8	2
1992	Nigel Mansell	39	GB	Williams	16	9	14	8
1993	Alain Prost	38	Fra	Williams	16	7	13	6
1994	Michael Schumacher	25	Ger	Benetton	16	8	6	8
1995	Michael Schumacher	26	Ger	Benetton	17	9	4	8
1996	Damon Hill	36	GB	Williams	16	8	9	5
1997	Jacques Villeneuve	26	Can	Williams	17	7	11	3
1998	Mika Hakkinen	30	Fin	McLaren	16	9	10	7

DRIVERS' WORLD CHAMPIONSHIP
WINS BY NUMBER 1950-98

Titles	Driver	Country	Year
5	Juan-Manuel Fangio	Argentina	1951, 1954, 1955, 1956, 1957
4	Alain Prost	France	1985, 1986, 1989, 1993
3	Jack Brabham	Australia	1959, 1960, 1966
3	Jackie Stewart	Great Britain	1969, 1971, 1973
3	Niki Lauda	Austria	1975, 1977, 1984
3	Nelson Piquet	Brazil	1981, 1983, 1987
3	Ayrton Senna	Brazil	1988, 1990, 1991
2	Alberto Ascari	Italy	1952, 1953
2	Graham Hill	Great Britain	1962, 1968
2	Jim Clark	Great Britain	1963, 1965
2	Emerson Fittipaldi	Brazil	1972, 1974
2	Michael Schumacher	Germany	1994, 1995
1	Giuseppe Farina	Italy	1950
1	Mike Hawthorn	Great Britain	1958
1	Phil Hill	USA	1961
1	John Surtees	Great Britain	1964
1	Denis Hulme	New Zealand	1967
1	Jochen Rindt	Austria	1970
1	James Hunt	Great Britain	1976
1	Mario Andretti	USA	1978

Titles	Driver	Country	Year
1	Jody Scheckter	USA	1979
1	Alan Jones	Australia	1980
1	Keke Rosberg	Finland	1982
1	Nigel Mansell	Great Britain	1992
1	Damon Hill	Great Britain	1996
1	Jacques Villeneuve	Canada	1997
1	Mika Hakkinen	Finland	1998

WORLD CHAMPIONSHIP DRIVERS WITH 100 POINTS OR MORE

Driver	Points	Driver	Points
Prost	768.5	Moss	186.5
Senna	610	Alboreto	185.5
Schumacher, M.	526	Arnoux	181
Piquet	481.5	Ickx	181
Mansell	480	Andretti	180
Lauda	420.5	Surtees	180
Berger	385	Villeneuve, J.	180
Stewart	359	Hunt	179
Hill, D.	353	Coulthard	173
Reutemann	298	Watson	169
E. Fittipaldi	281	Rosberg	159.5
Patrese	281	Depailler	139
G. Hill	270	Gurney	133
Clark	255	Boutsen	132
Brabham, J.	253	De Angelis	122
Scheckter	246	Farina	116.3
Hulme	248	Hawthorn	112.5
Fangio	245	Ascari	107.5
Alesi	234	Rindt	107
Laffite	228	Ginther	107
Hakkinen	217	Tambay	103
Regazzoni	209	Villeneuve, G.	101
Peterson	206	Pironi	101
Jones	199		
McLaren	188.5		

DRIVERS WITH FIVE OR MORE GRAND PRIX WINS

Wins	Driver
51	Alain Prost (France)
41	Ayrton Senna (Brazil)
33	Michael Schumacher (Germany)
31	Nigel Mansell (Great Britain)
27	Jackie Stewart (Great Britain),
25	Jim Clark (Great Britain), Niki Lauda (Austria)
24	Juan-Manuel Fangio (Italy)
23	Nelson Piquet (Brazil)
22	Damon Hill (Great Britain)
16	Stirling Moss (Great Britain)
14	Jack Brabham (Australia), Emerson Fittipaldi (Brazil), Graham Hill (Great Britain)
13	Alberto Ascari (Italy)
12	Mario Andretti (USA), Alan Jones (Australia), Carlos Reutemann (Argentina)
11	Jacques Villeneuve (Canada)
10	James Hunt (Great Britain), Ronnie Peterson (Switzerland), Jody Scheckter (USA), Gerhard Berger (Austria)
9	Mika Hakkinen (Finland)
8	Denis Hulme (New Zealand), Jacky Ickx (Belgium)
7	Rene Arnoux (France)
6	Tony Brooks (Great Britain), Jacques Laffite (France), Riccardo Patrese (Italy), Jochen Rindt (Austria), John Surtees (Great Britain), Gilles Villeneuve (Canada)
5	Michele Alboreto (Italy), Giuseppe Farina (Italy), Clay Regazzoni (Switzerland), Keke Rosberg (Finland), John Watson (Great Britain)

DRIVERS WITH FIVE OR MORE POLE POSITIONS

Poles	Driver
65	Ayrton Senna (Brazil)
33	Jim Clark (Great Britain), Alain Prost (France)
32	Nigel Mansell (Great Britain)
28	Juan-Manuel Fangio (Italy)

24	Niki Lauda (Austria), Nelson Piquet (Brazil)
20	Damon Hill (Great Britain), Michael Schumacher (Germany)
18	Mario Andretti (USA), Rene Arnoux (France)
17	Jackie Stewart (Great Britain)
16	Stirling Moss (Great Britain)
14	Giuseppe Farina (Italy), James Hunt (Great Britain), Ronnie Peterson (Switzerland)
13	Jack Brabham (Australia), Graham Hill (Great Britain), Jacky Ickx (Belgium), Jacques Villeneuve (Canada)
12	Gerhard Berger (Austria)
10	Jochen Rindt (Austria), Mika Hakkinen (Finland)
8	Riccardo Patrese (Italy), John Surtees (Great Britain), David Coulthard (Great Britain)
7	Jacques Laffite (France)
6	Emerson Fittipaldi (Brazil), Phil Hill (USA), Jean-Pierre Labouille (France), Alan Jones (Australia), Carlos Reutemann (Argentina)
5	Chris Amon (New Zealand), Giuseppe Farina (Italy), Clay Regazzoni (Switzerland), Keke Rosberg (Finland), Patrick Tambay (France)

DRIVERS WITH FIVE OR MORE FASTEST LAPS

No	Driver
41	Alain Prost (France)
35	Michael Schumacher (Germany)
30	Nigel Mansell (Great Britain)
28	Jim Clark (Great Britain)
25	Niki Lauda (Austria)
23	Juan-Manuel Fangio (Italy), Nelson Piquet (Brazil)
20	Stirling Moss (Great Britain), Gerhard Berger (Austria)
19	Ayrton Senna (Brazil), Damon Hill (Great Britain)
15	Clay Regazzoni (Switzerland), Jackie Stewart (Great Britain)
14	Jacky Ickx (Belgium)
13	Alan Jones (Australia), Riccardo Patrese (Italy)
12	Rene Arnoux (France)
11	Alberto Ascari (Italy), John Surtees (Great Britain)
10	Mario Andretti (USA), Jack Brabham (Australia), Graham Hill (Great Britain)

9		Denis Hulme (New Zealand), Ronnie Peterson (USA), Jacques Villeneuve (Canada)	
8		James Hunt (Great Britain), David Coulthard (Great Britain)	
7		Jacques Laffite (France), Gilles Villeneuve (Canada), Mika Hakkinen (Finland)	
6		Giuseppe Farina (Italy), Jose Gonzalez (Argentina), Dan Gurney (USA), Mike Hawthorn (Great Britain), Phil Hill (USA), Didier Pironi (France), Jody Scheckter (USA), Heinz-Harald Frentzen (Germany)	
5		Carlos Pace (Brazil), John Watson (Great Britain)	

DRIVERS WITH MORE THAN FIVE POLE POSITIONS IN A SEASON

Poles	Races	Driver	Year(s)
14	16	Mansell	1992
13	16/16	Senna	1988 and 1989
	16	Prost	1993
10	16	Senna	1990
	17	Villeneuve, J.	1997
9	15/14	Lauda	1974 and 1975
	15	Peterson	1973
	16	Piquet	1984
	16	Hill, Damon	1996
	16	Hakkinen	1998
8	16/16	Senna	1986 and 1991
	16	Hunt	1976
	16	Andretti	1978
	16	Mansell	1987
7	10	Clark	1963
	17	Andretti	1977
	16	Senna	1985
	17	Hill, Damon	1995
6	9/10/11	Clark	1962, 1965 and 1967
	9	Ascari	1953
	11	Stewart	1971
	17	Hunt	1977
	16	Schumacher, M.	1994

DRIVERS WITH THREE OR MORE SUCCESSIVE GRAND PRIX WINS

Wins	Driver	Year	Grand Prix
9	Ascari	1952/53	Bel, Fra, GB, Ger, Hol, Ita, Arg, Hol, Bel
5	Brabham	1960	Hol, Bel, Fra, GB, Por
	Clark	1965	Bel, Fra, GB, Hol, Ger
	Mansell	1992	SA, Mex, Bra, Esp, San
4	Senna	1988	GB, Ger, Hon, Bel
		1991	USA, Bra, San, Mon
	Fangio	1953/54	Ita/Arg, Bel, Fra
	Clark	1963	Bel, Hol, Fra, GB
	Brabham	1966	Fra, GB, Hol, Ger
	Rindt	1970	Hol, Fra, GB, Ger
	Prost	1993	Can, Fra, GB, Ger
	M. Schumacher	1994	Bra, Pac, San, Mon
3	Fangio	1954	Ger, Sui, Ita
		1957	Arg, Mon, Fra
	Stewart	1969	Hol, Fra, GB
		1971	Fra, GB, Ger
	Lauda	1975	Mon, Bel, Swe
		1975/76	USA/Bra, SA
	Jones	1979	Ger, Aut, Hol
		1980/81	Can, USAE/USAW
	Prost	1984/85	Eur, Por/Bra
		1990	Mex, Fra, GB
	Mansell	1991	Fra, GB, Ger
		1992	Fra, GB, Ger
	Moss	1957/58	Pes, Ita/Arg
	Clark	1967/68	USA, Mex/SA
	Senna	1989	San, Mon, Mex
	D. Hill	1993	Hun, Bel, Ita
		1994	Bel, Ita, Por
		1996	Aus, Bra, Arg
	M. Schumacher	1995	Eur, Pac, Jap
		1998	Can, Fra, GB

DRIVERS WHO HAVE CONTESTED 100 GRANDS PRIX OR MORE

No	Driver
256	Riccardo Patrese (Italy)
210	Gerhard Berger (Austria)
208	Andrea de Cesaris (Italy)
204	Nelson Piquet (Brazil)
199	Alain Prost (France)
194	Michele Alboreto (Italy)
187	Nigel Mansell (GB)
176	Graham Hill (GB), Jacques Laffite (France)
171	Niki Lauda (Austria)
163	Thierry Boutsen (Belgium)
161	Ayrton Senna (Brazil)
158	Martin Brundle (GB)
152	John Watson (GB)
151	Jean Alesi (France)
149	Rene Arnoux (France)
147	Derek Warwick (GB)
146	Carlos Reutemann (Argentina)
144	Emerson Fittipaldi (Brazil)
135	Jean-Pierre Jarier (France)
132	Eddie Cheever (USA), Clay Regazzoni (Switzerland)
129	Johnny Herbert (GB)
128	Mario Andretti (USA)
126	Jack Brabham (Australia)
123	Ronnie Peterson (USA)
119	Pierluigi Martini (Italy)
118	Michael Schumacher (Germany)
116	Jacky Ickx (Belgium), Alan Jones (Australia)
112	Denis Hulme (NZ), Jody Scheckter (USA), Mika Hakkinen (Finland)
111	John Surtees (GB)
109	Philippe Alliot (France)
108	Elio de Angelis (Italy)
105	Jochen Mass (Germany)
102	Joakim Bonnier (Switzerland)
101	Bruce McLaren (NZ)
100	Damon Hill (GB)

WORLD CHAMPIONSHIP LAST RACE DECIDERS

Year	GP	Circuit	Drivers
1950	Italian	Monza	Farina (30), Fangio (27), Fagioli (24)
1951	Spanish	Pedralbes	Fangio (31), Ascari (25)
1956	Italian	Monza	Fangio (30), Collins (25)*
1958	Morocco	Casablanca	Hawthorn (42), Moss (41)
1959	USA	Sebring	Brabham (31), Brooks (27), Moss (25.5)

1962	S. African	E. London	G. Hill (42), Clark (30)
1964	Mexican	Mexico City	Surtees (40), G. Hill (39), Clark (32)
1967	Mexican	Mexico City	Hulme (51), Brabham (46)
1968	Mexican	Mexico City	G. Hill (48), Stewart (36), Hulme (33)
1974	USA	Watkins Glen	E. Fittipaldi (55), Regazzoni (52), Scheckter (45)
1976	Japanese	Mount Fuji	Hunt (69), Lauda (68)
1981	USA	Las Vegas	Piquet (50), Reutemann (49), Laffite (46)
1982	USA	Las Vegas	Rosberg (44), Watson (39)†
1983	S. African	Kyalami	Piquet (59), Prost (57), Arnoux (49)
1984	Portuguese	Estoril	Lauda (72), Prost (71.5)
1986	Australian	Adelaide	Prost (72), Mansell (70), Piquet (69)
1994	Australian	Adelaide	M. Schumacher (92), D. Hill (91)
1996	Japanese	Suzuka	D. Hill (97), J. Villeneuve (78)
1997	European	Jerez	J. Villeneuve (81), M. Schumacher (78)
1998	Japanese	Suzuka	M. Hakkinen (90), M. Schumacher (86)

* *Finished third in Championship after Moss.* † *Finished joint second with Pironi. Numbers in brackets are final points total.*

DRIVERS TO WIN THEIR NATIONAL GRAND PRIX

Wins	Driver	Nat	Year(s)
6	Prost	French	1981, 1983, 1988, 1989, 1990, 1993
5	Clark	British	1962, 1963, 1964, 1965, 1967
4	Fangio	Argentine	1954, 1955, 1956, 1957
	Mansell	British	1986, 1987, 1991, 1992
2	Ascari	Italian	1951, 1952
	Moss	British	1955, 1957
	Stewart	British	1969, 1971
	Fittipaldi, E.	Brazilian	1973, 1974
	Piquet	Brazilian	1983, 1986
	Senna	Brazilian	1991, 1993
1	Farina	Italian	1950
	Collins	British	1958
	Scarfiotti	Italian	1966
	Pace	Brazilian	1975
	Scheckter	S. African	1975
	Andretti	American	1977
	Hunt	British	1977
	Villeneuve, G.	Canadian	1978
	Jabouille	French	1979
	Watson	British	1981
	Arnoux	French	1982
	Lauda	Austrian	1984
	Hill, Damon	British	1994
	Herbert	British	1995
	Schumacher, M.	German	1995

GRANDS PRIX WITH DRIVER FATALITIES

Year	GP	Venue	Driver	Car	During
1954	Germany	Nurburgring	O. Marimon	Maserati	P
1955	Indianapolis	Indianapolis	B. Vukovich		R
1958	France	Reims	L. Musso	Ferrari	R
1958	Germany	Nurburgring	P. Collins	Ferrari	R
1958	Morocco	Casablanca	S. Lewis-Evans	Vanwall	R
1959	Indianapolis	Indianapolis	J. Unser		R
			B. Cortner		R
1960	Belgium	Spa-Fran.	C. Bristow	Cooper	R
			A. Stacey	Lotus	R
1961	Italy	Monza	Von Trips	Ferrari	R
1964	Germany	Nurburgring	C. de Beaufort	Porsche	P
1966	Germany	Nurburgring	J. Taylor	Brabham	R
1967	Monaco	Monaco	L. Bandini	Ferrari	†R
1968	France	Rouen	J. Schlesser	Honda	R
1969	Germany	Nurburgring	G. Mitter		P
1970	Holland	Zandvoort	P. Courage	De Tomaso	R
1970	Italy	Monza	J. Rindt	Lotus	P
1973	Holland	Zandvoort	R. Williamson	March	R
1973	USA	Watkins Glen	F. Cevert	Tyrrell	P
1974	USA	Watkins Glen	H. Koinigg	Surtees	R
1975	Austria	Osterreichring	M. Donohue	M-Penske	P
1977	South Africa	Kyalami	T. Pryce	Shadow	R
1978	Italy	Monza	R. Peterson	Lotus	*R
1982	Belgium	Zolder	G. Villeneuve	Ferrari	P
1982	Canada	Montreal	R. Paletti	Osella Ford	R
1994	San Marino	Imola	R. Ratzenberger	Simtek	P
			A. Senna	Williams	R

P=Practice, R=Race
† Died three days after race from burns.
* Died the next day from injuries received during start of race.

CONSTRUCTORS' CUP WINNERS

Year	Team	Year	Team	Year	Team
1958	Vanwall	1973	Lotus	1988	McLaren
1959	Cooper	1974	McLaren	1989	McLaren
1960	Cooper	1975	Ferrari	1990	McLaren
1961	Ferrari	1976	Ferrari	1991	McLaren
1962	BRM	1977	Ferrari	1992	Williams
1963	Lotus	1978	Lotus	1993	Williams
1964	Ferrari	1979	Ferrari	1994	Williams
1965	Lotus	1980	Williams	1995	Benetton
1966	Brabham	1981	Williams	1996	Williams
1967	Brabham	1982	Ferrari	1997	Williams
1968	Lotus	1983	Ferrari	1998	McLaren
1969	Matra	1984	McLaren		
1970	Lotus	1985	McLaren		
1971	Tyrrell	1986	Williams		
1972	Lotus	1987	Williams		

CONSTRUCTORS' CUP BY CAR

Titles	Car	Year(s)
9	Williams	1980, 1981, 1986, 1987, 1992, 1993, 1994, 1996, 1997
8	Ferrari	1961, 1964, 1975, 1976, 1977, 1979, 1982, 1983
8	McLaren	1974, 1984, 1985, 1988, 1989, 1990, 1991, 1998
7	Lotus	1963, 1965, 1968, 1970, 1972, 1973, 1978
2	Cooper	1959, 1960
2	Brabham	1966, 1967
1	Vanwall	1958
1	BRM	1962
1	Matra	1969
1	Tyrrell	1971
1	Benetton	1995

GRAND PRIX WINS PER CAR TYPE

Wins	Car Type	Wins	Car Type	Wins	Car Type
119	Ferrari	15	Renault	2	Honda
116	McLaren	10	Alfa Romeo	1	Eagle,
103	Williams	9	Maserati,		Hesketh,
79	Lotus		Matra,		Jordan,
35	Brabham		Mercedes,		Penske,
27	Benetton		Vanwall,		Porsche,
23	Tyrrell		Ligier		Shadow
17	BRM	3	March,		
16	Cooper		Wolf		

GRANDS PRIX PARTICIPATED PER CAR TYPE

GP	Car Type	GP	Car Type	GP	Car Type
603	Ferrari	117	Surtees	33	Porsche
490	Lotus	112	Alfa Romeo		Stewart
476	McLaren	104	Fittipaldi,	30	Penske
418	Tyrrell		Shadow	28	Vanwall
394	Brabham	99	ATS	25	Eagle
359	Prost (Ligier)	98	Ensign	22	Pacific
332	Williams		Sauber	20	Rial
321	Arrows	78	Dallara	19	Lola Haas
267	Benetton	69	Maserati	17	Onyx, Forti
230	March	61	Matra	16	Simtek
221	Minardi	54	Zakspeed	15	Parnelli
197	BRM	48	AGS,	12	Mercedes
139	Lola		Larousse,	11	Forti
132	Osella		Wolf	10	Merzario
130	Jordan	40	Gordini	4	Lancia
129	Cooper	35	Honda		
123	Renault	34	Theodore		

GRAND PRIX POLE POSITIONS PER CAR TYPE

Poles	Car Type	Poles	Car Type
124	Ferrari	10	Maserati
108	Williams	9	Ligier
107	Lotus	8	Mercedes
92	McLaren	7	Vanwall
39	Brabham	5	March
31	Renault	4	Matra
16	Benetton	3	Shadow
14	Tyrrell	2	Lancia
12	Alfa Romeo	1	Arrows, Honda, Jordan,
11	BRM, Cooper		Lola, Porsche, Wolf

GRAND PRIX FASTEST LAPS PER CAR TYPE

Laps	Car Type	Laps	Car Type
130	Ferrari	9	Mercedes
109	Williams	7	March
80	McLaren	6	Vanwall
71	Lotus	4	Surtees
40	Brabham	2	Eagle, Honda,
39	Benetton		Shadow, Wolf,
20	Tyrrell		Jordan
18	Renault	1	Ensign, Gordini,
15	BRM, Maserati		Hesketh, Lancia,
14	Alfa Romeo		Parnelli
13	Cooper		
12	Matra		
11	Ligier		

Drivers 1999

Introduction

These pages contain an A-Z of drivers who have been named as teams'
major drivers for the 1999 Grand Prix season plus all the drivers who
featured in the 1998 Grand Prix season. While every attempt has been
made to ensure that this list is as accurate as possible, new drivers may
have come to light after this book went to press. Each entry lists a brief
resumé of each driver's F1 career to date and then provides a summary
of Grand Prix details. This is followed by a list of each of the Grand
Prix races he has competed in. Numbers in brackets after named Grands
Prix signify the number of points scored in the race in question.

Team and Driver Number Allocation 1999

No.	Driver	Team-Car
1	Mika Hakkinen	McLaren Mercedes MP4-14
2	David Coulthard	McLaren Mercedes MP4-14
3	Michael Schumacher (Ger)	Ferrari F301
4	Eddie Irvine (GB)	Ferrari F301
5	Alex Zanardi (Ita)	Williams Supertec FW21
6	Ralf Schumacher (Ger)	Williams Supertec FW21
7	Damon Hill (GB)	Jordan Mugen-Honda199
8	Heinz-Harald Frentzen (Ger)	Jordan Mugen-Honda199
9	Giancarlo Fisichella (Ita)	Benetton Supertec B199
10	Alexander Wurz (Aut)	Benetton Supertec B199
11	Jean Alesi (Fra)	Sauber Petronas C18
12	Pedro Diniz (Bra)	Sauber Petronas C18
14	Toranasuke Takagi	Arrows A20
15	Pedro de la Rosa	Arrows A20
16	Rubens Barrichello (Bra)	Stewart Ford SF3
17	Johnny Herbert (GB)	Stewart Ford SF3
18	Olivier Panis (Fra)	Prost Peugeot AP02
19	Jarno Trulli (Ita)	Prost Peugeot AP02
20	Luca Badoer	Minardi Ford M199
21	Marc Gené	Minardi Ford M199
22	Jacques Villeneuve (Can)	BAR Supertec 001
23	Ricardo Zonta (Bra)	BAR Supertec 001

ALESI, Jean   France

After seven seasons at the forefront of Formula 1 driving for the likes of Ferrari and Benetton, Jean Alesi started the 1998 season sitting in the cockpit of the more modest based and funded Sauber team. A new set-up perhaps but a degree of familiarity given the Swiss-based team's engines were Petronas badged Ferrari power-packs. That might go some way to explaining the relative success of the Frenchman with his new team in securing the team's only podium finish of the year, its only front row start and supplying all but one of its ten points. Alesi's tally of nine points was his lowest haul since his rookie year of 1989 when he scored eight for Tyrrell.

The season, though, started slowly with Alesi struggling to come to terms with his new car in racing conditions. Twelfth on the grid in Melbourne for the opening race, he had moved up to eighth before engine failure brought a premature end to his race. A ninth place finish in Brazil was achieved with the Frenchman complaining of a lack of grip which was instrumental in his struggle to achieve a reasonable grid position. Having qualified eleventh in Argentina, the raining race conditions suited the Frenchman, who made a great start and was in seventh place almost immediately. An airgun tangling with one of the new winglets on the car nearly had disastrous effects at one of his two pit stops but he still managed to secure the team's first points of the season when he took the flag in fifth place.

Alesi took the success with him to San Marino where sixth place earned another point but in the Spanish Grand Prix he was forced out of the race a handful of laps from home when he faced engine problems. At the time of the Canadian Grand Prix, Alesi set his best grid position – ninth – to date but was taken out of the race by Trulli at its restart. Back on home soil for the French Grand Prix, he rose as high as fifth while other drivers were taking their stops but had only lost two places when the pit stops sorted themselves out.

Improvements in qualifying were more than apparent in the next two races. For the British race, Alesi started on the fourth row for only the second time of the season but electrical problems forced a retirement just a few laps from the flag. In Austria Alesi gave Sauber its best ever qualifying position in second place behind Giancarlo Fisichella. In the race he was involved in a tangle with Fisichella who was rejoining the track, and as Alesi tried to hold his ground, he found himself pushed off. Two eleventh place qualifications in Germany and Hungary couldn't be converted into points and when he secured tenth position on the grid in

71

Belgium it looked as though it was a case of more of the same. Alesi, who had made a good start at the first off, managed to do so again in the second start and coasted up into fourth place. Schumacher Senior's shunt into Coulthard elevated the Sauber driver into third place where he stayed to earn his team's only podium position of the season and to equal the best ever finish by a Sauber car.

For the Italian Grand Prix he qualified in eighth place and then drove well enough to move up to fifth by the flag. He came back down to earth for the Luxembourg Grand Prix where he eventually came home down the field in tenth place in his 150th Grand Prix race. He improved on this in the season's final race in Japan by finishing seventh.

Alesi remains with Sauber for 1999 in what will likely be a landmark year for the Frenchman as the Swiss team will be looking for him to supply its first victory in F1. If that is to happen he will need to recover that care free driving attitude that seemed to have deserted him in 1998.
Born: 11/6/64, Avignon, France. Single, one daughter.

Grand Prix 1998 Record

Grand Prix	Grid	Qual Time	Fin	Laps	Race Time	Reason
Australian	12	1:33.240	–	41		Engine
Brazilian	15	1:19.449	9	71	1:37:42.228	
Argentinian	11	1:27.839	5	72	1:49:54.461	
San Marino	12	1:28.191	6	61	1:34.30.693	
Spanish	14	1:23.327	10	63	1:33:47.986	
Monaco	11	1:22.257	12	72		Engine
Canadian	9	1:19.693	–	0		Accident
French	11	1:16.827	7	70	1:34:54.330	
British	8	1:25.081	–	53		Electrics
Austrian	2	1:30.317	–	21		Accident
German	11	1:43.663	10	45	1:21:36.355	
Hungarian	11	1:19.210	7	76	1:45:41.961	
Belgian	10	1:51.189	3	44	1:43:54.647	
Italian	8	1:26.637	5	53	1:18:11.544	
Luxembourg	11	1:20.493	10	66	1:32:29.424	
Japanese	12	1:39.448	7	51	1:28:58.588	

1998 Position Summary

Contested:	16	Finished:	12
Pole Positions:	0	Fastest Laps:	0
Points:	9		
1st:	0	2nd:	0
3rd:	1	4th:	0
5th:	2	6th:	1

Grand Prix Career Record

Contested:	151	(1989-1998)
Points:	234	1989 (8), 1990 (13), 1991 (21), 1992 (18), 1993 (16), 1994 (24), 1995 (42), 1996 (47), 1997 (36), 1998 (9)
Point Finishes:	64	42.38%
Pole Positions:	2	1994 (Ita), 1997 (Ita)
Fastest Laps:	4	1991 (USA), 1995 (Mon), 1996 (Arg, Mon)
1st:	1	1995 (Can)
2nd:	16	1990 (USA, Mon), 1993 (Ita), 1994 (GB), 1995 (Arg, San, GB, Eur), 1996 (Bra, Esp, Ger, Ita), 1997 (Can, GB, Ita, Lux)
3rd:	15	1991 (Mon, Ger, Por), 1992 (Esp, Can), 1993 (Mon), 1994 (Bra, Can, Jap), 1996 (Arg, Can, Fra, Hun), 1997 (Esp), 1998 (Bel)
4th:	11	1989 (Fra, Esp), 1991 (Fra, Esp), 1992 (Bra, Aus), 1993 (Por, Aus), 1994 (Esp), 1996 (Bel, Por)
5th:	14	1989 (Ita), 1991 (Hun), 1992 (Ger, Jap), 1994 (Mon), 1995 (Bra, Fra, Por, Pac), 1997 (San, Fra, Jap), 1998 (Arg, Ita)
6th:	7	1990 (San), 1991 (Bra), 1994 (Aus), 1996 (San), 1997 (Bra, Ger), 1998 (San)

Year	Team	No.	Grand Prix
1989	Tyrrell Ford	8	Fra (3), GB, Ger, Hun, Ita (2), Esp (3), Jap, Aus
1990	Tyrrell Ford	15	USA (6), Bra, San (1), Mon (6), Can, Mex, Fra, GB, Ger, Hun, Bel, Ita, Por, Esp, Aus
1991	Ferrari	16	USA, Bra (1), San, Mon (4), Can, Mex, Fra (3), GB, Ger (4), Hun (2), Bel, Ita, Por (4), Esp (3), Jap, Aus
1992	Ferrari	16	SA, Mex, Bra (3), Esp (4), San, Mon, Can (4), Fra, GB, Ger (2), Hun, Bel, Ita, Por, Jap (2), Aus (3)
1993	Ferrari	16	SA, Bra, Eur, San, Esp, Mon (4), Can, Fra, GB, Ger, Hun, Bel, Ita (6), Por (3), Jap, Aus (3)
1994	Ferrari	14	Bra (4), Mon (2), Esp (3), Can (4), Fra, GB (6), Ger, Hun, Bel, Ita, Por, Eur, Jap (4), Aus

1995	Ferrari	42	17	Bra (2), Arg (6), San (6), Esp, Mon, Can (10), Fra (2), GB (6), Ger, Hun, Bel, Ita, Por (2), Eur (6), Pac (2), Jap, Aus
1996	Benetton Renault	47	16	Aus, Bra (6), Arg (4), Eur, San (1), Mon, Esp (6), Can (4), Fra (4), GB, Ger (6), Hun (4), Bel (3), Ita (6), Por (3), Jap
1997	Benetton Renault	36	17	Aus, Bra (1), Arg, San (2), Mon, Esp (4), Can (6), Fra (2), GB (6), Ger (1), Hun, Bel, Ita (6), Aut, Lux (6), Jap (2), Eur
1998	Sauber Petronas	9	16	Aus, Bra, Arg (2), San (1), Esp, Mon, Can, Fra, GB, Aut, Ger, Hun, Bel (4), Ita (2), Lux, Jap

BARRICHELLO, Rubens   Brazil

1998: Stewart Ford   *1999: Stewart Ford*

Good on a good day – bad on a bad day. The 1998 season was one when the phrase 'When the going gets tough, the tough gets going' didn't apply to Rubens Barrichello, unless, that is, it applies to the rumours that he was seeking a move away from Team Stewart.

Having finished just three races out of 17 in 1997, the 1998 season had to offer the Brazilian more in his second year with the fledgling Stewart team. Indeed it did, with five finishes from his 15 starts. Although his points haul wasn't as much as 1997, the four points he did score came courtesy of two fifth places while his chases to the chequered flag were consistent in terms of position – tenth or eleventh. Qualifying on the seventh row of the grid was a favourite starting point – on two occasions he did break into the top five rows, with a ninth at Barcelona being the starting point for the two fifth place finishes, and this was bettered in Austria where he qualified fifth.

The continued development of the SF-2 played a large part in Barrichello's season and the decision by the team to plump for the development of a carbon-fibre gearbox was a key factor in his ability to finish. In terms of reliability, gearbox problems accounted for four of those non-finishes.

For the first race of the season, Rubens failed to complete the first lap when he was unable to select a gear at the start. In Brazil things were going much better and from fourteenth on the grid he was running in ninth place, when rising temperatures in the gearbox caused concern and he retired after 56 laps. The Argentinian race provided Barrichello with his first really satisfying performance of the season with a steady race home to tenth. His seventeenth place on the grid in San Marino was the worst of the season and his team-mate Jan Magnussen ran into his rear at the first chicane to finish him off. In Spain Rubens qualified in ninth and took advantage of retirements to grab a fifth place finish.

There is never any likelihood of Barrichello following up on his second place of 1997 for Monaco and a suspension failure after 11 laps was probably not the best way for him to celebrate his 26th birthday. The trip to Canada for the next race brought more fifth place joy, however, and after a spin at Silverstone, he suffered with reliability at the next three races and was a victim of the mêlée at the start of the Belgium Grand Prix.

The season looked to be finishing on a more positive note – tenth at Monza was followed by eleventh at the Nurburgring. A hydraulics failure after 25 laps brought the season to the non-finishing close that had started it.

Rubens enters the final year of his three-year Stewart deal and unless he can turn in the sort of performances he did in his early Jordan days, by scoring points a little more consistently, then he may find extending his contract with his current team even more difficult than finding another drive. The arrival of Gary Anderson will no doubt help his cause in a season where he will mark his 100th Grand Prix race.
Born: 23/5/72, Sao Paulo, Brazil. Single.

Grand Prix 1998 Record

Grand Prix	Grid	Qual Time	Fin	Laps	Race Time	Reason
Australian	14	1:33.383	–	0		Gearbox
Brazilian	13	1:19.344	–	56		Gearbox
Argentinian	14	1:29.249	10	70	1:49:03.354	
San Marino	17	1:29.641	–	0		Accident
Spanish	9	1:22.860	5	64	1:33:54.435	
Monaco	14	1:22.540	–	11		Suspension
Canadian	13	1:19.953	5	69	1:42:18.868	
French	14	1:17.024	10	69	1:34:46.884	
British	16	1:26.990	–	39		Spin
Austrian	5	1:31.005	–	8		Brakes
German	13	1:44.776	–	27		Gearbox
Hungarian	14	1:19.876	–	54		Gearbox
Belgian	14	1:52.670	dns	0		Accident
Italian	13	1:27.247	10	52	1:18:22.050	
Luxembourg	12	1:20.530	11	65	1:32:28.610	
Japanese	16	1:40.502	–	25		Hydraulics

1998 Position Summary

Contested:	16	Finished:	6
Pole Positions:	0	Fastest Laps:	0
Points:	4		
1st-6th:	0	2nd:	0
3rd:	0	4th:	0
5th:	2	6th:	0

Grand Prix Career Record

Contested:	97	(1993-1998)
Points:	54	1993 (2), 1994 (19), 1995 (11), 1996 (14), 1997 (6), 1998 (4)
Point Finishes:	21	21.65%
Pole Positions:	1	1994 (Bel)
Fastest Laps:	1	
1st:	0	
2nd:	2	1995 (Can), 1997 (Mon)
3rd:	1	1994 (Aus)
4th:	8	1994 (Bra, GB, Ita, Por, Aus), 1995 (Eur), 1996 (Arg, GB)
5th:	6	1993 (Jap), 1996 (Eur, San, Ita), 1998 (Spa, Can)
6th:	4	1995 (Fra, Bel), 1996 (Ger, Hun)

Year	Team	No.	Grand Prix
1993	Jordan Hart	16	SA, Bra, Eur, San, Esp, Mon, Can, Fra, GB, Ger, Hun, Bel, Ita, Por, Jap (2), Aus
1994	Jordan Hart	15	Bra (3), Pac (4), Mon, Esp, Can, Fra, GB (3), Ger, Hun, Bel, Ita (3), Por (3), Eur, Jap, Aus (3)
1995	Jordan Peugeot	17	Bra, Arg, San, Esp, Mon, Can (6), Fra (1), GB, Ger, Hun, Bel (1), Ita, Por, Eur (3), Pac, Jap, Aus
1996	Jordan Peugeot	16	Aus, Bra, Arg (3), Eur (2), San (2), Mon, Esp, Can, Fra, GB (3), Ger (1), Hun (1), Bel, Ita (2), Por, Jap
1997	Stewart Ford	17	Aus, Bra, Arg, San, Mon (6), Esp, Can, Fra, GB, Ger, Hun, Bel, Ita, Aut, Lux, Jap, Eur
1998	Stewart Ford	16	Aus, Bra, Arg, San, Esp (2), Mon, Can (2), Fra, GB, Aut, Ger, Hun, Bel, Ita, Lux, Jap

1998: McLaren Mercedes   *1999: McLaren Mercedes*

Any other season and David Coulthard might have been celebrating his first Drivers' World Championship title at the end of 1998. As it was he came home third, having played the supporting role to his team-mate Mika Hakkinen for much of the season. As hard as it seems on the face of it, 1998 has to be classified as a disappointing season for the Scot. In an identical car to his team-mate he was outqualified and out-raced for most of the season. He gained one win compared to Hakkinen's eight while he only out-qualified the Finn on three occasions. There are mitigating circumstances though. At the start of the season McLaren manager Ron Dennis seemed to indicate that whoever was in the lead after the first few races would start to get the advantage of team orders – team orders would not come into play in those early few races. Even with that in mind Coulthard was sometimes well off the pace of his team-mate. What did shine through though was the Scot's sense of honour.

The start of the season got underway at Melbourne with the Scot securing the first of two successive front row starting positions. The McLarens had been dominant in Australia and showed it in the race with Coulthard following team-mate Mika Hakkinen into the first corner. At that point the race destiny had been set as the two drivers had a private pact that stated whoever got into the first corner first would be allowed to win the race from the front by the other driver. On lap 36 Hakkinen pitted for what was to be a phantom stop – the result of a radio problem. As such the Finn found himself behind the Scot, only for Coulthard to honour their agreement late in the race and allow the Finn past and home to victory. Did honour exist in F1? The answer was clear even if the action was not seen by the FIA as something they wanted to encourage.

It was largely the same again in Brazil – second on the grid and second on the podium. In Argentina Coulthard secured his first pole position in a McLaren and his first since driving for Williams in 1995. Despite the good omens, gearbox problems took their toll and the Scot had to be satisfied with a single point by the end of the afternoon.

It went even better for the first European race of the year. Having secured pole, Coulthard got ahead at the start and held his lead throughout the race to secure his first McLaren victory and the fourth race win of his career. Unfortunately it was to be his only win of the season. In Spain it was second and second again for the third time in just five races and it looked to continue when second on the grid was achieved at Monaco – but reliability came into question when his engine blew as early as lap 18 as he exited the tunnel. A throttle linkage problem restricted Coulthard to half power early in the Canadian race and so the Scot had to retire after having secured his third pole position of the season.

A point secured in France at least looked to kick-start matters but a spin at Silverstone as early as the fourth lap effectively ended any real chances the Scot had of taking the Drivers' title – he was already 26 points behind Hakkinen. At the A1-Ring the Scot attacked the field positively and was up in second before the race was halfway through! Second places in Germany and Hungary followed, only for the run to be blighted by a seventh place at Spa. During his qualifying runs for the German GP at Hockenheim, Coulthard set what is thought to be the fastest speed by an F1 car on a race circuit. He went through one of the speed traps at 221.49 mph.

Engine failure meant no points in Italy, followed by a third place in Luxembourg. A third place grid and finish rounded off the season in Japan and confirmed his third place in the Drivers' Championship.

Team orders will no doubt be the same from McLaren in 1999. That makes it vital for Coulthard to get off to the sort of blistering start that Hakkinen did. A World Championship title is probably there for Coulthard if he wants it – but not by playing the supporting role. Big season for David.

Born: 27/3/71, Twynholm, Scotland. Single.

Grand Prix 1998 Record

Grand Prix	Grid	Qual Time	Fin	Laps	Race Time	Reason
Australian	2	1:30.053	2	58	1:31:46.698	
Brazilian	2	1:17.757	2	72	1:37:12.849	
Argentinian	1	1:25.852	6	72	1:49:55.826	
San Marino	1	1:25.973	1	62	1:34:24.593	
Spanish	2	1:20.996	2	65	1:33:47.060	
Monaco	2	1:20.137	–	17		Engine
Canadian	1	1:18.213	–	18		Throttle linkage
French	3	1:15.333	6	70	1:34:52.416	fl
British	4	1:24.310	–	37		Spin
Austrian	14	1:32.399	2	71	1:30:49.375	fl
German	2	1:42.347	2	45	1:20:48.410	fl
Hungarian	2	1:17.131	2	77	1:45:34.983	
Belgian	2	1:48.845	7	39	1:43:51.512	
Italian	4	1:25.987	–	16		Engine
Luxembourg	5	1:19.169	3	67	1:32:48.952	
Japanese	3	1:37.496	3	51	1:27:50.197	

1998 Position Summary

Contested:	16	Finished:	12
Pole Positions:	3	Fastest Laps:	3
Points:	56		
1st:	1	2nd:	6
3rd:	2	4th:	0
5th:	0	6th:	2

Grand Prix Career Record

Contested:	74	(1994-1998)
Points:	173	1994 (14), 1995 (49), 1996 (18), 1997 (36), 1998 (56)
Point Finishes:	37	50.00%
Pole Positions:	8	1995 (Arg, Ita, Por, Eur, Pac), 1998 (Arg, San, Can)
Fastest Laps:	8	1994 (Ger, Por), 1995 (Bel, Por), 1997 (Can), 1998 (Fra, Aut, Ger)
1st:	4	1995 (Por), 1997 (Aus, Ita), 1998 (San)
2nd:	14	1994 (Por), 1995 (Bra, Ger, Hun, Pac), 1996 (Mon), 1997 (Aut, Eur), 1998 (Aus, Bra, Esp, Aut, Ger, Hun)
3rd:	6	1995 (Fra, GB, Eur), 1996 (Eur), 1998 (Lux, Jap)
4th:	4	1994 (Bel), 1995 (San), 1996 (Can), 1997 (GB)
5th:	4	1994 (Can, GB), 1996 (GB, Ger)
6th:	5	1994 (Ita), 1996 (Fra), 1997 (Esp), 1998 (Arg, Fra)

Year	Team	No.	Grand Prix
1994	Williams Renault	8	Esp, Can (2), GB (2), Ger, Hun, Bel (3), Ita (1), Por (6)
1995	Williams Renault	17	Bra (6), Arg, San (3), Esp, Mon, Can, Fra (4), GB (4), Ger (6), Hun (6), Bel, Ita, Por (10), Eur (4), Pac (6), Jap, Aus
1996	McLaren Mercedes	16	Aus, Bra, Arg, Eur (4), San, Mon (6), Esp, Can (3), Fra (1), GB (2), Ger (2), Hun, Bel, Ita, Por, Jap
1997	McLaren Mercedes	17	Aus (10), Bra, Arg, San, Mon, Esp (1), Can, Fra, GB (3), Ger, Hun, Bel, Ita (10), Aut (6), Lux, Jap, Eur (6)
1998	McLaren Mercedes	16	Aus (6), Bra (6), Arg (1), San (10), Esp (6), Mon, Can, Fra (1), GB, Aut (6), Ger (6), Hun (6), Bel, Ita, Lux (4), Jap (4)

DINIZ, Pedro   Brazil

1998: Arrows   *1999: Sauber Petronas*

In his third year as a Grand Prix driver Pedro Diniz bettered his previous points tallies by one. His three point total was the same as his more experienced team-mate Mika Salo and indicated once again that he brings more than just a big sponsorship budget to the team that he drives for, a fact that might have been noticed by Sauber who have secured his services for the 1999 season.

Straight line speed was always a problem and qualifying positions were normally limited to the last couple of rows on the grid – his best performance being twelfth, which was achieved at Silverstone and the Hungaroring. Hydraulic problems hampered Diniz in his preparation for the opening race of the season and hit again in the warm-up lap so that the Brazilian had to start the race from the pit lane. After just two laps of the Melbourne track they proved terminal to his race.

It was then a further four races without a finish. After a trip across the gravel he was forced to start the Brazilian Grand Prix from the back of the grid. Gear box problems finished Brazil and Argentina. In San Marino and Spain it was the engine that played up, forcing him out well before the halfway stage in both races.

After all the early problems with gearboxes, the journey to Monaco – where over 3,000 gear changes are needed in a race – might have been viewed with some apprehension. But with a season's best twelfth on the grid he kept plugging away and was rewarded with his first point of the season when finishing sixth. In Canada he rose up the ranks and held ninth spot even after spinning off. A disappointing fourteenth place came in France which he drove with a very sore neck suffered in a qualifying crash. The next three races, Silverstone, A1-Ring and Hockenheim all brought retirements. In Hungary Diniz gained one place to finish eleventh and in Belgium he avoided the pre-race pile-up to finish in fifth place and match his best ever completion. It was the last of the points for the season and the last of the finishes.

Pedro Diniz has come a long way in four years. Retirements are now largely down to mechanical problems rather than the spins that were prominent in his early career with Forti and Minardi. He has never finished higher than fifth in his 66 race career. He could well improve on that record in 1999 and add more points finishes to his record.

Born: 22/5/70, Sao Paulo, Brazil. Single.

Grand Prix 1998 Record

Grand Prix	Grid	Qual Time	Fin	Laps	Race Time	Reason
Australian	20	1:35.140	–	2		Hydraulics

Brazilian	22	1:20.847	–	26		Gearbox
Argentinian	18	1:30.022	–	13		Gearbox
San Marino	18	1:29.932	–	18		Engine
Spanish	15	1:23.704	–	20		Engine
Monaco	12	1:22.355	6	77	1:52:06.752	
Canadian	19	1:21.301	9	68	1:43:19.361	
French	17	1:17.880	14	69	1:36:03.194	
British	12	1:26.376	–	45		Spin
Austrian	13	1:32.206	–	3		Accident damage
German	18	1:45.588	–	2		Throttle
Hungarian	12	1:19.706	11	74	1:45:27.272	
Belgian	16	1:53.037	5	44	1:44:39.089	
Italian	20	1:28.387	–	10		Spin
Luxembourg	17	1:21.258	–	6		Hydraulics
Japanese	18	1:40.687	–	2		Spin

1998 Position Summary

Contested:	16	Finished:	5
Pole Positions:	0	Fastest Laps:	0
Points:	3		
1st:	0	2nd:	0
3rd:	0	4th:	0
5th:	1	6th:	1

Grand Prix Career Record

Contested:	66	(1995-98)
Points:	7	1996 (2), 1997 (2), 1998 (3)
Point Finishes:	3	4.55%
Pole Positions:	0	
Fastest Laps:	0	
1st:	0	
2nd:	0	
3rd:	0	
4th:	0	
5th:	2	1997 (Lux), 1998 (Lux)
6th:	3	1996 (Esp, Ita), 1998 (Mon)

Year	Team	No.	Grand Prix
1995	Forti Ford	17	Bra, Arg, San, Esp, Mon, Can, Fra, GB, Ger, Hun, Bel, Ita, Por, Eur, Pac, Jap, Aus
1996	Minardi Ford	16	Aus, Bra, Arg, Eur, San, Mon, Esp (1), Can, Fra, GB, Ger, Hun, Bel, Ita (1), Por, Jap

| 1997 Arrows Yamaha | 17 | Aus, Bra, Arg, San, Mon, Esp, Can, Fra, GB, Ger, Hun, Bel, Ita, Aut, Lux (2), Jap, Eur |
| 1998 Arrows | 16 | Aus, Bra, Arg, San, Esp, Mon (1), Can, Fra, GB, Aut, Ger, Hun, Bel, Ita, Lux (2), Jap |

FISICHELLA, Giancarlo   Italy

1998: Benetton Playlife   *1999: Benetton Supertec*

For the third time in as many years the likeable, ever-smiling Giancarlo Fisichella started the Grand Prix season with a new team. Half a season with Minardi, a full season with Jordan and now the first of contractually a few at Benetton. As a season it was one that showed that the Italian possesses the potential to be able to succeed. It also proved that he has the nerves to fail. Out on his own, he showed he could drive fast and aggressively, but when push came to shove he was too easily displaced from winning situations when pressed. Experience should solve the latter and if it does then the 1999 season could see Gianny win his first Formula 1 Grand Prix. As it was he came close with two second places and in Austria recorded his first ever pole position.

Despite the pole position it was the grid that was often the stumbling block. When Giancarlo qualified on the front couple of rows then he produced finishes to match. Too often, though, he found himself on the fourth and fifth rows with finishes to match. On the other hand it must be remembered that he was competing with a new team and a new car. In Melbourne a rear wing failure forced him out as the race entered its final stages while at Interlagos he recorded his first point.

In Argentina he looked to be converting his drive into another point but a late off lost it and a finishing position. Handling at Imola looked difficult and culminated in a heavy crash after just 17 laps. Gianny was held responsible for the crash in Spain and was levied a fine of £4,500.

In Monaco third place was secured on the grid and then he showed that he could handle some of the pressures by holding off Michael Schumacher for much of the race and closing the gap on the flying Finn, Hakkinen. Confidence continued to ooze in Canada as he came home a creditable second for only the third time of his career.

In France the blinding pace of Fisichella's Benetton seemed to have been left in North America. Two points at Silverstone with a fifth place finish was achieved from tenth on the grid and Giancarlo secured his first ever pole position at the A1-Ring. The advantage of pole wasn't pushed home as Coulthard and Michael Schumacher flew past him at the start. His race came to an end after 21 laps when he tangled with his front row partner Alesi for an unsatisfactory end to what had been a promising weekend for the Italian.

Fisichella struggled to recapture that spate of form in the closing stages of the season, during which he was at sevens and eights, both in terms of grid and finishing positions. In Germany and Hungary he started on the fourth row and wasn't able to get in the points. A lack of grip effectively brought the Belgian race to an end after 26 laps when he ran into the back of Nakano in wet conditions at the Bus Stop. Italy again left Giancarlo out of the points. The first point in six races did finally come at the Nurburgring for the Luxembourg Grand Prix and he might have been fourth had he not lost time sliding over Ricardo Rosset's oil late on. His season ended on a disappointing note in Japan with an eighth place finish.

A year's worth of experience under him, Giancarlo will surely benefit from the fact that he is not changing team. 1999 will see him race in his 50th Grand Prix and will maybe yield up his first win in the same. The potential is there for him to do so if he can conquer the pressure.
Born: 14/1/73, Roma, Italy. Single.

Grand Prix 1998 Record

Grand Prix	Grid	Qual Time	Fin	Laps	Race Time	Reason
Australian	7	1:31.733	–	43		Rear wing
Brazilian	7	1:18.652	6	71	1:37:19.574	
Argentinian	10	1:27.836	7	72	1:50:04.612	
San Marino	10	1:27.937	–	17		Accident
Spanish	4	1:21.894	–	28		Accident
Monaco	3	1:20.388	2	78	1:51:35.070	
Canadian	4	1:18.826	2	69	1:41:14.071	
French	9	1:16.375	9	70	1:35:53.089	
British	10	1:25.654	5	59	1:47:30.546	
Austrian	1	1:29.598	–	21		Accident
German	8	1:43.396	7	45	1:21:19.010	
Hungarian	8	1:19.050	8	76	1:45:56.357	
Belgian	7	1:50.462	–	26		Accident
Italian	11	1:26.817	8	52	1:17:11.752	
Luxembourg	4	1:19.048	6	67	1:33:16.148	
Japanese	10	1:39.080	8	51	1:29.03.837	

1998 Position Summary

Contested:	16	Finished:	11
Pole Positions:	1	Fastest Laps:	0
Points:	16		
1st:	0	2nd:	2

| 3rd: | 0 | 4th: | 0 |
| 5th: | 1 | 6th: | 2 |

Grand Prix Career Record

Contested:	41	(1996-1998)
Points:	36	1997 (20), 1998 (16)
Point Finishes:	11	26.83%
Pole Positions:	1	1998 (Aut)
Fastest Laps:	0	
1st:	0	
2nd:	3	1997 (Bel), 1998 (Mon, Can)
3rd:	1	1997 (Can)
4th:	3	1997 (San, Ita, Aut)
5th:	1	1998 (GB)
6th:	3	1997 (Mon), 1998 (Bra, Lux)

Year	Team	No.	Grand Prix
1996	Minardi Ford	8	Aus, Eur, San, Mon, Esp, Can, Fra, GB
1997	Jordan Peugeot	17	Aus, Bra, Arg, San (3), Mon (1), Esp, Can (4), Fra, GB, Ger, Hun, Bel (6), Ita (3), Aut (3), Lux, Jap, Eur
1998	Benetton Playlife	16	Aus, Bra (1), Arg, San, Esp, Mon (6), Can (6), Fra, GB (2), Aut, Ger, Hun, Bel, Ita, Lux (1), Jap

---

FRENTZEN, Heinz-Harald   Germany

1998: Williams Mecachrome   1999: Jordan Mugen Honda
He showed at Nurburgring what he can do – he just didn't do it often enough and is therefore not at Williams any more.

Heinz-Harald was spoken of as a potential World Champion when he arrived at Williams for the start of the 1997 season. He went some way to backing that claim with a second spot in the Drivers' Championship in his first year. But it has to be said that 1998 saw any talk in that direction totally evaporate as the German seemed to live more on the fringe of events and like team-mate Villeneuve, struggled to come to terms with the new Williams regulation-enforced design changes.

Within the team Frentzen won the early battle, finishing ahead of Villeneuve in the first three races. The first of those came in Australia and, despite having to battle against high oil temperatures, Frentzen took his car from sixth on the grid to a third place finish. Having secured four successive thirds towards the end of 1997, the German must have thought that he was simply carrying on where he had left off the previous season. That was not to be but the number three was prominent in Brazil in marking his starting position on the grid. Despite holding the position for some time he lost two places in the final stages to finish fifth – but still amongst the points. A good start in Argentina from the third row saw him begin competitively but mistakes crept in as he stalled the car in the pit lane and then got a stop-go penalty for speeding in the same area.

Two points in San Marino meant that Heinz-Harald had scored points in three of his first four races – albeit just eight – but the fifth in San Marino marked the start of seven outings without a point-scoring position.

Things started to look bleak in Spain. Having qualified in thirteenth, he spun on the first lap and then lost time having a new nose fitted to his Williams. With this in mind, his finish in eighth place could be regarded as an impressive performance and his technique in passing Ralf Schumacher and Jean Alesi went to underline the potential that lies within.

Accident, accident, accident, spin, engine problem. The five reasons that saw Frentzen fail to reach the chequered flag in the following five races – yet in qualifying there was a degree of consistency. In Monaco he started fifth but only completed nine laps when he slid off and out at Loews. Seventh in the T-car in Canada lasted 21 laps when he spun on to the grass after Schumacher bolted from the pits. In France, he made a bad start and slipped three places to eleventh from the off. Although he was classified in fifteenth place he was already retired in the pits after an attempt to overtake Alesi had resulted in a coming together which damaged his car.

The races in Britain and Austria provided similar tales. At his home Grand Prix in Germany, although the performance was poor he did at least manage to get past the chequered flag to finish ninth, a position achieved by his late passing of Wurz. Illness plagued Heinz-Harald in Hungary but two points were reward for his efforts to combat an upset stomach. Three points came in Belgium but a podium third place was very much on the cards until a detour through a gravel trap.

Finishing seventh from a twelfth starting position at Monza came on the back of having agreed to join the Jordan team in 1999. However, the German was somewhat fortunate in making it into the pits to implement his one-stop race strategy – having returned on fumes after staying out longer than planned. Although it wasn't his best finish of the season, Luxembourg produced probably the best race of the season for Frentzen, which saw him involved in an enticing battle with the two Benetton cars as he converted his seventh place on the grid to two points by finishing fifth. He brought his Williams career to an end in Suzuka where he qualified and finished fifth.

1999 will be a huge year for Frentzen and he will need to show in a potentially challenging Jordan team that he is the sort of driver his Sauber days suggested he was. Twelve more points will bring him to his century in F1 driving – but that is a barrier he needs to burst through and be well clear of before the season is out.

Born: 18/5/67, Mönchengladbach, Germany. Single.

Grand Prix 1998 Record

Grand Prix	Grid	Qual Time	Fin	Laps	Race Time	Reason
Australian	6	1:31.397	3	57	+1 lap	
Brazilian	3	1:18.109	5	71	1:37:14.445	
Argentinian	6	1:26.876	9	71	1:49:43.772	
San Marino	8	1:27.645	5	62	1:35:42.069	
Spanish	13	1:23.197	8	63	1:33:42.553	
Monaco	5	1:20.729	–	9		Accident
Canadian	7	1:19.614	–	20		Accident
French	8	1:16.319	15	68		Accident damage
British	6	1:24.442	–	15		Spin
Austrian	7	1:31.515	–	16		Engine
German	10	1:43.467	9	45	1:21:20.768	
Hungarian	7	1:19.029	5	77	1:46:22.060	
Belgian	9	1:50.686	4	44	1:44:19.650	
Italian	12	1:26.836	7	52	1:17:11.164	
Luxembourg	7	1:19.522	5	67	1:33:15.036	
Japanese	5	1:38.272	5	51	1:28:36.392	

1998 Position Summary

Contested:	16	Finished:	12
Pole Positions:	0	Fastest Laps:	0
Points:	17		
1st:	0	2nd:	0
3rd:	1	4th:	1
5th:	5	6th:	0

Grand Prix Career Record

Contested:	81	(1994-1998)
Points:	88	1994 (7), 1995 (15), 1996 (7), 1997 (42), 1998 (17)
Point Finishes:	31	38.27%
Pole Positions:	1	1997 (Mon)
Fastest Laps:	6	1997 (Aus, San, Hun, Lux, Jap, Eur)
1st:	1	1997 (San)
2nd:	2	1997 (Fra, Jap)

3rd:	6	1995 (Ita), 1997 (Bel, Ita, Aus, Lux), 1998 (Aus)
4th:	6	1994 (Fra), 1995 (Bel), 1996 (Mon, Esp), 1997 (Can), 1998 (Bel)
5th:	8	1994 (Pac), 1995 (Arg, Hun), 1998 (Bra, San, Hun, Lux, Jap)
6th:	8	1994 (Eur, Jap), 1995 (San, Mon, GB, Por), 1996 (Jap), 1997 (Eur)

Year	Team	No.	Grand Prix
1994	Sauber Mercedes	15	Bra, Pac (2), San, Esp, Can, Fra (3), GB, Ger, Hun, Bel, Ita, Por, Eur (1), Jap (1), Aus
1995	Sauber Ford	17	Bra, Arg (2), San (1), Esp, Mon (1), Can, Fra, GB (1), Ger, Hun (2), Bel (3), Ita (4), Por (1), Eur, Pac, Jap, Aus
1996	Sauber Ford	16	Aus, Bra, Arg, Eur, San, Mon (3), Esp (3), Can, Fra, GB, Ger, Hun, Bel, Ita, Por, Jap (1)
1997	Williams Renault	17	Aus, Bra, Arg, San (10), Mon, Esp, Can (3), Fra (6), GB, Ger, Hun, Bel (4), Ita (4), Aut (4), Lux (4), Jap (6), Eur (1)
1998	Williams Mecachrome	16	Aus, Bra, Arg, San, Esp, Mon, Can, Fra, GB, Aut, Ger, Hun, Bel, Ita, Lux, Jap

HAKKINEN, Mika   Finland

1998: McLaren Mercedes   *1999: McLaren Mercedes*

What a difference a win makes! For Mika Hakkinen Grand Prix success was just like waiting for a bus. Wait ages for one then they all come along together. The start of it, though, was all a little contrived. Career race number 96 came in Jerez in the final race of 1997 – you may recall as Jacques Villeneuve was winging his way to the Drivers' Championship. After a pit wall discussion the McLarens came in one-two for Hakkinen's maiden victory. A new season and a new start but this time in Melbourne it was team-mate David Coulthard who allowed his team-mate to pass early on and fly his way to another victory. It kick-started the campaign and set the trend for the Flying Finn to dominate the early stages of the season and, despite a few wobbles late on, drive to his first World Championship.

While other teams seemed to struggle with the new regulations and new tyres, McLaren and in particular Hakkinen did not. In fact, in the early part of the season he positively dominated the scene in a car he looked as though he had been driving for ever. There were four wins and one second place from his first six starts coupled with four pole positions in the same span.

In Melbourne for the first race of the season, Hakkinen vied with team-mate Coulthard for the pole position and won the race by just 0.043 seconds. It was to be the fractional difference at the chequered flag – not the margin of victory, but the right of way. Hakkinen got to the first corner in the lead and stayed there until he came in for a pitstop that never was: somewhere along the line there had been mis-communication. Coulthard took the lead but with two laps to go moved aside for Hakkinen to retake the lead because of a gentleman's agreement. The two had shook hands to agree that whoever led into the first corner would be allowed to win the race. There was FIA uproar with subsequent orders coming down from on high that it shouldn't be allowed to happen again. The net result was a pole and win for Hakkinen, thereby doubling his previous totals in these credit columns.

It was more of the same in Brazil with Hakkinen tripling his win and pole count – the Finn was in outstanding form and for this race no-one could argue that he wasn't the best on the circuit. Having looked largely invincible in the opening races, a few chinks in the armour started to appear in Argentina. Third on the grid was improved for his fourth second place finish of his career and the first since 1995.

The return to Europe saw some frustration as a gearbox problem brought the San Marino Grand Prix to a premature end, but successive poles and successive wins in Spain and at Monaco confirmed Mika's racing excellence if his 46 point Drivers' Championship tally (from a possible 60) did not.

Canadian gremlins halted Mika's charge in Montreal when his McLaren got stuck in first gear at the second race start and retired him right away. The fifth and sixth pole positions of the year came at Magny-Cours and Silverstone but victories were more elusive. In France a spin late on was recovered and Mika seemed more than happy to run home in third place and take the points on offer. For the British Grand Prix the weather conspired against him when the safety car reduced his lead over Schumacher Senior and the pressure at the restart proved too great. Mika came home in second place and his lead was reduced to just two points. The pressure was well and truly on.

A win was the best way to relieve this and two in succession came at the A1-Ring and in Hockenheim. Third place on the grid in Austria was converted into a flying start lead which Mika held for full points and the same was true in Germany where he had secured his seventh pole of the season. The pole position marked the first of a hat-trick but only converted into a single Championship point. Sixth place in Hungary was due to handling problems after the Finn had led for a large part of the race. In Belgium, despite the pole, Hakkinen was outed on the first lap at the race restart.

Matters looked bleaker come the finish of the Italian Grand Prix where Hakkinen could only manage fourth. This was despite hitting the front from the start from the second row of the grid. The Finn cited handling problems for lack of pace – more distressingly Hakkinen now found himself level on 80 points with Michael Schumacher.

The question mark against Hakkinen's ability to handle pressure was blown away by the end of the Luxembourg race, as were the opposition. Simply, Mika drove the race of his life and arguably the race of the season. It was electrifying, with the Finn knowing that if he won and Schumacher failed to score at least a point he would be crowned World Champion. Hakkinen maintained his third place at the start and moved into second place ahead of Irvine in the early stages. Driving home some stunning laps Hakkinen closed the gap on Schumi and two stunning pit stops got him out ahead of his rival. With Schumacher coming home second, Hakkinen had established a four-point lead going into the final race of the season.

Hakkinen arrived in Japan knowing that a first or second place finish would crown him World Champion regardless of what Michael did. After his rival outqualified him to gain pole it must have seemed like Christmas when his challenger stalled his car on the grid and had to start from the back. When Schumacher retired at mid-point, Mika was crowned World Champion as he held his comfortable lead to take the ninth victory of his 112 race career.

Finishing on a round 100 points the Finn had almost doubled his previous points total and he will surely be one of the main contenders for the title in 1999.

Born: 28/9/68, Helsinki, Finland. Married.

Grand Prix 1998 Record

Grand Prix	Grid	Qual Time	Fin	Laps	Race Time	Reason
Australian	1	1:30.010	1	58	1:31:45.996	fl
Brazilian	1	1:17.092	1	72	1:37:11.747	fl
Argentinian	3	1:26.632	2	72	1:48:69.173	
San Marino	2	1:26.075	–	17		Gearbox
Spanish	1	1:20.262	1	65	1:33:37.621	fl
Monaco	1	1:19.798	1	78	1:51:23.595	fl
Canadian	2	1:18.282	–	0		Gearbox

French	1	1:14.929	3	71	1:35:04.773	
British	1	1:23.271	2	60	1:47:24.915	
Austrian	3	1:30.517	1	71	1:30:44.086	
German	1	1:41.838	1	45	1:20:47.984	
Hungarian	1	1:16.973	6	76	1:45:29.932	
Belgian	1	1:48.682	–	0		Accident
Italian	3	1:25.679	4	53	1:18:05.343	fl
Luxembourg	3	1:18.940	1	67	1:32:14.789	fl
Japanese	2	1:36.471	1	51	1:27:22.535	

fl=fastest lap

1998 Position Summary

Contested:	16	Finished:	13
Pole Positions:	9	Fastest Laps:	6
Points:	100		
1st:	8	2nd:	2
3rd:	1	4th:	1
5th:	0	6th:	0

Grand Prix Career Record

Contested:	112	(1991-1998)
Points:	217	1991 (2), 1992 (11), 1993 (4), 1994 (25), 1995 (17), 1996 (31), 1997 (27), 1998 (100)
Point Finishes:	48	42.86%
Pole Positions:	10	1997 (Lux), 1998 (Aus, Bra, Esp, Mon, Fra, GB, Ger, Hun, Bel)
Fastest Laps:	7	1997 (Ita), 1998 (Aus, Bra, Esp, Mon, Ita, Lux)
1st:	9	1997 (Eur), 1998 (Aus, Bra, Esp, Mon, Aut, Ger, Lux, Jap)
2nd:	5	1994 (Bel), 1995 (Ita, Jap), 1998 (Arg, GB)
3rd:	12	1993 (Jap), 1994 (San, GB, Bel, Por), 1996 (GB, Bel, Ita, Jap), 1997 (Aus, Ger), 1998 (Fra)
4th:	8	1992 (Fra, Hun), 1994 (GB), 1996 (Bra, Hun), 1997 (Bra, Jap), 1998 (Ita)
5th:	8	1991 (San), 1992 (Por), 1995 (San), 1996 (Aus, Esp, Can, Fra), 1997 (Arg)
6th:	6	1992 (Mex, GB, Bel), 1996 (Mon), 1997 (San), 1998 (Hun)

| Year | Team | No. | Grand Prix |
| 1991 | Lotus Judd | 15 | USA, Bra, San (2), Mon, Can, Mex, GB, Ger, Hun, Bel, Ita, Por, Esp, Jap, Aus |

90

1992	Lotus Ford	15	SA, Mex (1), Bra, Esp, Mon, Can, Fra (3), GB (1), Ger, Hun (3), Bel (1), Ita, Por (2), Jap, Aus
1993	McLaren Ford	3	Por, Jap (4), Aus
1994	McLaren Peugeot	15	Bra, Pac, San (4), Mon, Esp, Can, Fra, GB (3), Ger, Bel (6), Ita (4), Por (4), Eur (4), Jap, Aus
1995	McLaren Mercedes	15	Bra (3), Arg, San (2), Esp, Mon, Can, Fra, GB, Ger, Hun, Bel, Ita (6), Por, Eur, Jap (6)
1996	McLaren Mercedes	16	Aus (2), Bra (3), Arg, Eur, San, Mon (1), Esp (2), Can (2), Fra (2), GB (4), Ger, Hun (3), Bel (4), Ita (4), Por, Jap (4)
1997	McLaren Mercedes	17	Aus (4), Bra (3), Arg (2), San (1), Mon, Esp, Can, Fra, GB, Ger (4), Hun, Bel, Ita, Aut, Lux, Jap (3), Eur (10)
1998	McLaren Mercedes	16	Aus (10), Bra (10), Arg (6), San, Esp (10), Mon (10), Can, Fra (4), GB (6), Aut (10), Ger (10), Hun (1), Bel, Ita (3), Lux (10), Jap (10)

HERBERT, Johnny   Great Britain

1998: Sauber Petronas   *1999: Stewart Ford*

Judged by his recent achievements the 1998 season was a huge disappointment for Johnny Herbert. His solitary World Championship point was his lowest total since he failed to score during his seven drives for Lotus in 1991. In 1998 in the six other Grands Prix he managed to finish he was only just outside the points on four occasions – although that is scant reward for his efforts in the season. Having scored 19 points in the previous two years for Sauber in what seemed to be a good-spirited relationship, the arrival of Jean Alesi as his co-driver seemed to turn it all sour, especially as Alesi was apparently awarded the mantle of the Swiss team's number one.

The season had looked to start on a bright note though. Despite not being too enthusiastic about his chances in the build-up to the Australian opener, Herbert qualified in fifth place. The Englishman drove a typically gutsy battle and it was only in the pit stops that he ultimately lost his place and had to settle for sixth and a point. Unfortunately for Herbert, it was to prove the highlight of the season.

All sorts of problems and a heavy crash were not the best preparation for the qualifying session in Brazil and given the circumstances he did well to get fourteenth on the grid in the spare car. The sore neck he had as a reminder of those early problems finally took its toll and forced him to retire late in the race when he was running eleventh.

In Argentina Herbert once again found himself having to qualify in the T-car but managed to get up to twelfth with a one-stop strategy although he was forced to retire when he was hit by Damon Hill. It was a third successive retirement when the spotlight moved to Europe and the San Marino Grand Prix – this time he suffered a puncture as a result of avoiding a separate incident on the track. His excursion through the gravel led the pit crew to think he had suspension damage. In fact he didn't and, but for a tyre replacement, he could have continued with the race! This incident in many respects summed up Johnny's season to a T (-car).

Spain and Monaco offered some brighter moments. At Barcelona he qualified seventh only to lose two places at the start. A battling performance saw him regain the lost places but come home three seconds out of the points. Another one-stop strategy had a very similar result in Monaco where understeer was causing havoc. Qualifying in ninth, Herbert again pulled back two places to finish seventh a full half minute outside of the points.

Using a new SPE02D Petronas engine in his C17, he qualified twelfth for the Canadian outing but had to start the race from the pit lane after the original start had been aborted. Twelve laps later, though, it was over when he spun off while trying to outmanoeuvre Jan Magnussen's Stewart. The French Grand Prix provided the fourth finish in his eighth outing and was well achieved from a disappointing thirteenth place on the grid. Given a gravel excursion, a stall in the pit lane and a semi spin on oil laid down on the track from one of the back-markers, it perhaps wasn't a bad result. A fully fledged spin at Luffield put paid to Herbert's chances at Silverstone before the race had run half its course, but another eighth place was secured at the Austrian Grand Prix from what was a very disappointing qualifying performance.

Gearbox problems played havoc throughout the weekend of the German Grand Prix and after 37 laps of the race it forced the engine to stall for his sixth retirement of the season. For the sixth race in a row Herbert found himself outqualified by his team-mate Jean Alesi at the Hungarian Grand Prix. Starting from fifteenth he drove home in tenth place despite missing a heartbeat or two when he spun in the final stages of the race.

Accident, spin, engine were the three factors that meant three successive non-finishes. The first was at Spa – which coincided with the news that he would drive for Stewart in 1999 – when he was involved in the thick of the action at the initial pile-up and then on the restart when he was involved with Hakkinen. After the start at Monza, Herbert found he had a pair of pliers spinning around inside his cockpit! Being plagued with them in his footwell, they eventually proved too much of a distraction and he spun out after 12 laps. Johnny was not a happy man. Thirteenth on the grid proved unlucky in Luxembourg and engine problems just after the halfway stage of the race forced him out of the race. Herbert's Sauber career finished in Suzuka where he managed his seventh finish of the season – coming home tenth.

A year ago it would have been difficult to see Johnny Herbert moving from Sauber, but such was the change in relationships – it seems due to the arrival of Alesi – a move was on the cards even midway through 1998. With Team Stewart dumping Jan Magnussen in mid-season, and his replacement Jos Verstappen hardly setting the world alight, Herbert was the obvious choice. However, it seems unlikely that, as number two, he will be as competitive as he might have been had he had the chance to remain at Sauber. Johnny has risen to more than a few challenges in his driving career and this is another big one for him.

Born: 27/6/64, Brentwood, Essex, England. Married with two daughters.

Grand Prix 1998 Record

Grand Prix	Grid	Qual Time	Fin	Laps	Race Time	Reason
Australian	5	1:31.384	6	57	1:31:46.420	
Brazilian	14	1:19.375	–	67		Neck injury
Argentinian	12	1:28.016	–	46		Accident damage
San Marino	11	1:28.111	–	12		Puncture
Spanish	7	1:22.794	7	64	1:33:58.147	
Monaco	9	1:22.157	7	77	1:52:36.186	
Canadian	12	1:19.845	–	18		Spin
French	13	1:16.977	8	70	1:35:37.415	
British	9	1:25.084	–	27		Spin
Austrian	18	1:33.205	8	70	1:30:56.888	
German	12	1:44.599	–	37		Gearbox
Hungarian	15	1:19.878	10	76	1:46:20.059	
Belgian	12	1:51.851	–	0		Accident
Italian	15	1:27.510	–	12		Spin
Luxembourg	13	1:20.650	–	37		Engine
Japanese	11	1:39.234	10	50	1:27:43.035	

1998 Position Summary

Contested:	16	Finished:	7
Pole Positions:	0	Fastest Laps:	0
Points:	1		

1st:	0	2nd:	0
3rd:	0	4th:	0
5th:	0	6th:	1

Grand Prix Career Record

Contested:	129	(1989-1998)
Points:	83	1989 (5), 1992 (2), 1993 (11), 1995 (45), 1996 (4), 1997 (15), 1998 (1)
Point Finishes:	26	20.26%
Pole Positions:	0	
Fastest Laps:	1	1995 (Ita)
1st:	2	1995 (GB, Ita)
2nd:	1	1995 (Esp)
3rd:	3	1995 (Jap), 1996 (Mon), 1997 (Hun)
4th:	10	1991 (Bra), 1993 (Bra, Eur, GB) 1995 (Arg, Mon, Ger, Hun), 1997 (Arg, Bel)
5th:	5	1989 (USA), 1993 (Bel), 1995 (Eur), 1997 (Esp, Can)
6th:	5	1992 (SA, Fra), 1995 (Pac), 1997 (Jap), 1998 (Aus)

Year	Team	No.	Grand Prix
1989	Benetton Ford	5	Bra (3), San, Mon, Mex, USA (2)
	Tyrrell Ford	1	Bel
1990	Lotus Lamborghini	2	Jap, Aus
1991	Lotus Judd	7	Mex, Fra, GB, Bel, Por, Jap, Aus
1992	Lotus Ford	16	SA (1), Mex, Bra, Esp, San, Mon, Can, Fra (1), GB, Ger, Hun, Bel, Ita, Por, Jap, Aus
1993	Lotus Ford	16	SA, Bra (3), Eur (3), San, Esp, Mon, Can, Fra, GB (3), Ger, Hun, Bel (2), Ita, Por, Jap, Aus
1994	Lotus Mugen Honda	13	Bra, Pac, San, Mon, Esp, Can, Fra, GB, Ger, Hun, Bel, Ita, Por
	Ligier Renault	1	Eur
	Benetton Ford	2	Jap, Aus
1995	Benetton Renault	17	Bra, Arg (3), San, Esp (6), Mon (3), Can, Fra, GB (10), Ger (3), Hun (3), Bel, Ita (10), Por, Eur (2), Pac (1), Jap (4), Aus
1996	Sauber Ford	16	Aus, Bra, Arg, Eur, San, Mon (4), Esp, Can, Fra, GB, Ger, Hun, Bel, Ita, Por, Jap

| 1997 | Sauber Petronas | 17 | Aus, Bra, Arg (3), San, Mon, Esp (2), Can (2), Fra, GB, Ger, Hun (4), Bel (3), Ita, Aut, Lux, Jap (1), Eur |
| 1998 | Sauber Petronas | 16 | Aus (1), Bra, Arg, San, Esp, Mon, Can, Fra, GB, Aut, Ger, Hun, Bel, Ita, Lux, Jap |

HILL, Damon OBE   Great Britain

1998: Jordan Mugen Honda   *1999: Jordan Mugen Honda*

Even when Damon Hill joined Tom Walkinshaw's Arrows team for the 1997 season it always seemed likely that he would ultimately end up driving a Jordan (well, to me, at least). Eddie and Damon seemed the perfect match and so it proved. After a very disappointing first half of the season things gradually started to snap into place for the partnership and in amongst four point-scoring races there was the pulsating first ever win for a Jordan car. What Hill had come so close to doing for Arrows at the Hungaroring in 1997 he achieved at Spa and deservedly so.

The first nine races of the season provided few highlights. In fact, on reflection it was awful. Three eighth place finishes, a disqualification, four retirements due to mechanical problems and a spin made for pretty miserable reading. For the opening race in Melbourne, Hill complained the car wasn't quick enough but still managed to pick up a $2,500 fine for speeding! Having qualified tenth the race started slowly but the former World Champion was able to push the car in the later stages of the race to move up two places for an eighth spot finish. Matters got worse in Brazil where he came home a disappointing tenth, only then to find his car an amazing 7kg underweight and therefore disqualified by the marshals. Hill, who had lost 4kg in weight since the start of the season, counted for over half of this discrepancy!

In Argentina things looked to be improving, especially in qualifying, where Hill looked on pace to get up the grid only to suffer a spin on the last corner of his flying lap. He had to settle for ninth and despite having to pit for a new nose cone following a collision with Herbert's Sauber, he ran home for his second eighth finish of the season.

Despite suffering a blown engine during qualifying for the San Marino race, Hill secured his best grid position so far of seventh. The engine problem was a forerunner of what was to come when his engine started to fail a few laps from the chequered flag while running in eighth place. The engine problems continued to Spain where it gave up on lap 47. Monaco came and went with Damon still dreaming of his first win in the principality. A lack of grip didn't help on the curvaceous circuit where fifteenth on the grid was a huge disappointment. Working his way through the back markers and by a process of natural wastage he managed his third eighth place of the season.

With a new specification engine for the Canadian Grand Prix there was optimism for the race. Spins cost Hill dear in qualifying but during the race he moved through the field and was a steady third and a second place for two laps while the pit stops sorted themselves out. With his first points of the season looking guaranteed, his 198 developed electrical problems and forced him to retire with a third of the race remaining. It was the first of three successive retirements for the Englishman. In the ensuing races at Magny-Cours and Silverstone, qualifying was more encouraging with seventh place starts on both grids. But hydraulic problems forced Hill out after 19 laps in France while at Silverstone he spun his car out and stalled the engine at Brooklands on lap 14.

Although it didn't quite seem that way at the start of the Austrian Grand Prix, Damon's season was just turning the proverbial corner. In qualifying the team misread the weather conditions and put in the laps on wets early on, only missing out on the chance to run more laps on intermediates as the track started to dry out late in the qualifying hour. Fifteenth position didn't bode well. An encouraging start put him up through the field and, but for some untimely pit stops which brought him out in traffic, he would have probably finished in the points – as it was he came home seventh.

Hockenheim and Hungaroring saw great improvement. For the German race Damon qualified fifth and was on the pace all the way through the race, securing his first points of the season and only just missing out on a podium finish. His fourth place was just over seven seconds behind race winner Mika Hakkinen.

Optimism was high for the Hungarian Grand Prix, where Damon had never finished outside the top two, and the previous year had probably driven the race of his life for Arrows only to be denied victory at the death. The improvement in qualifying continued, with Damon getting on to the second row of the grid for the first time in 1998. Another solid race earned him his second successive fourth and in the latter stages he did well to hold off the challenge of Heinz-Harald Frentzen. The best was still to come.

With an ever-improving package and bubbling with confidence, Hill found another place in qualifying and a season's best third place on the grid in Spa. After the aborted first start Hill got off to a flyer at the second start and raced into the lead. He held off Schumacher Senior for the first eight laps but when the German took the lead at the Bus Stop he looked on his way to victory. Then, in terrible conditions, the German ran into Coulthard and allowed Damon back into the lead, which he held on to for his first victory since he won the Championship at Suzuka in 1996. The celebrations showed the relief.

Frustration returned briefly at Monza, where qualifying traffic interfered with Hill's attempts to set competitive times, and he had to settle for a disappointing fourteenth place. The race was a different matter, though, as his two-stop plan worked perfectly and by the flag he had worked his way into a point-winning sixth. For the Luxembourg Grand Prix Damon again looked uneasy with his Jordan and never looked like drastically improving on his qualifying position and, despite running in the points at one stage, he came home a disappointing ninth.

In the final race of the season – his 100th Grand Prix – Damon qualified eighth and with the rest of the world watching the battle for the Championship, Hill drove splendidly. Pushing hard in fifth place, Damon somehow got past Frentzen at the very last corner to gain a last-gasp fourth place and the points his Jordan team needed to secure their best ever Constructors' Cup position outright.

Going into the close season, confidence was high at Jordan and with Hill in particular. The win at Spa – his twenty-second in total – has proved he can win races on his driving ability alone. If he can start the 1999 season the way he finished the 1998 season and maintain his momentum then Damon will get the sort of coverage he likes best – from the podium.

Born: 17/9/60, Hampstead, London, England. Married with two daughters and one son.

Grand Prix 1998 Record

Grand Prix	Grid	Qual Time	Fin	Laps	Race Time	Reason
Australian	10	1:32.399	8	57	1:31:47.279	
Brazilian	11	1:18.955	dq	70	1:37:29.652	
Argentinian	9	1:27.483	8	71	1:49:17.781	
San Marino	7	1:27.592	–	57		Engine
Spanish	8	1:22.835	–	46		Engine
Monaco	15	1:23.151	8	76	1:51:47.513	
Canadian	10	1:19.717	–	42		Electrics
French	7	1:16.245	–	19		Hydraulics
British	7	1:24.542	–	13		Spin
Austrian	15	1:32.718	7	71	1:31:57.710	
German	5	1:43.183	4	45	1:20:55.169	
Hungarian	4	1:18.214	4	77	1:46:20.626	
Belgian	3	1:49.728	1	44	1:43:47.407	

Italian	14	1:27.362	6	53	1:18:16.360
Luxembourg	10	1:19.807	9	66	1:32:22.990
Japanese	8	1:38.603	4	51	1:28:36.026

1998 Position Summary

Contested:	16	Finished:	11
Pole Positions:	0	Fastest Laps:	0
Points:	20		
1st:	1	2nd:	0
3rd:	0	4th:	3
5th:	0	6th:	1

Grand Prix Career Record

Contested:	100	(1992-1998)
Points:	353	1993 (69), 1994 (91), 1995 (69), 1996 (97), 1997 (7), 1998 (20)
Point Finishes:	52	52.00%
Pole Positions:	20	1993 (Fra, Por), 1994 (Fra, GB), 1995 (Bra, Mon, Fra, GB, Ger, Hun, Aus), 1996 (Bra, Arg, Eur, Esp, Can, GB, Ger, Ita, Por)
Fastest Laps:	19	1993 (GB, Ita, Por, Aus), 1994 (San, Fra, GB, Bel, Ita, Jap), 1995 (Esp, Hun, GB, Aus), 1996 (Bra, Eur, San, Ger, Hun)
1st:	22	1993 (Hun, Bel, Ita), 1994 (Esp, GB, Bel, Ita, Por, Jap), 1995 (Arg, San, Hun, Aus), 1996 (Aus, Bra, Arg, San, Can, Fra, Ger, Jap), 1998 (Bel)
2nd:	15	1993 (Bra, Eur, Mon, Fra), 1994 (Bra, Can, Fra, Hun, Eur), 1995 (Mon, Fra, Bel), 1996 (Hun, Por), 1997 (Hun)
3rd:	5	1993 (Can, Por, Aus), 1995 (Por, Pac)
4th:	6	1993 (Jap), 1995 (Esp), 1996 (Eur), 1998 (Ger, Hun, Jap)
5th:	1	1996 (Bel)
6th:	3	1994 (San), 1997 (GB), 1998 (Ita)

Year	Team	No.	Grand Prix
1992	Brabham Judd	2	GB, Hun
1993	Williams Renault	16	SA, Bra (6), Eur (6), San, Esp, Mon (6), Can (4), Fra (6), GB, Ger, Hun (10), Bel (10, Ita (10, Por (4), Jap (3), Aus (4)
1994	Williams Renault	16	Bra (6), Pac, San (1), Mon, Esp (10), Can (6), Fra (6), GB (10), Ger, Hun

			(6), Bel (10), Ita (10), Por (10), Eur (6), Jap (10), Aus
1995	Williams Renault	17	Bra, Arg (10), San (10), Esp (3), Mon (6), Can, Fra (6), GB, Ger, Hun (10), Bel (6), Ita, Por (4), Eur, Pac (4), Jap, Aus (10)
1996	Williams Renault	16	Aus (10), Bra (10), Arg (10), Eur (3), San (10), Mon, Esp, Can (10), Fra (10), GB, Ger (10), Hun (6), Bel (2), Ita, Por (6), Jap (10)
1997	Arrows	17	Aus, Bra, Arg, San, Mon, Esp, Can, Fra, GB (1), Ger, Hun (6), Bel, Ita, Aut, Lux, Jap, Eur
1998	Jordan Mugen Honda	16	Aus, Bra, Arg, San, Esp, Mon, Can, Fra, GB, Aut, Ger (4), Hun (4), Bel (10), Ita (1), Lux, Jap (4)

IRVINE, Eddie   Great Britain

1998: Ferrari   *1999: Ferrari*

By the end of the 1998 season Eddie Irvine was in danger of becoming called The Third Man. Having recorded just three third placed finishes throughout his 65 race career coming into the 1998 season, the Irishman produced no less than five in 1998 along with three (!) second places in what was a quite outstanding season for him. His tally of 47 points was his best haul ever and was almost double the total he secured with Ferrari in 1996.

Playing the perfect number two to Schumacher Senior, Eddie helped the German in no small way in his challenge to regain his World Championship crown. But looking further you sense that Irvine had also got to grips with the red machine and, had team orders not come into play, the Ulsterman might well have recorded a few ten-pointers himself. Don't forget that the Ferrari effort was always behind Michael's drive and what Irvine himself achieved was done with that in mind. Eleven points-scoring races showed great consistency but apart from the Luxembourg race these were all from behind the front row of the grid. Eddie found himself consigned to the second, third and fourth row of the grid throughout the season and improvement in this area would certainly enhance the chances of him recording his first ever Formula 1 victory.

Engine failures in the lead-up to the opening race in Melbourne meant that he was starting eighth on the grid (his worst position of the season –

but one that would be repeated on a couple more occasions). A blistering start saw him jump up the placings but his race was frustrating when he found himself behind Frentzen and unable to pass in what looked a quicker car and he had to settle for fourth. Qualifying was better in Brazil but this time there were no points as he drove home eighth. It was the first of only two races in which he finished but failed to score points.

Consistency in Argentina and San Marino saw two fourth place starts and two third place finishes. In Spain an accident on lap 29 when he tangled with Fisichella was a disappointing end to a great start which saw him jump from sixth on the grid to a running third place.

Two more third place finishes came in Monaco and Montreal. In the principality Eddie crashed during qualifying and then secured seventh place on the grid in the T-car which was set up for Schumacher. Frentzen again proved an obstacle to Irvine early on but after passing him he was able to fight his way through the field to the podium. In Canada qualifying again proved problematic and he finished a lowly eighth for the second time. Third place this time was even more impressive considering he at one point trailed last following a puncture. Steady Eddie again weaved his way through the backfield and attacked the frontrunners for his podium.

The run of fine driving form was rewarded in France. At Magny-Cours Eddie qualified fourth but drove superbly to record what was then only his second ever second place finish in what proved to be a one-two finish for Ferrari. The key to this was the restart to the race when Eddie made an electrifying start to reach the first corner just behind Michael.

The good start deserted him at Silverstone as he fell from fifth to tenth in the early stages. Once again, though, he attacked the cars in front of him to record his fifth third place of the season. Another eighth place on the grid was halved by the finish in Austria with Irvine giving up yet another third place by allowing team-mate Schumacher to pass three laps from the flag. In Germany Irvine equalled his worst finish of the season, eighth, after again struggling to record a really competitive time in qualifying. There should have been at least a point at Hockenheim but a poor pit stop cost him time when he looked set to come home with a point.

Hungaroring and Spa produced successive fifth places on the grid but a broken gearbox put him out at the former after 13 laps while running fourth and in Belgium he spun off whilst looking uncomfortable in Schumacher's T-car after his original had been lost in the multiple pile-up at the original start.

For Ferrari's home race in Monza, Irvine produced his third fifth place start in succession and looked to be coming home third again behind Hakkinen until the Finn's McLaren developed problems and allowed him through to record his second second of the season and another one-two for Ferrari.

Eddie translated his second place finish in Italy into the front row of the grid to give the Ferrari team a different kind of one-two. Lining up alongside Schumacher on the front row, Irvine made the better start and got into the lead at the first corner before clipping the kerb into the chicane to allow Michael to pass him (again). Pit stops saw Irvine lose places to the two McLarens as he drove home fourth.

Japan's Suzuka track is a firm favourite of Irvine's and he finished the season on a high, coming home second from fourth on the grid. Team-mate Schumacher's failure to secure the Championship did little to help Irvine's chances of actually being able to race his team-mate in 1999 as he will certainly be consigned to the number two role once more. Most impartial observers will be hoping he records his first ever win at some point in 1999. One thing is certain, though, – his next point will be his 100th in Formula 1 racing.

Born: 10/11/65, Newtownards, Northern Ireland. Single.

Grand Prix 1998 Record

Grand Prix	Grid	Qual Time	Fin	Laps	Race Time	Reason
Australian	8	1:31.767	4	57	1:31:47.075	
Brazilian	6	1:18.449	8	71	1:37:28.184	
Argentinian	4	1:26.780	3	72	1:49:33.920	
San Marino	4	1:27.169	3	62	1:35:16.368	
Spanish	6	1:22.350	–	28		Accident
Monaco	7	1:21.712	3	78	1:52:04.973	
Canadian	8	1:19.616	3	69	1:41:57.414	
French	4	1:15.527	2	71	1:35:04.601	
British	5	1:24.436	3	60	1:47:31.649	
Austrian	8	1:31.651	4	71	1:31:28.062	
German	6	1:43.270	8	45	1:21:19.633	
Hungarian	5	1:18.325	–	13	Gearbox	
Belgian	5	1:50.189	–	25	Spin	
Italian	5	1:26.159	2	53	1:17:47.649	
Luxembourg	2	1:18.907	4	67	1:33.12.971	
Japanese	4	1:38.197	2	51	1:27:29.026	

1998 Position Summary

Contested:	16	Finished:	13
Pole Positions:	0	Fastest Laps:	0

Points:	47		
1st:	0	2nd:	3
3rd:	5	4th:	3
5th:	0	6th:	0

Grand Prix Career Record

Contested:	81	(1993-1998)
Points:	99	1993 (1), 1994 (6), 1995 (10), 1996 (11), 1997 (24), 1998 (47)
Point Finishes:	27	33.33%
Pole Positions:	0	
Fastest Laps:	0	
1st:	0	
2nd:	4	1997 (Arg), 1998 (Fra, Ita, Jap)
3rd:	9	1995 (Can), 1996 (Aus), 1997 (San, Mon, Fra, Jap), 1998 (Aus, Aut, Lux)
4th:	6	1994 (Eur), 1995 (Jap), 1996 (San), 1998 (Aus, Aut, Lux)
5th:	5	1994 (Jap), 1995 (Esp), 1996 (Arg, Por), 1997 (Eur)
6th:	3	1993 (Jap), 1994 (Esp), 1995 (Eur)

Year	Team	No.	Grand Prix
1993	Jordan Hart	2	Jap (1), Aus
1994	Jordan Hart	13	Bra, Esp (1), Can, Fra, GB, Ger, Hun, Bel, Ita, Por, Eur (3), Jap (2), Aus
1995	Jordan Peugeot	17	Bra, Arg, San, Esp (2), Mon, Can (4), Fra, GB, Ger, Hun, Bel, Ita, Por, Eur (1), Pac, Jap (3), Aus
1996	Ferrari	16	Aus (4), Bra, Arg (2), Eur, San (3), Mon, Esp, Can, Fra, GB, Ger, Hun, Bel, Ita, Por (2), Jap
1997	Ferrari	17	Aus, Bra, Arg (6), San (4), Mon (4), Esp, Can, Fra (4), GB, Ger, Hun, Bel, Ita, Aut, Lux, Jap (4), Eur (2)
1998	Ferrari	16	Aus (3), Bra, Arg (4), San (4), Esp, Mon (4), Can (4), Fra (6), GB (4), Aut (3), Ger, Hun, Bel, Ita (6), Lux (3), Jap (6)

MAGNUSSEN, Jan   Denmark

1998: Stewart Ford   *1999: –*

The signs were there in his debut season and they were really confirmed in 1998. The rumours about Jan Magnussen's position at Stewart were doing the rounds during the latter stages of the 1997 season and they were quick to resurface in 1998 before being proved correct after the Dane had completed the Canadian Grand Prix. Perhaps the heightening of the whispers did something to spur him on and it was ironic that he secured his first ever F1 point in what proved to be his last race for the Stewart team! He was never able to translate his F3 success into the F1 cockpit.

Qualifying was a problem. In his seven races in 1998 the best starting position was sixteenth. Just three finishes came from those races although in fairness the tenth and twelfth positions he achieved in two of them were on a par with the team's number one, Rubens Barrichello. Perhaps the Dane's biggest problem in terms of his place with the team came in San Marino where, with the Ford Powermen in attendance for the race, he careered into the back of team-mate Rubens Barrichello at the start. The collision forced the Brazilian out of the race and, after losing time while he pitted for a new nose, Magnussen retired after eight laps with gearbox problems.

The first races of the season lasted just one lap for Magnussen. Lack of testing miles no doubt hindered qualification but, having toured the gravel early on, he then span off terminally after clashing with Ralf Schumacher on the second lap. A more measured race in Brazil meant that Magnussen provided his team with their first finish of the season. Although he finished eleventh at the flag, he was promoted to tenth when Damon Hill was excluded from the result for a weight infringement. Lack of testing on the Friday due to mechanical problems was not the best preparation for the qualifying in Argentina for the Dane. After going off early on in qualifying he had to rush to get the spare and ultimately found himself last on the grid for race day. A frustrating weekend ended when he was forced to retire early on with transmission problems.

After the trials and tribulations of Imola, Magnussen ran home twelfth in Spain, having gained five places on his starting position. Suspension problems bounced him out at Monaco before he made that ironic last drive in Montreal where he had run as high as fourth at one point. Following the race the Stewart team announced the departure of the Dane, citing his lack of improvement in qualifying as the principle reason.

Born: 4/7/73, Roskilde, Denmark. Single. One son.

Grand Prix 1998 Record

Grand Prix	Grid	Qual Time	Fin	Laps	Race Time	Reason
Australian	18	1:34.906	–	1		Accident
Brazilian	16	1:19.644	10	70	1:37:41.719	
Argentinian	22	1:31.178	–	17		Transmission
San Marino	20	1:31.017	–	8		Gearbox
Spanish	18	1:24.112	12	63	1:34:01.002	
Monaco	17	1:23.411	–	30		Suspension
Canadian	20	1:21.629	6	68	1:42:26.707	

1998 Position Summary

Contested:	7	Finished:	3
Pole Positions:	0	Fastest Laps:	0
Points:	1		
1st:	0	2nd:	0
3rd:	0	4th:	0
5th:	0	6th:	1

Grand Prix Career Record

Contested:	25	(1995-1998)
Points:	1	1998 (1)
Point Finishes:	1	4.00%
Pole Positions:	0	
Fastest Laps:	0	
1st:	0	
2nd:	0	
3rd:	0	
4th:	0	
5th:	0	
6th:	1	1998 (Can)

Year	Team	No.	Grand Prix
1995	McLaren Mercedes	1	Pac
1997	Stewart Ford	17	Aus, Bra, Arg, San, Mon, Esp, Can, Fra, GB, Ger, Hun, Bel, Ita, Aut, Lux, Jap, Eur
1998	Stewart Ford	7	Aus, Bra, Arg, San, Esp, Mon, Can (1)

NAKANO, Shinji   Japan

1998: Minardi Ford   *1999: –*

Having learned his trade with Prost in 1997, Nakano came into the
Minardi team relatively late in the pre-season but still managed to turn

in an overall good performance on the season. He improved his race completions by two to ten and, despite not adding to the two points he scored for Prost, he produced a couple of performances, notably at Silverstone and Spa, that on other days might have registered some.

Qualifying positions were generally at the back end of the grid with eighteenth being his best position, coming in Brazil and Canada. For the first race of the season, having to use the T-car, he found himself on the back of the grid and out of the race after just eight laps when the transmission went. Brazil brought a better qualifying performance but on the fourth lap of the race the Japanese spun off at the first turn. It was third time lucky in Argentina, though, and despite being plagued with brake problems he managed to bring the car home in a lucky thirteenth place.

At San Marino Nakano must have thought someone had put a curse on his car's engines – he suffered a couple of blow-outs with the most catastrophic coming in lap 28 of the race. Following that disappointment there was huge encouragement as he produced six successive race completions. Fourteenth in Spain in the first of these (where he had acute oversteer problems) saw gradual improvements in Monaco (ninth) and a season's best in Canada where he finished just a second outside of a point in a race where he ran as high as fifth.

Although he was classified as having finished seventeenth in France, Nakano actually didn't reach the chequered flag because his engine failed in the final stages of the race while he was running one place higher. At Silverstone, it was back with another good performance, finishing eighth despite starting from the back row. The sequence of finishes came to a temporary halt in Austria where he finished eleventh. A gearbox failure forced him out of the race in Germany where he was never that competitive anyway and his fifteenth place in the next race in Hungary would have been bettered had a jammed refuelling valve not added an extra half minute to his second pit stop.

Nakano managed to survive the first start pile-up and made the restart to race home as the last of the eight finishes. This was another instance where he might have done even better had he not lost vital time in the pits – this time though it was for repairs after he had been hit by Giancarlo Fisichella's Benetton. A gradually failing engine finally gave up the ghost for Nakano on lap 14 of the Italian GP while a one-stop strategy in Luxembourg didn't really help the Minardi driver, who finished fifteenth. In Japan it was electrical problems that brought his season to an end after 40 laps.

Born: 1/4/71, Osaka, Japan. Single.

Grand Prix 1998 Record

Grand Prix	Grid	Qual Time	Fin	Laps	Race Time	Reason
Australian	22	1:35.301	–	8		Transmission
Brazilian	18	1:20.390	–	3		Spin
Argentinian	19	1:30.054	13	69	1:49:18.217	
San Marino	21	1:31.255	–	27		Engine
Spanish	20	1:24.538	14	63	1:34:11.328	
Monaco	19	1:23.957	9	76	1:51:48.485	
Canadian	18	1:21.230	7	68	1:42:27.937	
French	21	1:18.273	17	65		Engine
British	19	1:28.123	8	58	1:48:26.357	
Austrian	21	1:34.536	11	70	1:31:44.313	
German	20	1:46.713	–	36		Gearbox
Hungarian	19	1:20.635	15	74	1:47:45.727	
Belgian	21	1:55.084	8	39	1:46:01.069	
Italian	21	1:29.101	–	13		Engine
Luxembourg	20	1:22.078	15	65	1:32:56.589	
Japanese	20	1:41.315	–	40		Electrics

1998 Position Summary

Contested:	16	Finished:	10
Pole Positions:	0	Fastest Laps:	0
Points:	0		
1st:	0	2nd:	0
3rd:	0	4th:	0
5th:	0	6th:	0

Grand Prix Career Record

Contested:	31	(1997-1998)
Points:	2	1997 (2), 1998 (0)
Point Finishes:	2	6.45%
Pole Positions:	0	
Fastest Laps:	0	
1st:	0	
2nd:	0	
3rd:	0	
4th:	0	
5th:	0	
6th:	2	1997 (Can, Hun)

Year Team

Year	Team	No.	Grand Prix
1997	Prost Mugen Honda	17	Aus, Bra, Arg, San, Mon, Esp, Can (2), Fra, GB, Ger, Hun (2), Bel, Ita, Aut, Lux, Jap, Eur

1998	Minardi Ford	16	Aus, Bra, Arg, San, Esp, Mon, Can, Fra, GB, Aut, Ger, Hun, Bel, Ita, Lux, Jap

PANIS, Olivier   France

1998: Prost Peugeot   *1999: Prost Peugeot*

Whatever happened to Olivier Panis? Two years ago in these pages I suggested he could be the next great driver and the man to take the then newly named Prost team into the millennium as one of the Championship challengers. He went some way towards that before breaking his legs at the Canadian Grand Prix in 1997. Perhaps that sapped some of his confidence – perhaps. Problems, though, lay within the overall package and the AP01 was never a contender in 1998. For the first time in five years as an F1 driver Panis failed to score a point.

The opening race of the season in Australia didn't provide the best of starts. An experienced driver, Panis should know better than to abandon his car in gear after spinning and causing the qualifying session to be red-flagged, but that's what he did and as such lost his best times as punishment and found himself on the last row of the grid. Problematic gearboxes didn't help matters over the weekend and, given his starting position, perhaps a ninth place finish wasn't an overly bad weekend's work. The gearbox was still proving problematic in Brazil and when it seized late in the race it put paid to a reasonable race by the Frenchman given that he had to drive it in the spare car after writing off his own in a Sunday morning crash. The only highlight from Brazil was the ninth place on the grid – that was to be his highest position of the year although he was to match it in Italy. Argentina brought little more joy. Fifteenth on the grid was perhaps more reward for a better-looking set-up and with a heavy fuel load Panis was driving reasonably well in seventh place. Then an engine blow-out on lap 66 finished the race for him although he was classified fifteenth.

With the gearbox becoming more reliable Panis now had a problem with his engine which expired during the race in San Marino. Hydraulic engine problems were the cause for a third successive non-finish – this time in Spain. Monaco and Canada were the next two venues that provided two more non-finishes. In Monaco the gremlins bit at him all weekend and if it could go wrong it did. The net result was very few laps and an almost guessed-at set-up. Not surprisingly he qualified at the rear of the grid and then was forced out of the race after 49 laps with what turned out to be nothing more than a loose wheel nut. As I said, if it could go wrong it did…

The Canadian race was one of the first where Panis was able to go through the weekend without too many problems. Qualifying though was hampered by lack of grip and the inability to get the tyres up to running temperature. At the scene of his big accident in 1997 he managed to stay relatively clear of the shunt at the first start and by staying out on a full load of fuel after the restart he actually ran as high as third as other drivers went through their pit stops. Then on lap 40 his engine gave up the ghost and spun him into the gravel and out of the race.

Despite having moved from Magny-Cours to Paris prior to the start of the 1998 season, the French circuit is still very much home court for the Prost team and their engine suppliers Peugeot. Clutch problems hampered Panis's qualifying run and he had to be disappointed with a sixteenth place on the grid. After six races without reaching the chequered flag he must have been relieved that his car stayed the course this time, although he didn't make up too many places to finish eleventh.

At Silverstone Panis found himself starting the race once again on the back row. The demotion was only a few places behind what he had achieved and came when the car was found to be underweight. As in Australia, Panis started to weave his way through the field and was in the middle order when he went into a slow speed pirouette after aquaplaning through water at Priory. He was out of the race. Clutch problems returned at the A1-Ring – he couldn't get the car into gear at the start and, despite a push and a shove, couldn't get the car engaged and was forced to stop before he had started.

Having failed to finish eight of the previous ten races, two successive finishes in Germany and Hungary came as a great relief. Starting sixteenth on the grid, Panis made his way through the other back markers early on but then suffered a stop-go penalty because of a jump start. He was also forced to make an additional pit stop for a puncture which took further toll and he came home fifteenth. The Hungarian Grand Prix came with the news that Panis would be staying with the team for the 1999 season. It did little to inspire in what was a very poor showing. Twentieth on the grid – this time without being demoted there – was converted into a marginally more positive twelfth place – bettered only by his ninth place in the opening race of the season.

Spa came and went for Panis, who was involved with team-mate Trulli in the massive pile-up at the initial start. With Trulli two places better off in qualification he was awarded the T-car and so Panis had to sit the race out. Monza produced a better qualifying performance where he equalled his season's best of ninth on the grid. Vibrations throughout the car spelled trouble at the start and after two unscheduled pit stops to try and locate the cause of the trouble (to no avail) the Frenchman retired after 15 laps.

After the generally positive progress made over the weekend of the Italian race, it seemed to evaporate for the Luxembourg Grand Prix. Transmission problems and understeer reaction did help and with a one-stop strategy he made up only three places and finished twelfth. There was a one-place improvement five weeks later for the final race of the season at Suzuka.

At the end of November Panis went into hospital to remove the metal plate that had been put there after his 1997 accident. That meant virtually no testing time with the team during the last couple of months of 1998. Another year's experience with Peugeot may help and certainly as far as the 1999 season goes Panis has more than a few records to set straight. All aficionados will no doubt be watching with interest – certainly this one will – but deep down you have to wonder if the Frenchman has made the right decision in standing with Prost. The 1999 season might have been the time for a new team and a new challenge. Another poor showing this time round might damage his chances for good.

Born: 2/9/66, Lyon, France. Married with one son.

Grand Prix 1998 Record

Grand Prix	Grid	Qual Time	Fin	Laps	Race Time	Reason
Australian	21	1:35.215	9	57	1:32:03.548	
Brazilian	9	1:18.753	–	63		Gearbox
Argentinian	15	1:29.320	15	65		Engine
San Marino	13	1:28.270	–	56		Engine
Spanish	12	1:22.963	16	60		Engine
Monaco	18	1:23.536	–	49		Loose wheel
Canadian	15	1:20.303	–	39		Engine
French	16	1:17.671	11	69	1:35:02.913	
British	22	no time	–	40		Spin
Austrian	10	1:32.081	–	0		Clutch
German	16	1:45.197	15	44	1:21:52.283	
Hungarian	20	1:20.663	12	74	1:45:29.999	
Belgian	15	1:52.784	–	0		Accident at first start
Italian	9	1:26.681	–	15		Vibrations
Luxembourg	15	1:21.048	12	65	1:32:29.872	
Japanese	13	1:40.037	11	50	1:28:20.327	

1998 Position Summary

Contested:	16	Finished:	8
Pole Positions:	0	Fastest Laps:	0
Points:	0		

1st:	0	2nd:	0
3rd:	0	4th:	0
5th:	0	6th:	0

Grand Prix Career Record

Contested:	75	(1994-1998)
Points:	54	1994 (9), 1995 (16), 1996 (13), 1997 (16), 1998 (0)
Point Finishes	17	22.67%
Pole Positions:	0	
Fastest Laps:	0	
1st:	1	1996 (Mon)
2nd:	3	1994 (Ger), 1995 (Aus), 1997 (Esp)
3rd:	1	1997 (Bra)
4th:	3	1995 (Can, GB), 1997 (Mon)
5th:	4	1994 (Aus), 1995 (Jap), 1996 (Hun), 1997 (Aus)
6th:	5	1994 (Hun), 1995 (Esp, Hun), 1996 (Bra), 1997 (Lux)

Year	Team	No.	Grand Prix
1994	Ligier Renault	16	Bra, Pac, San, Mon, Esp, Can, Fra, GB, Ger (6), Hun (1), Bel, Ita, Por, Eur, Jap, Aus (2)
1995	Ligier Mugen Honda	17	Bra, Arg, San, Esp (1), Mon, Can (3), Fra, GB (3), Ger, Hun (1), Bel, Ita, Por, Eur, Pac, Jap (2), Aus (6)
1996	Ligier Mugen Honda	16	Aus, Bra (1), Arg, Eur, San, Mon (10), Esp, Can, Fra, GB, Ger, Hun (2), Bel, Ita, Por, Jap
1997	Prost Mugen Honda	10	Aus (2), Bra (4), Arg, San, Mon (3), Esp (6), Can, Lux (1), Jap, Eur
1998	Prost Peugeot	16	Aus, Bra, Arg, San, Esp, Mon, Can, Fra, GB, Aut, Ger, Hun, Bel, Ita, Lux, Jap

ROSSET, Ricardo   Brazil

1998: Tyrrell Ford   *1999: –*

It was a pretty awful season for Ricardo Rosset. The fact that he only managed to finish four of his races was not as damning as the fact that he failed to qualify for three by virtue of being outside the 107% qualifying rule. (You may recall that he also fell foul of the 107% rule while racing for the Lola F1 team in their abortive 1996 season.) If this wasn't bad enough for the Brazilian, he was largely outraced and out-qualified by the team's rookie 'Tiger' Takagi and it is difficult to believe that he will be able to secure another drive in F1 without bringing with him a large sponsorship deal to the team that takes his services.

Despite all the negative points, he did actually manage to provide the team with their best finish of the year when, starting from the back of the grid, he ran home in eighth place at the Canadian Grand Prix, having avoided the problems of the first start and taking advantage of the safety car to reduce his race pit-stop time.

Gearbox problems plagued him at the first two races of the season, but in Argentina he came home in fourteenth place. A compressor problem terminated his race at Imola and this was followed by qualifying failures in Spain and Monaco. After the success in Canada came two more non-finishes – an engine failure in France and a spin after tangling with Esteban Tuero's Minardi at Silverstone. Twelfth from another last place start in Austria provided some respite before a hat-trick of non-starts. In Germany a practice accident led to him being ruled out of the race by Professor Watkins and in Hungary he missed the 107% cut by over three-quarters of a second. In Belgium he seemed to ignore the problems of the first start and simply drove into the cars in front of him to leave him car less for the second start!

Another twelfth place came in Italy, where his qualifying position of eighteenth matched his best grid position of the season. An engine failure after 36 laps brought the Brazilian's Luxembourg GP to an end and with it almost certainly Ricardo Rosset's career as a Formula 1 driver.
Born: 27/7/68, Sao Paulo, Brazil. Single.

Grand Prix 1998 Record

Grand Prix	Grid	Qual Time	Fin	Laps	Race Time	Reason
Australian	19	1:35.119	–	25		Gear selection
Brazilian	21	1:20.748	–	52		Gearbox
Argentinian	21	1:30.437	14	68	1:48:49.538	
San Marino	22	1:31.482	–	48		Engine
Spanish	–	1:25.946	dnq	–		
Monaco	–	1:25.737	dnq	–		
Canadian	22	1:21.824	8	68	1:43:17.371	
French	18	1:17.908	–	16		Engine
British	20	1:28.608	–	29		Spin
Austrian	22	1:34.910	12	69	1:33:28.193	
German	–	–	–	–		Practice accident
Hungarian	–	1:23.140	dnq	–		
Belgian	20	1:54.850	–	0		Accident at first start
Italian	18	1:28.286	12	51	1:18:12.566	

| Luxembourg | 22 | 1:22.822 | – | 36 | | Engine |
| Japanese | – | 1:43.259 | dnq | | | |

1998 Position Summary

Contested:	12	Finished:	4
Pole Positions:	0	Fastest Laps:	0
Points:	0		
1st-6th:	0	Best Finish:	8th

Grand Prix Career Record

Contested: 28   (1996-1998)
Points: 0
Pole Positions: 0
Fastest Laps: 0
1st-6th: 0
Best Finish: 8th   1996 (Hun), 1998 (Can)

Year	Team	No.	Grand Prix
1996	Arrows Hart	16	Aus, Bra, Arg, Eur, San, Mon, Esp, Can, Fra, GB, Ger, Hun, Bel, Ita, Por, Jap
1997	Lola Ford	–	*Failed to qualify for Australian GP*
1998	Tyrrell Ford	12	Aus, Bra, Arg, San, Can, Fra, GB, Aut, Ger, Bel, Ita, Lux

SALO, Mika   Finland

1998: Arrows   *1999: Arrows*

Finland's other Mika has never been short on confidence. He has always been heralded as one of the quicker drivers in F1 but once again he failed to impress and the reputation he established with Tyrrell is starting to wane. Perhaps he was never going to fulfil the said potential at Arrows. His fourth full season in Formula 1, he did maintain his record of having scored points in each of those seasons.

It wasn't a great season by any stretch of the imagination, however, with just five finishes from the 16 races. The best performance came in Monaco where his problem-struck car lasted the pace and took advantage of the attrition being suffered by others. Having looked good in pre-qualifying, he had to take the T-car for the session and expressed his disappointment at only being eighth on the grid. He held his place at the start and came home a reasonably impressive fourth – his best ever finish in F1 – for what were to be his only points of the season.

Eighth on the grid at Monaco was not to be his best starting point of the season. He moved one row up for the Austrian Grand Prix to start sixth, and it might have been even better had he not encountered traffic on his last flying lap in qualifying. As it was it was team-mate Pedro Diniz who helped the Finn to an early finish when he shunted into him at the start. Salo came home for repairs but soon found out they were not possible and had to retire after just one lap.

The season had got underway with three successive failures. A transmission problem in Australia was followed by engine maladies in Brazil and a gradual loss of gearbox function in Argentina. Ninth place marked a first finish at San Marino and it might have been a lot better had a fuel hose problem not forced him to make an extra pit stop.

A blown engine a third of the way through the race in Spain brought proceedings to an end there and after the success of Monaco, his steering was damaged in the start at Canada. This was followed by what appeared to be a suspension failure that led to him crashing into the wall and out of the race on lap 19. A poor start at Magny-Cours marred his race in France. Having dropped to twenty-first he worked his way through the back field and eventually finished thirteenth.

A spin at Silverstone and the accident at the A1-Ring added two more non-finishes for the Finn. Clutch problems hampered his progress in Germany but he still managed to gain three places on his start and finished in fourteenth. The gearbox problems of South America rearose in Hungary and Salo missed the restart at Spa after his car had been badly damaged in the first start – team-mate Diniz getting the spare. In Italy the problems continued when throttle troubles after just 14 laps ended the race for him.

A lack of grip was one problem Salo reported for the Luxembourg Grand Prix but the extra diligence that inspired on his behalf seemed to help get him home in a second successive fourteenth place finish. That same number figured in his race in Japan when a hydraulic failure ended his race on that lap.

Salo did provide one memorable moment, though, by delivering probably the quote of the year after the Brazilian race, when he said, "We had a lot of problems this weekend, and I am looking forward to getting to the next race so we can have some more".

Born: 30/11/66, Helsinki, Finland. Single.

Grand Prix 1998 Record

Grand Prix	Grid	Qual Time	Fin	Laps	Race Time	Reason
Australian	16	1:33.927	–	23		Transmission
Brazilian	20	1:20.481	–	18		Engine

Argentinian	17	1:29.617	–	18		Gearbox
San Marino	14	1:28.798	9	60	1:35:55.865	
Spanish	17	1:23.887	–	21		Engine
Monaco	8	1:22.144	4	78	1:52:23.958	
Canadian	17	1:20.536	–	18		Steering/accident
French	19	1:17.970	13	69	1:35:43.315	
British	13	1:26.487	–	27		Spin
Austrian	6	1:31.028	–	1		Accident damage
German	17	1:45.276	14	44	1:21:13.440	
Hungarian	13	1:19.712	–	18		Gearbox
Belgian	18	1:53.207	–	0		Accident at first start
Italian	16	1:27.744	–	32		Throttle
Luxembourg	16	1:21.120	14	65	1:32:53.413	
Japanese	15	1:40.387	–	14		Hydraulics

1998 Position Summary

Contested:	16	Finished:	5
Pole Positions:	0	Fastest Laps:	0
Points:	3		
1st:	0	2nd:	0
3rd:	0	4th:	1
5th:	0	6th:	0

Grand Prix Career Record

Contested:	68	(1994-1998)
Points:	15	1995 (5), 1996 (5), 1997 (2), 1998 (3)
Point Finishes:	8	11.76%
Pole Positions:	0	
Fastest Laps:	0	
1st:	0	
2nd:	0	
3rd:	0	
4th:	1	1998 (Mon)
5th:	5	1995 (Ita, Por), 1996 (Bra, Mon), 1997 (Mon)
6th:	2	1995 (Jap), 1996 (Aus)

Year	Team	No.	Grand Prix
1994	Lotus Mugen Honda	2	Jap, Aus
1995	Tyrrell Yamaha	17	Bra, Arg, San, Esp, Mon, Can, Fra, GB, Ger, Hun, Bel, Ita (2), Por, Eur, Pac, Jap (1), Aus (2)
1996	Tyrrell Yamaha	16	Aus (1), Bra (2), Arg, Eur, San, Mon (2), Esp, Can, Fra, GB, Ger, Hun, Bel, Ita, Por, Jap

| 1997 | Tyrrell Ford | 17 | Aus, Bra, Arg, San, Mon (2), Esp, Can, Fra, GB, Ger, Hun, Bel, Ita, Aut, Lux, Jap, Eur |
| 1998 | Arrows | 16 | Aus, Bra, Arg, San, Esp, Mon (3), Can, Fra, GB, Aut, Ger, Hun, Bel, Ita, Lux, Jap |

SCHUMACHER, Michael   Germany

1998: Ferrari   *1999: Ferrari*

On his own time scale then 1998 was the year by which the prancing horse would reign supreme. It didn't quite happen that way and there was no third World Championship title for the German in '98 but Schumacher Senior pushed all the way and was only thwarted in the end by Mika Hakkinen having the drive of his life. Schumacher will return to Ferrari for a fourth season where the hopes will be high and also in the knowledge that in team-mate Eddie Irvine he has a driver committed to his cause.

Apart from one aberration, surprisingly at his home Grand Prix, Schumacher's Ferrari was never off the front two rows of the starting grid. On paper that sounds great but the red machine's qualifying performance was never quite the ultimate experience for Michael – he often seemed to be driving his car beyond its real limits. Indeed, he had to wait until Italy to record his first pole of the season, a position he would maintain for the final races of the season. His tally of three poles was the same as for 1997.

Schumacher always pushes to the limit but in the opening race in Melbourne it often looked as though he was overstepping that invisible line – spinning and slipping off throughout the weekend and having his race come to an end on lap six when his engine failed. It was to be the first of only two FTF (Failures To Finish) in the season. The next races provided excursions to different steps on the podium. In Brazil it was third from a place fourth on the grid despite stalling the engine on his second pit stop. In Argentina the first of his season's wins came from the front row of the grid and the track seemed particularly suited to the new tyres supplied by Goodyear, manifested by a half-minute lead at the flag. Third on the grid in San Marino and Spain produced a second and third. The former, with Schuey's car sporting sidewings for the first time, saw him chasing Coulthard for the win in the final laps. The wings were gone in Spain and a stop-go penalty almost cost him dear. Monaco brought the German his worst result of the year. It wasn't the result of a bad drive, but bad luck that saw a coming together with

Wurz providing him with a broken rear suspension that needed repair and the loss of too many seconds in the pit lane.

The trip to Canada saw Michael start to eat into Hakkinen's Championship lead in real style and provided the first of three successive victories which was achieved with another stop-go penalty coming when he had beached Frentzen on the grass after emerging from the pit lane. The win lifted him into second place in the Drivers' Championship. France and Britain saw starts from the number two spot on the grid. At Magny-Cours the race restart helped and with team-mate Irvine slotted in behind him, Michael was able to build a lead that he maintained for all but one lap. At Silverstone the safety car helped the German get up behind Hakkinen and then overtake him at the restart. There was confusion at the end relating to a yellow flag stop-go penalty which saw Schumi come in for his ten second fine on his last lap, and crossing the line in the pit lane. The victory was confirmed (after a McLaren appeal) and Michael was now just two points behind Hakkinen.

By previous standards the Austrian and German races were let-downs. At the A1-Ring a gravel trip and the need for a new nose cone hindered his progress but nevertheless a podium third place was secured – but only after team-mate Eddie Irvine had controversially let him pass three laps from the chequered flag. At Hockenheim a disastrous qualifying session meant a ninth place on the grid (his worst of the season) which was at least converted into a couple of points by the end. The gap in the Drivers' Championship was now stretched to 16 points with just five races remaining for Michael to pull it back. And that he did immediately with a win in Hungary. An accident on lap 26 at Spa meant no points which was made all the more unbearable because the German was well in the lead and about to lap Coulthard. In heavy rain, visibility was bad and Schuey ran into the back of the Scot who kept an inside line to let him pass. Michael was furious after the race and tried to confront Coulthard in his garage when both had returned to the paddock – he had to be physically restrained. Most believed it was down to the German, though, something that was upheld by the race stewards and the subsequent Ferrari appeal was rightly turned down.

Three races to go and seven points down, Michael fired in his first pole position of the season at the Ferrari home Grand Prix in Italy and recorded his sixth win of the season in front of the tifosi. More importantly, with Hakkinen finishing fourth, it meant that the two protagonists were equal on points going into the penultimate race of the season. With points level Hakkinen remained ahead courtesy of more wins and more second places so it was imperative that Michael record a win in Luxembourg. It was also a race where Schuey had to finish otherwise the title could go to the Finn. It was Michael at his best in qualifying as he recorded his second successive pole. In the race, though, tyre wear and a jerky car ultimately took their toll. Despite taking the lead at the start, Ferrari's pit stops were just fractionally slower than McLaren's and Michael had to suffer second place behind Hakkinen.

So to Japan with Michael trailing Hakkinen by four points. A win was needed with the hope that Hakkinen would not finish in the top two. Having qualified for a third successive pole, the German's car stalled on the grid at what was a second restart. Technical problem or driver error – the rumours persist but the fact was that he had to start from the back of the grid. He went to the back and so did any real thoughts of winning the title. The charge was on but despite a demon drive in which he set the race's fastest lap, tyre wear took its toll and he suffered a puncture. With that went the race and Championship hopes.

Schumacher now has 526 Championship points and moves to third in the all-time points list – only Senna and Prost have scored more. Those two drivers are also ahead in the list of victories while only Prost has recorded more fastest laps. 1999 will almost certainly mirror 1998 for Schumacher and it will be a surprise if the battle plans are not the same. Regarded by most as the best driver on the grid, he is blatantly prone to making errors on the big occasions.

Born: 3/1/69, Kerpen, Germany. Married with one child.

Grand Prix 1998 Record

Grand Prix	Grid	Qual Time	Fin	Laps	Race Time	Reason
Australian	3	1:30.767	–	5		Engine
Brazilian	4	1:18.250	3	72	1:38:12.297	
Argentinian	2	1:26.251	1	72	1:48:36.175	
San Marino	3	1:26.437	2	62	1:34:29.147	fl
Spanish	3	1:21.785	3	65	1:34:24.715	
Monaco	4	1:20.702	10	76	1:52:16.789	
Canadian	3	1:18.497	1	69	1:40:57.355	fl
French	2	1:15.159	1	71	1:34:45.026	
British	2	1:23.720	1	60	1:47:12.450	fl
Austrian	4	1:30.551	3	71	1:31:23.178	
German	9	1:43.459	5	45	1:21:00.597	
Hungarian	3	1:17.366	1	77	1:45:25.550	fl
Belgian	4	1:50.027	–	25		Accident – fl
Italian	1	1:25.298	1	53	1:17:09.672	
Luxembourg	1	1:18.561	2	67	1:32:17.000	
Japanese	1	1:36.293	–	31		Puncture – fl

1998 Position Summary

Contested:	16	Finished:	13
Pole Positions:	3	Fastest Laps:	6
Points:	86		
1st:	6	2nd:	2
3rd:	3	4th:	0
5th:	1	6th:	0

Grand Prix Career Record

Contested:	118	
Points:	526	1991 (4), 1992 (53), 1993 (52), 1994 (92), 1995 (102), 1996 (59), 1997 (78), 1998 (86)
Point Finishes:	79	66.95%
Pole Positions:	20	1994 (Mon, Esp, Can, Hun, Eur, Jap), 1995 (San, Esp, Can, Jap), 1996 (San, Mon, Fra, Hun), 1997 (Can, Fra, Hun), 1998 (Ita, Lux, Jap)
Fastest Laps:	35	1992 (Bel, Aus), 1993 (Bra, Esp, Can, Fra, Ger), 1994 (Bra, Pac, Mon, Esp, Can, Hun, Eur, Aus), 1995 (Bra, Arg, Mon, Fra, Ger, Bel, Eur, Pac, Jap), 1996 (Esp, Ita), 1997 (Mon, Fra, GB), 1998 (San, Can, GB, Hun, Bel, Jap)
1st:	33	1992 (Bel), 1993 (Por), 1994 (Bra, Pac, San, Can, Mon, Ger, Hun, Eur), 1995 (Bra, Esp, Mon, Fra, Ger, Bel, Eur, Pac, Jap), 1996 (Esp, Bel, Ita), 1997 (Mon, Can, Fra, Bel, Jap), 1998 (Arg, Can, Fra, GB, Hun, Ita)
2nd:	19	1992 (Esp, Can, Aus), 1993 (San, Can, GB, Ger, Bel), 1994 (Esp, Jap), 1995 (Por), 1996 (Eur, San, Jap), 1997 (Aus, San, Ger), 1998 (San, Lux)
3rd:	13	1992 (Mex, Bra, Ger, Ita), 1993 (Bra, Esp, Fra), 1995 (Arg), 1996 (Bra, Por), 1998 (Bra, Esp, Aut)
4th:	6	1992 (SA, Mon, GB), 1996 (Ger), 1997 (Esp, Hun)
5th:	4	1991 (Ita), 1995 (Can), 1997 (Bra), 1998 (Ger)
6th:	4	1991 (Por, Esp), 1997 (Ita, Aut)

Year	Team	No.	Grand Prix
1991	Jordan Ford	1	Bel
	Benetton Ford	5	Ita (2), Por (1), Esp (1), Jap, Aus
1992	Benetton Ford	16	SA (3), Mex (4), Bra (4), Esp (6), San, Mon (3), Can (6), Fra, GB (3), Ger (4), Hun, Bel (10), Ita (4), Por, Jap, Aus (6)

1993	Benetton Ford	16	SA, Bra (4), Eur, San (6), Esp (4), Mon, Can (6), Fra (4), GB (6), Ger (6), Hun, Bel (6), Ita, Por (10), Jap, Aus
1994	Benetton Ford	14	Bra (10), Pac (10), San (10), Mon (10), Esp (6), Can (10), Fra (10), GB, Ger, Hun (10), Bel, Eur (10), Jap (6), Aus
1995	Benetton Renault	17	Bra (10), Arg (4), San, Esp (10), Mon (10), Can (2), Fra (10), GB, Ger (10), Hun, Bel (10), Ita, Por (6), Eur (10), Pac (10), Jap (10), Aus
1996	Ferrari	16	Aus, Bra (4), Arg, Eur (10), San (6), Mon, Esp (10), Can, Fra, GB, Ger (3), Hun, Bel (10), Ita (10), Por (4), Jap (6)
1997	Ferrari	17	Aus (6), Bra (2), Arg, San (6), Mon (10), Esp (4), Can (10), Fra (10), GB, Ger (6), Hun (4), Bel (10), Ita (1), Aut (1), Lux, Jap (10), Eur
1998	Ferrari	16	Aus, Bra (4), Arg (10), San (6), Esp (4), Mon, Can (10), Fra (10), GB (10), Aut (4), Ger (2), Hun (10), Bel, Ita (10), Lux (6), Jap

SCHUMACHER, Ralf   Germany

1998: Jordan Mugen-Honda   *1999: Williams Supertec*

In his second and last season driving for Jordan, Ralf Schumacher improved on his 1997 points tally and recorded his best ever Grand Prix finish when he came home in second place behind team-mate Damon Hill at Spa. The German's fortunes mirrored that of the team in general, having a disappointing first half of the year when he only managed two finishes in his first seven races. In fact, in the opening two races Schumacher Junior only managed to record one complete lap. That came in the season's opener in Melbourne, where having started ninth on the grid, and having survived one spin, he twisted off again. Having been hit by Takagi's Tyrrell in the process there was no chance of redemption. Qualifying went one position better in Brazil but this time the spin-out came on the very first lap.

Things looked more encouraging two weeks later in Argentina when on new format Goodyear tyres Schumi Junior qualified fifth, only to blow it at the start where he dropped to an unlucky thirteenth. A spin in the early stages forced him to pit and within four laps his rear wishbone failed and he was out of the race for the third time in succession.

The European start to the season saw his first finish. At San Marino he qualified ninth – not helped by a spin on his final qualifying run – and fuel flap problems made for a couple of iffy pit stops which he got through to come home in seventh place. Another terrible start in Spain saw him fall further behind but by the end of the race he had at least regained his eleventh starting position, despite some very dodgy moments involving grassy areas of the track. Monaco proved even more problematic with a paltry sixteenth place on the grid and when he clipped the barrier at Ste Devote on his forty-fifth lap he was forced out with suspension problems.

In Canada Ralf matched his performance in Argentina by qualifying fifth again. He got a reprieve, having stalled at the start when the race was red-flagged, but the clutch was still troubling him at the second start and he spun early on for his fifth non-finish of the season. Not surprisingly a revised clutch was part of Schumacher's new set-up for the French Grand Prix and it helped him to the third row of the grid. He held on to his sixth place at the start but a collision with Wurz after his first pit stop lost him over two minutes in repair time and resulted in a final sixteenth place.

For the British Grand Prix, Schumacher Jnr found himself starting from the back of the grid after he had forfeited his quickest time by overtaking under yellow flags in the morning's practice and then failed a scrutineering check. His start from the back row was clean and he weaved his way through the other back markers early on. Before the race was half run he was already up to sixth place which he maintained to be rewarded with his, and his team's, first point of the season. The Austrian Grand Prix saw a one-place improvement to fifth with his best drive of the season to date, this despite a disappointing performance in qualifying when he finished ninth. A place on the second row was the reward for a good qualifying run in the German Grand Prix and he might have matched that for the finish had he not pitted for what he thought was a broken damper. It transpired there was no damage and Ralf came home in sixth.

After three successive point finishes Hungary proved to be a disappointment. Tenth on the starting grid resulted in a ninth place finish and could have been worse given his spin. Eighth on the grid for the start of the Belgium Grand Prix did little to indicate what was in store. After the restart, Schumacher then took advantage of the appearance of the safety car before settling in behind team-mate Damon Hill to record his first ever second place finish – his first podium of the year – and Jordan's first ever one-two.

It was a second podium in Monza this time for a third place. Schumi Junior qualified sixth place in changing conditions and, using a one-stop strategy, secured third place with just a few laps to go. It was another sixth place at the Nurburgring for the conveniently named Luxembourg Grand Prix. With the race two-thirds gone, the German had squeezed into fifth place and looked certain to record his sixth points finish before a front brake failure sent him careering out of the contest. Engine problems ended his last race in the Jordan yellow after completing an unlucky 13 laps.

A new season with one of the top teams has been the reward for Ralf Schumacher for 1999. In his first two seasons he has proved he is not just in F1 because of his brother's name. However, as fellow German Heinz-Harald has proved, unless Ralf produces the goods and does so on a consistent basis, his time as part of the Williams set-up could be limited.

Born: 30/6/75, Huerth, Germany. Single.

Grand Prix 1998 Record

Grand Prix	Grid	Qual Time	Fin	Laps	Race Time	Reason
Australian	9	1:32.392	–	1		Accident
Brazilian	8	1:18.735	–	0		Spin
Argentinian	5	1:26.827	–	22		Suspension/spin
San Marino	9	1:27.866	7	60	1:34:34.790	
Spanish	11	1:22.927	11	63	1:33:49.657	
Monaco	16	1:23.283	–	44		Accident damage
Canadian	5	1:19.242	–	0		Loss of drive
French	6	1:15.926	16	68	1:35:42.686	
British	21	no time	6	59	1:47:54.075	
Austrian	9	1:31.917	5	71	1:31:34.740	
German	4	1:42.994	6	45	1:21:17.722	
Hungarian	10	1:19.171	9	76	1:46:15.311	
Belgian	8	1:50.501	2	44	1:43:48.339	
Italian	6	1:26.309	3	53	1:17:50.824	
Luxembourg	6	1:19.455	–	53		Brakes
Japanese	7	1:38.461	–	13		Engine

1998 Position Summary

Contested:	16	Finished:	9
Pole Positions:	0	Fastest Laps:	0
Points:	14		
1st:	0	2nd:	1
3rd:	1	4th:	0
5th:	1	6th:	2

Grand Prix Career Record

Contested:	33	(1997-1998)
Points:	27	1997 (13), 1998 (14)
Point Finishes:	11	40.74%
Pole Positions:	0	
Fastest Laps:	0	
1st:	0	
2nd:	1	1998 (Bel)
3rd:	2	1997 (Arg), 1998 (Ita)
4th:	0	
5th:	5	1997 (GB, Ger, Hun, Aut), 1998 (Aut)
6th:	3	1997 (Fra), 1998 (GB, Ger)

Year	Team	No.	Grand Prix
1997	Jordan Peugeot	17	Aus, Bra, Arg (4), San, Mon, Esp, Can, Fra (1), GB (2), Ger (2), Hun (2), Bel, Ita, Aut (2), Lux, Jap, Eur
1998	Jordan Mugen Honda	16	Aus, Bra, Arg, San, Esp, Mon, Can, Fra, GB (1), Aut (2), Ger (1), Hun, Bel (6), Ita (4), Lux, Jap

TAKAGI, Toranosuke   Japan

1998: Tyrrell Ford   *1999: –*

When he joined the Tyrrell team for the 1998 season many independent observers described the rookie Japanese as having the potential to become one of the all-time greats. Although securing his drive as part of a sponsorship deal with one of Tyrrell's backers – Nakajima Planning – the signs were there that 'Tiger' Takagi indeed has a bright future. His eight finishes from his first ever 16 F1 races were as good as the Tyrrell drivers he replaced and he got as good a performance from the 026 as was probably possible. Indeed, he outshone his team-mate, the more experienced Ricardo Rosset, virtually all season. The one aspect of Takagi's season that stood out was his apparent ability to learn circuits quickly.

His first Grand Prix didn't go according to plan. Qualifying a very commendable thirteenth in Melbourne, he was a victim of Ralf Schumacher's early digression and spun on the gravel the German's Jordan had left after its own excursion, going out of the race on the second lap. His performance in his first GP qualifying session may well have brought red faces to the Stewart drivers Barrichello and Magnussen, given that they were supposedly running a better Ford engine package and found themselves on the grid several spots behind him!

Engine failure brought a premature end to his run at the Brazilian Grand Prix after he had settled in towards the rear of the field. The Argentine race brought the Japanese driver's first career finish. He equalled his best position on the grid and gained one position on this to come home comfortably in twelfth place.

Another engine problem ended his race when the show returned to Europe for the San Marino Grand Prix. The Barcelona track was one that Takagi had previous experience of, yet it brought his worst qualifying performance of the season as he started at the back of the grid. Nevertheless, he made a fine start and by the end of the first lap had gained six places and finished the race a further two laps up in thirteenth. The Monaco race provided an even better finish – eleventh place. Although once again qualifying was disappointing, Tiger compensated by having another great start to gain places from his lowly twentieth.

Mechanical problems besieged his next two starts. A loss of drive on the first lap of the Canadian Grand Prix put him out at the start while in France, having to race in the spare with an old P7 engine, it gave up the ghost on lap 61 when it blew. Silverstone held more luck and was the scene of Takagi's best result of the season, finishing ninth and learning how to use the safety car to best advantage, and allowing him to come in for an extra change of tyres in the changeable conditions. The rain in Britain had created some problems for him and it proved his undoing in Austria where the conditions saw him spin out at the very first turn.

The weekend of the German meeting saw Takagi have a large crash and spin off during the practice sessions. Despite the problems he managed to qualify fifteenth and produced one of the best drives of his season, coming home in thirteenth place but holding off a number of challenges, in particular from Mika Salo, in the final stages of the race. Given the positive nature of his drive it was in stark contrast that he took a cautious approach in Hungary and fell to last place at the start although he climbed back to finish fourteenth.

Having survived both starts at Spa, Takagi's Belgium Grand Prix lasted just ten laps when he spun out at La Source. The race in Monza provided him with the chance to equal his best ever finish – ninth – which he achieved despite having started in a disappointing grid position. He bettered that position by two places for the Luxembourg race but seemed to have trouble getting past the slower cars around him and came home as the last finishing car in sixteenth place. The final race of the season at 'home' in Japan – which also earmarked the last Tyrrell Grand Prix race – didn't quite follow to the sort of plan he would have wished for, when he was shunted out of the race by Esterban Tuero after 28 laps.

Despite the lack of points Takagi did more than enough to prove his worth in a team that was in a run-down situation. Hopefully he will get his chance again in 1999.

Born: 12/2/74, Shizuoka, Japan. Single.

Grand Prix 1998 Record

Grand Prix	Grid	Qual Time	Fin	Laps	Race Time	Reason
Australian	13	1:33.291	–	1		Spin
Brazilian	17	1:20.203	–	19		Engine
Argentinian	13	1:28.811	12	70	1:50:15.941	
San Marino	15	1:29.073	–	40		Engine
Spanish	21	1:24.722	13	63	1:34:37.820	
Monaco	20	1:24.024	11	76	1:52:31.704	
Canadian	16	1:20.328	–	0		Loss of drive
French	20	1:18.221	–	60		Engine
British	17	1:27.061	9	56	1:47:37.746	
Austrian	20	1:34.090	–	0		Spin
German	15	1:44.961	13	44	1:21:07.369	
Hungarian	18	1:20.354	14	74	1:46:08.141	
Belgian	19	1:53.237	–	10		Spin
Italian	19	1:28.346	9	52	1:18:15.640	
Luxembourg	17	1:21.525	16	65	1:32:57.269	
Japanese	17	1:40.619	–	28		Accident

1998 Position Summary

Contested:	16	Finished:	8
Pole Positions:	0	Fastest Laps:	0
Points:	0		
1st-6th:	0	Best Finish:	9th

Grand Prix Career Record

Contested:	16	(1998)
Points:	0	
Pole Positions:	0	
Fastest Laps:	0	
1st-6th:	0	
Best:	9th	1998 (GB, Ita)

Year	Team	No.	Grand Prix
1998	Tyrrell Ford	16	Aus, Bra, Arg, San, Esp, Mon, Can, Fra, GB, Aut, Ger, Hun, Bel, Ita, Lux, Jap

TRULLI, Jarno   Italy

1998: Prost Peugeot   *1999: Prost Peugeot*

Jarno Trulli won his place at Prost courtesy of the drives he made for the team when standing in for the injured Olivier Panis for the second half of the 1997 season – during which he led the Austrian Grand Prix. In 1998 he, like Panis, struggled to come to terms with the new set-up and the new engine but at least provided one moment of joy when he scored the team's only points of the season after he survived the early carnage at Spa to come home in sixth place.

Only two finishes in the first nine races tell the tale – the first four failures being down to reliability problems. Low race finishes in the final stages, apart from the relative success of Spa, were not aided by the inability to get the car round the circuit quick enough to enable a fighting chance from the grid. The highest starting point – tenth – was achieved only twice and more often that not Trulli found himself starting either fourteenth or sixteenth. Despite this fact he still managed to outqualify his more experienced team-mate Panis by 9-7.

Gearbox development hadn't gone smoothly in the lead-up to Melbourne and it forced Trulli out of the race after just 26 laps. In Brazil, fuel pressure was a problem almost from the start of the race and forced the Italian out after 17 laps. The season's first finish came in Argentina where he improved five places on his grid position to come home in eleventh place. A stuck throttle brought a premature end to the San Marino Grand Prix and a third successive sixteenth place was his starting point in Spain. Trulli finished ninth and might have done better had he not mistakenly thought blue flags were being waved at him and consequently let Frentzen past and ahead of him!

The next four meetings all resulted in non-finishes. At Monaco Trulli made it on to the fifth row of the grid – his highest all season. He held his position of tenth before gear selection maladies forced him to retire two-thirds of the way through the race. Accidents at the two starts to the Canadian Grand Prix didn't see the Italian make it round the first corner and successive spins at the French and British races simply added to his woe. Finishes in tenth and twelfth at the Austrian and German meetings followed with the latter a more encouraging performance while he was holding off the challenge of Wurz in the first part of proceedings. Engine failure after 28 laps at the Hungaroring brought the Hungary meeting to an early close.

Having been part of the multiple car pile-up at the first start to the Belgium Grand Prix, Trulli was awarded the T-car over equally piled up team-mate Olivier Panis because his thirteenth place on the grid was better. It was a move that worked well for the Prost team and by just over the halfway point the Italian moved into sixth place and held on to it to the finish to claim his and his team's only point of the season. Buoyed by this success, he equalled his best qualifying performance in the next race at Monza but he lost places in the latter stages of the race due to a loose-fitting wheel and took the chequered flag in thirteenth place. After two races where positive progress could be measured, set-up proved to be problematic for the Luxembourg Grand Prix. Starting from the back half of the grid Trulli was hampered by transmission problems and was forced to retire on the track when it finally gave up the ghost after six laps. In the final race of the season Trulli did not finish but was classified twelfth.

As first seasons go Trulli was in at the deep end and for large parts he must have felt as though he was drowning. He has agreed to stay with Prost until the end of the year 2000 and it may well be then that Benetton take up their option on him which they can implement in 2001. Trulli is contracted to Benetton until the year 2003.

Born: 13/7/74, Pescara, Italy. Single.

Grand Prix 1998 Record

Grand Prix	Grid	Qual Time	Fin	Laps	Race Time	Reason
Australian	15	1:33.739	–	26		Gearbox
Brazilian	12	1:19.069	–	17		Fuel pressure
Argentinian	16	1:29.352	11	70	1:49:18.377	
San Marino	16	1:29.584	–	34		Throttle
Spanish	16	1:23.748	9	63	1:33:46.888	
Monaco	10	1:22.238	–	56		Gearbox
Canadian	14	1:20.188	–	0		Accident
French	12	1:16.892	–	55		Spin
British	14	1:26.808	–	37		Spin
Austrian	16	1:32.906	10	70	1:31:33.536	
German	14	1:44.844	12	44	1:20:53.714	
Hungarian	16	1:20.042	–	28		Engine
Belgian	13	1:52.572	6	42	1:44:42.230	
Italian	10	1:26.794	13	50	1:17:27.397	
Luxembourg	14	1:20.709	–	6		Transmission
Japanese	14	1:40.111	12	48		dnf

1998 Position Summary

Contested:	16	Finished:	7
Pole Positions:	0	Fastest Laps:	0
Points:	1		
1st:	0	2nd:	0

| 3rd: | 0 | 4th: | 0 |
| 5th: | 0 | 6th: | 1 |

Grand Prix Career Record

Contested:	30	
Points	4	1997 (3), 1998 (1)
Point Finishes:	2	6.67%
Pole Positions:	0	
Fastest Laps:	0	
1st:	0	
2nd:	0	
3rd:	0	
4th:	1	1997 (Ger)
5th:	0	
6th:	1	1998 (Lux)

Year	Team	No.	Grand Prix
1997	Minardi Hart	7	Aus, Bra, Arg, San, Mon, Esp, Can
1997	Prost Mugen Honda	7	Fra, GB, Ger (3), Hun, Bel, Ita, Aut
1998	Prost Peugeot	16	Aus, Bra, Arg, San, Esp, Mon, Can, Fra, GB, Aut, Ger, Hun, Bel, Ita, Lux (1), Jap

TUERO, Esterban   Argentina

1998: Minardi Ford   *1999: Minardi Ford*

The Argentinian Esterban Tuero, at 19 the youngest driver in F1 for the 1998 season, got his chance of a drive with Minardi having reported to have taken close on £4 million to the Italian team in sponsorship monies. His debut season was a mixed bag – given his age and inexperience it was largely expected that he would have his problems. Indeed he did, but not all of his own making. Of his 16 starts he managed to complete just four races and the majority of his non-finishes were down to car problems. There were, however, several driver-induced errors.

For the opening race of the season, Tuero qualified in seventeenth place ahead of several more experienced drivers and that proved to be his best starting position of the season and the only time he forced his way off the back two rows. After 22 laps his engine blew and his debut race was over. In Brazil it was electrical problems, having gained four positions at the start to run fifteenth, while in Argentina he had a hard crash at the first corner of the circuit with under eight laps remaining in the race.

The return to Europe brought the rookie his first finish in a Formula 1 car when he did excellently to finish eighth although he was some time away from a potential points position. The result was achieved just a few days after his twentieth birthday. It became a second finish a couple of weeks later in Spain with a final fifteenth – this might have been bettered had he not been given a ten-second stop-go penalty for blocking Frentzen when the German was coming into the pits.

The next five races were frustrating. At Monaco he clipped the barrier at Casino to put him out on the very first lap while spins brought premature ends to his races at the British and Austrian races. At Silverstone the luck was largely against him when he got caught up in Ricardo Rosset's own spin problems while at the A1-Ring he was forced to take the spare car when his own car had engine problems just before the start. In between these disappointments came retirements in Canada and France due to car problems.

His third finish of the season came in what was his eleventh start as he was the last of the classified finishers in Germany. Engine and electrical problems prevailed in Hungary and Spa. At Monza, Tuero made a great start from the back of the grid to pass a number of cars, only to be passed by them all again during the first series of laps and find himself back in last place! He managed to claw back a couple of places before the end when he came home ahead of Rosset and Trulli to finish eleventh.

In the penultimate race of the season – the Luxembourg Grand Prix – Tuero found himself finishing the race but was not classified for the simple fact that he was no less than 12 laps down on race winner Mika Hakkinen. This was not the result of some pretty poor driving but more down to miracle working by his mechanics who managed to repair the broken drive shaft he suffered at the start. By the time the car was back on the track he was already ten laps down!

For the final race of the season at Suzuka he had the advantage of at least knowing the track. However, it came to an end when his foot apparently slipped from the brake peddle causing him to ram into the back of Takagi's Tyrrell – the debris from which caught Michael Schumacher's car and resulted in the burst tyre that ended his Championship charge.

Young and inexperienced, you can't help thinking that Tuero hasn't done himself any favours by entering the sport so early. But money talks and if he has a big sponsorship cashbook then the lower ranked teams will always be willing to enter into a conversation.

Grand Prix 1998 Record

Grand Prix	Grid	Qual Time	Fin	Laps	Race Time	Reason
Australian	17	1:34.646	–	22		Engine
Brazilian	19	1:20.459	–	44		Electrics
Argentinian	20	1:30.158	–	63		Accident

San Marino	19	1:30.649	8	60	1:35:48.285	
Spanish	19	1:24.265	15	63	1:34:42.163	
Monaco	21	1:24.024	–	0		Accident
Canadian	21	1:21.822	–	53		Electrics
French	22	1:19.146	–	41		Gearbox
British	18	1:28.051	–	29		Spin
Austrian	19	1:33.399	–	30		Spin
German	21	1:47.265	16	43	1:22:35.459	
Hungarian	21	1:21.725	–	13		Engine
Belgian	22	1:55.520	–	17		Electrics
Italian	22	1:29.417	11	51	1:17:59.838	
Luxembourg	21	1:22.146	–	56	nc	
Japanese	21	1:42.358	–	28		Accident

1998 Position Summary

Contested:	16	Finished:	4
Pole Positions:	0	Fastest Laps:	0
Points:	0		
1st-6th	0	Best: 8th	

Grand Prix Career Record

Contested:	16	
Points	0	
Pole Positions:	0	
Fastest Laps:	0	
1st-6th:	0	
Best:	8th	1998 (San)

Year	Team	No.	Grand Prix
1998	Minardi Ford	16	Aus, Bra, Arg, San, Esp, Mon, Can, Fra, GB, Aut, Ger, Hun, Bel, Ita, Lux, Jap

VERSTAPPEN, Jos   Holland

1998: Stewart Ford   *1999: –*

Despite his retirement from F1 at the end of 1997, Jos Verstappen was
always the likely go-to man for teams in trouble or looking for a
replacement for struggling drivers. Having helped out with Benetton
with some test drives in the early part of the season, it was no real
surprise when the Dutchman took the seat in a Stewart SF-2 for the start
of the French Grand Prix after the team had removed Jan Magnussen
from their line-up. But for contractual negotiations, Verstappen might

well have been driving for the team much earlier in the season – San Marino had been an original target.

Verstappen had been brought into the team in an effort to improve on the second car's grid position. It worked. Despite virtually no testing – he missed Friday's run-out due to car problems – he managed fifteenth on the grid alongside team-mate Barrichello and brought the car home in twelfth place. This was after having caused the race to be restarted. Verstappen made his qualifying point at Silverstone by pipping his team-mate but an engine failure midway through ended his race. Engine problems and then transmission difficulties meant two further non-finishes. At the A1-Ring Verstappen managed the best qualifying run of his nine races in the Stewart by qualifying twelfth.

The next four races saw two finishes, both in thirteenth place, and two non-finishes. Having survived the two starts at Spa, his engine gave up as early as the ninth lap and at Monza the car's gearbox malady reared its ugly head once again. In retrospect Verstappen probably did worse than the driver he was replacing in the team. He secured a contract with Honda to test drive for them during 1999 as the Japanese team prepare for a return to Formula 1 in 2000.

Born: 4/3/72, Montford, Holland. Married with one son.

Grand Prix 1998 Record

Grand Prix	Grid	Qual Time	Fin	Laps	Race Time	Reason
French	15	1:17.604	12	69	1:35:21.800	
British	15	1:26.948	–	38		Engine
Austrian	12	1:32.099	–	51		Engine
German	19	1:45.623	–	24		Transmission
Hungarian	17	1:20.918	13	74	1:45:53.909	
Belgian	17	1:53.149	–	8		Engine
Italian	17	1:28.212	–	39		Gearbox
Luxembourg	18	1:21.501	13	65	1:32:52.806	
Japanese	19	1:40.943	–	21		Gearbox

1998 Position Summary

Contested:	9	Finished:	3
Pole Positions:	0	Fastest Laps:	0
Points:	0		
1st-6th:	0	Best Finish:	12th

Grand Prix Career Record

Contested: 57   (1994-1998)
Pole Positions: 0
Fastest Laps: 0

Points:	11	1994 (10), 1996 (1)
1st:	0	
2nd:	0	
3rd:	2	1994 (Hun, Bel)
4th:	0	
5th:	1	1994 (Por)
6th:	1	1996 (Arg)

Year	Team	No.	Grand Prix
1994	Benetton Ford	10	Bra, Pac, Fra, GB, Ger, Hun (4), Bel (4), Ita, Por (2), Eur
1995	Simtek Ford	5	Bra, Arg, San, Esp, Mon
1996	Arrows Hart	16	Aus, Bra, Arg (1), Eur, San, Mon, Esp, Can, Fra, GB, Ger, Hun, Bel, Ita, Por, Jap
1997	Tyrrell Ford	17	Aus, Bra, Arg, San, Mon, Esp, Can, Fra, GB, Ger, Hun, Bel, Ita, Aut, Lux, Jap, Eur
1998	Stewart Ford	9	Fra, GB, Aut, Ger, Hun, Bel, Ita, Lux, Jap

VILLENEUVE, Jacques   Canada

1998: Williams Mecachrome   *1999: BAR Supertec*

Jacques Villeneuve arrived at Melbourne for the first race of the season as reigning World Champion having built on a pretty successful debut year in 1996. With that in mind 1998 was a let-down for the French-Canadian, but while it was clear early on that he had little hope of defending his crown, Villeneuve deserves some praise for the professional way he approached each race, never giving less than 100% and without a bad word for anyone. The smile was normally there and when it wasn't the wry humour was never too far behind.

The enforced specification changes to the cars for the 1998 season seemed to affect Williams more than most and Villeneuve, despite all his circuitry skills, was never able to mount a serious challenge on the Championship. It was a case of third time unlucky for him. Having won four races in his debut season in 1996 and seven on the way to the Championship in 1997 he would mount the podium just twice with two third place wins in 1998, in his last season with Williams. There were no wins, no pole positions and no fastest laps to record in 1998.

From the second row Jacques picked up two points in Australia and was introduced to the concept of being lapped – an experience that would become a little too familiar before the season was done. The move to South America for the next two races did little more than confirm that this was going to be a year that would test the Canadian all the way. Seventh place in Brazil was achieved from tenth on the grid – at that point Jacques' worst in F1. He improved his starting point in Argentina and at one point was travelling in fourth spot before a tangle with David Coulthard 20 laps from home forced him out.

Back in Europe, qualifying was again a struggle with understeer taking over from oversteer as the main problem. San Marino provided some positive points after South America with a final fourth position that might and probably would have been bettered had a stuck fuel filler, followed by an open fuel filler cap, not prolonged successive pit stops. In Spain, Jacques made one of his best starts of the season to climb from tenth to sixth, where he stayed, while in Monaco the climb was even better from thirteenth (his worse ever starting point) to fifth. Eight points came from six races compared to 30 points at the same point in the previous season.

If anything was going to kick-start his season it was the trip to his homeland. In Canada his Williams was sporting some important modifications but the changes proved troublesome. Starting sixth on the grid he pushed hard and was vying for the lead which he attempted to take after a safety car restart. It didn't pay off and a subsequent tangle with Tuero cost him four laps' worth of repairs, giving him a final tenth position.

Moving back to Europe, with the pressure and spotlight off him now, Villeneuve started to improve in qualifying and in finishing. At Magny-Cours, aggressive driving gained him fifth place on the grid and this was improved during the race where he finished fourth. Two weeks later, at Silverstone, a third place starting point provided more optimism but the weather played its part and his tyre strategy was not the best, ultimately costing him time and position – seventh.

Villeneuve announced he had signed for the new BAR team for 1999 prior to the Austrian Grand Prix where he started in a lowly eleventh position, but this was largely due to a spin during qualifying which cost him time and another race to get the T-car out to ensure a time. Despite a bad start, he worked hard and was rewarded with a point come the chequered flag.

The next two races provided him with his only two podium finishes of the year. In Germany he matched his performance in Britain by qualifying third and was competitive throughout the race to finish with six points. In Hungary a similar third came despite steering problems in the latter stage of the race. At Spa Villeneuve struggled on intermediate tyres in the changeable weather conditions and his second spin of the race put him out of it. It was a similar result at Monza despite the fine weather and the encouragement of a front row starting position – his only one of the year – achieved with a superb series of drives that unfortunately didn't translate to the Sunday.

Luxembourg saw the gremlins thwart Villeneuve for the second time in the season. Having qualified ninth, the Canadian went for a one-stop race strategy which looked to be paying off in terms of race position. But one turned into two when the refuelling rig developed a fault and his fifth position at the first stop became ninth after the second. A point at Suzuka in the final race of the season brought his Williams career to a close.

Given that the MD of BAR and Villeneuve's manager Craig Pollock are one and the same it was no real surprise when he announced he would be driving for the new organisation in 1999. His first drive for them will be the 50th of his Grand Prix career. BAR has predicted that they can be race winners in 1999 and clearly they will be looking to Jacques to deliver that particular prize. Easier said than done and in reality one can only suggest that 1999 will be a season of consolidation for him. Stranger things have happened though.

Born: 9/4/71, St Jean-sur-Richelieu, Quebec, Canada. Single.

Grand Prix 1998 Record

Grand Prix	Grid	Qual Time	Fin	Laps	Race Time	Reason
Australian	4	1:30.919	5	57	1:32:20.799	
Brazilian	10	1:18.761	7	71	1:37:23.653	
Argentinian	7	1:29.941	–	52		Accident
San Marino	6	1:27.390	4	62	1:35:19.183	
Spanish	10	1:22.885	6	64	1:33:55.147	
Monaco	13	1:22.488	5	77	1:51:58.811	
Canadian	6	1:19.588	10	63	1:42:14.604	
French	5	1:15.630	4	71	1:35:51.991	
British	3	1:24.102	7	59	1:48:20.879	
Austrian	11	1:32.083	6	71	1:31:37.288	
German	3	1:42.365	3	45	1:20:50.561	
Hungarian	6	1:18.337	3	77	1:46:09.994	
Belgian	6	1:50.204	–	16		Accident
Italian	2	1:25.965	–	37		Spin
Luxembourg	9	1:19.631	8	66	1:32:20.762	
Japanese	6	1:38.448	6	51	1:28:38.402	

1998 Position Summary

Contested:	16	Finished:	13
Pole Positions:	0	Fastest Laps:	0
Points:	21		
1st:	0	2nd:	0

| 3rd: | 2 | 4th: | 2 |
| 5th: | 2 | 6th: | 3 |

Grand Prix Career Record

Contested:	49	(1996-1998)
Points:	180	1996 (78), 1997 (81), 1998 (21)
Point Finishes:		
Pole Positions:	13	1996 (Aus, Bel, Jap), 1997 (Aus, Bra, Arg, San, Esp, GB, Bel, Aut, Jap, Eur)
Fastest Laps:	9	1996 (Aus, Can, Fra, GB, Por, Jap), 1997 (Bra, Bel, Aut)
1st:	11	1996 (Eur, GB, Hun, Por), 1997 (Bra, Arg, Esp, GB, Hun, Aut, Lux)
2nd:	5	1996 (Aus, Arg, Can, Fra, Bel)
3rd:	5	1996 (Esp, Ger), 1997 (Eur), 1998 (Ger, Hun)
4th:	3	1997 (Fra), 1998 (San, Fra)
5th:	4	1997 (Bel, Ita), 1998 (Aut, Mon)
6th:	3	1998 (Esp, Aut, Jap)

Year	Team	No.	Grand Prix
1996	Williams Renault	16	Aus (6), Bra, Arg (6), Eur (10), San, Mon, Esp (4), Can (6), Fra (6), GB (10), Ger (4), Hun (10), Bel (6), Ita, Por (10), Jap
1997	Williams Renault	17	Aus, Bra (10), Arg (10), San, Mon, Esp (10), Can, Fra (3), GB (10), Ger, Hun (10), Bel (2), Ita (2), Aut (10), Lux (10), Jap, Eur (3)
1998	Williams Mecachrome	16	Aus (2), Bra, Arg, San (3), Esp (1), Mon (2), Can, Fra (3), GB, Aut (1), Ger (4), Hun (4), Bel, Ita, Lux, Jap (1)

WURZ, Alexander   Austria

1998: Benetton Playlife   *1999: Benetton Supertec*

The lanky Austrian shot to the forefront of the F1 world when he came in for three races on cover for fellow national Gerhard Berger. Despite having just three races to prove himself, he secured third place in only his third race. As such it was no real surprise when he was announced in the Benetton starting line-up for the 1998 season. And as first seasons go it was a positive response, especially in the first half of the season when he scored points consistently with some mature performances.

The Australian Grand Prix provided Alexander with a slow start – new car design and new tyres testing him, especially in qualifying when a spin ultimately meant he started his first full season from eleventh position. By the chequered flag he had worked his way through a bit of the field to claim a final seventh place.

The switch to South America produced the start of what would be six finishes from eight races that all scored points – including six fourth places and one fifth position. Two non-finishes, one mechanical and one error, completed the sequence. In Brazil, Wurz qualified fifth and was fully worth the first fourth of the series with a positive performance. It was an even better performance in Argentina where fourth this time came off eighth place on the grid, again after an off in qualifying. More importantly he recorded his first ever fastest race time.

A jammed gearbox thanks to a shunt by Damon Hill brought the San Marino race to a premature end but a repeat qualifying performance in Spain saw Wurz again starting fifth. Starting steadily Wurz ran as high as third before the pit stops sorted final positions out with his third fourth of the season. In Monaco Wurz again experienced a non-finish, this time thanks to Schumacher Senior who clashed wheels with him to lead to a race-ending accident in the tunnel that saw the Austrian career into the barriers at 155 mph.

The Canadian Grand Prix was where Wurz had made his debut a year earlier and as then he qualified eleventh on the grid but went better by finishing and scoring points with yet another fourth place, but only after he had settled into the spare car at the race restart, having bounced over a few cars at the original off!

Tenth and eleventh on the grid at Magny-Cours and Silverstone again converted into points via fifth and fourth place finishes. The Austrian's three-stop race strategy in France helped his cause.

After the points at Silverstone Wurz's season took a dip for the worse as he failed to score any more points in the remaining races. Some say this was because Bridgestone were concentrating their tyre efforts on the McLaren team. In Austria spins and clutch problems beset him throughout the weekend – his seventeenth starting position his worst ever. In Hungary he was classified sixteenth but failed to make the finishing line when his gearbox, not for the first time in the season, proved problematic. It was a hat-trick of non-finishes by the time the Spa and Monza weekends had passed. At Spa Wurz ended up in the pit wall at the first start and then got caught up with Coulthard on the restart before the first lap was run. Monza brought another gearbox problem 25 laps into the event.

For the penultimate race of the season, Wurz's Benetton looked to be in better shape but could only improve by one place on his grid position by the end of the race and he fared little better in Japan, starting and finishing ninth.

A true talent, Wurz's first full season in F1 was impressive indeed. His 17 points were one more than his Benetton team-mate Fisichella but earned him two positions better in the Drivers' Championship. He can expect to improve on his points total in 1999.

Born: 15/2/74, Waithofen, Austria.

Grand Prix 1998 Record

Grand Prix	Grid	Qual Time	Fin	Laps	Race Time	Reason
Australian	11	1:32.726	7	57	1:31:48.637	
Brazilian	5	1:18.261	4	72	1:38:19.200	
Argentinian	8	1:27.198	4	72	1:49:44.309	fl
San Marino	5	1:27.273	–	17		Gearbox
Spanish	5	1:21.965	4	65	1:34:40.159	
Monaco	6	1:20.855	–	42		Accident
Canadian	11	1:19.765	4	69	1:42:00.587	
French	10	1:16.460	5	70	1:34:47.515	
British	11	1:25.760	4	59	1:47:29.402	
Austrian	17	1:33.185	9	70	1:30:58.611	
German	7	1:43.341	11	45	1:21:45.978	
Hungarian	9	1:19.063	16	69		dnf/Gearbox
Belgian	11	1:51.648	–	0		Accident
Italian	7	1:26.567	–	24		Gearbox
Luxembourg	8	1:19.569	7	67	1:33:19.578	
Japanese	9	1:38.959	9	50	1:27:37.673	

1998 Position Summary

Contested:	16	Finished:	12
Pole Positions:	0	Fastest Laps:	1
Points:	17		
1st:	0	2nd:	0
3rd:	0	4th:	5
5th:	1	6th:	0

Grand Prix Career Record

Contested:	19	(1997-1998)
Points:	21	1997 (4), 1998 (17)
Point Finishes:	7	77.78%
Pole Positions:	0	
Fastest Laps:	1	1998 (Arg)
1st:	0	
2nd:	0	

3rd:	1	1997 (GB)
4th:	5	1998 (Bra, Arg, Esp, Can, GB)
5th:	1	1998 (Fra)
6th:	0	

Year	Team	No.	Grand Prix
1997	Benetton Renault	3	Can, Fra, GB (4)
1998	Benetton Playlife	16	Aus, Bra (3), Arg (3), San, Esp (3), Mon, Can (3), Fra (1), GB (3), Aut, Ger, Hun, Bel, Ita, Lux, Jap

ZANARDI, Alex   Italy

1999: Williams Supertec

Alessandro Zanardi is not a newcomer to Formula 1 racing. He made his debut in Spain in 1991 when filling the Jordan seat vacated by Michael Schumacher. He drove the Ford powered car home to ninth place, which was made all the more impressive as it was achieved without any pre-race testing and in driving rain! A retirement in Japan and another ninth place in the final race in Australia earned him a job as Benetton's test driver in 1992 – during which he lined up three times for Minardi (as replacement for the injured Christian Fittipaldi), but only managed to qualify once, for the British Grand Prix.

In 1993 he joined Team Lotus where, in his second race for the team, he secured his only Championship point prior to the 1999 season with a sixth place in Brazil. Zanardi competed in 11 races in that season but was replaced in the team after he was involved in a practice accident in Belgium which left him with concussion and spinal nerve damage. He returned to Lotus for 1994, starting the season as test driver and got his chance to drive again when Pedro Lamy was injured. He raced five times that season for the then cash-strapped team.

With Lotus going into receivership at the start of the 1995 season, Alex found himself without an F1 drive and, after racing in the GT2 category, he started 1996 in the States as a member of the Chip Ganassi Racing team driving Indy Cars where he was named Rookie of the Year. It was a major turning point for the Italian and in 1997 and 1998 he secured the PPG CART World Series Championship.

At 33-years of age, the chance to drive an F1 Williams comes late in his career and no doubt Zanardi will be looking to follow in former William's drivers Villeneuve and Mansell's footsteps by winning championships on both sides of the Atlantic.

Born: 23/10/66. Bologna, Italy. Married with one son.

Grand Prix Career Record

Contested:	20	(1992-94)
Pole Positions:	0	
Fastest Laps:	0	
Points:	1	1994 (1)
1st:	0	
2nd:	0	
3rd:	0	
4th:	0	
5th:	0	
6th:	1	1994 (Bra)

Year	Team	No.	Grand Prix
1991	Jordan-Ford	3	Esp, Jap, Aus
1992	Minardi-Lamborghini	1	(GB), Ger, (Hun)
1993	Lotus-Ford	11	SA, Bra (1), Eur, San, Esp, Mon, Can, Fra, GB, Ger, Hun, (Bel)
1994	Lotus-Mugen Honda	5	Fra, GB, Ger, Hun, Ita

Races in brackets: Failed to qualify for race.

ZONTA, Ricardo   Brazil

1999: BAR Supertec

Ricardo Zonta may be new to the Formula 1 scene but the 22 year old Brazilian has experienced competitive racing at all levels. His performances during the 1997 season attracted attention from a variety of sources and ultimately provided him with his limited experience in an F1 car when he was contracted to be test driver for the McLaren-Mercedes F1 team last season and also an integral member of one of the two AMG-Mercedes teams competing in the FIA's Grand Touring Championship in 1998.

Zonta began racing karts and after experiencing his first win at the age of 11 was a karting champion in Brazil just four years later! In 1995 he took the Brazilian and South American F3 Drivers' Championship before moving to Europe to contest the FIA International Formula 3000 Championship in 1996 where he recorded a couple of victories. In 1997 he joined Britain's Super Nova team and was subsequently crowned series champion.

He completed the 1998 season by clinching the GT1 Championship title with team-mate Klaus Ludwig as part of the AMG Mercedes-Benz 'second team'. Zonta will start as the second to Jacques Villeneuve in the BAR line-up for 1999 but will be looking to continue the impressive run of form he has shown in the past few years.

Born: 23/3/76. Curibita, Brazil. Single.

Arrows

Danka Arrows
Arrows Grand Prix International
TWR Group Ltd, Leafield Technical Centre,
Leafield, Witney, Oxon, OX8 5PF
Tel: +44 (0)1993 871000   Fax : +44 (0)1993 871100

Chairman/CEO:	Tom Walkinshaw
Designer:	Frank Dernie
Team Manager:	John Walton
Chief Mechanic:	Les Jones
Drivers:	~~Mika Salo~~
	~~tba~~
Test Driver:	–

(handwritten annotations: Brian Hart (engine); Takagi, de la Rosa)

Sponsors: Danka, Zepter International, Parmalat, Power
House, Yamaha Motor Co., Bridgestone Corporation, Brastemp,
Remus, Quest International, Cadcentre, Kibon, Arisco, Reporter
Parfum, Amik, Packplast.

Brief History

1977: Arrows Grand Prix founded. 1978: Riccardo Patrese scores
Arrows' first point with sixth at Long Beach; Patrese takes second in
Sweden – the team's best finish to date; Patrese banned for involvement
in the accident that killed Ronnie Peterson. 1981: Patrese takes only
pole position to date at Long Beach. 1984: Arrows switch to BMW
Turbo engines. 1987: Megatron supply engines to Arrows after BMW
pulls out. 1989: Arrows open new $10 million technical centre in
Milton Keynes. 1989: Arrows are bought by Wataru Ohashi's Footwork
Corporation. 1995: Jackie Oliver takes control after Footwork pull out.
1996: Tom Walkinshaw buys controlling interest in team and relocates
works; reigning World Champion Damon Hill signs for team. 1997:
Damon Hill equals team's best ever finish – 2nd after leading
Hungarian Grand Prix.

Grand Prix Record

Contested:	321	
Victories:	0	(Best Finish: 2nd – 5 times)
Pole Positions:	1	

Fastest Laps:	0	
Constructors' World Titles:	0	(Best: 4th 1988)
Drivers' World Championships:	0	(Best: =7th 1988)
Most Points in a Season:	23	(1988)
Total Constructors' Cup Points:	156	
Average Points/Grand Prix:	0.49	

Review

After a second full year in charge of the Arrows team a measly ten finishes from 32 starts was probably not the sort of form that Tom Walkinshaw was looking for from his team. It offered no improvement on the 1997 season and for the most part the cars seemed to be hampered with a variety of reliability problems. Indeed the team didn't manage to get a car to the chequered flag until the fourth race of the season in San Marino when Mika Salo ran home in ninth place.

At the start of the season the team moved away from the use of Yamaha engines and went with its own V10 powerpack built with the help of Brian Hart who had supplied engines to the team in past seasons. The A19 though had the advantage of the influence of designer John Bernard and probably won handsdown in the looks stakes. Power from the in-house engine was always a problem, as indicated by straight line speeds which were generally on the low side, as the speed trap lists for most of the tracks indicated. The car tended to look more impressive at circuits where this was less of an issue, as proved the case in Monaco.

Mika Salo joined the team for the outgoing Damon Hill, and his driving ability, as with Damon Hill in 1997, showed that when the car lasted the distance it was quite capable of being amongst the front half of the course. The highlight of the Arrows' season came in Monaco where both drivers, Salo and Diniz, scored points. Salo was in fourth place and Diniz in sixth. Curiously, it was also the first race in which the team got both drivers to the finish line! Salo had looked good in qualifying, reaching eighth on the grid, a position he bettered at the A1-Ring by moving up a row to start the Austrian Grand Prix in sixth place.

Monaco marked the first finish of the season for Diniz after hydraulics, gearbox (twice) and engine (twice) halted his progress in the early part of those first five races. Transmission, engine and gearbox terminated Salo in his first three races. Salo's finish in San Marino came after he had toyed with a new spec engine but abandoned it for qualifying and the race. The Spanish race was the fourth double non-finish for the team but with the arrival at Monaco there was only one failure to finish in the next six starts at the Grands Prix of Monaco, Canada and France. The successes in the principality were perhaps not surprising because straight-line speed is not a benefit there. What was surprising was the effective cornering of the cars, given that both drivers had often commented on a lack of grip.

The British Grand Prix saw the introduction of an upgraded engine and perhaps the additional power was too much as both drivers retired after spins. The Belgium race had mixed emotions for the drivers. After both spun out at the first start Diniz was able to take the spare and lasted the course to score two points in fifth position. That was to prove to be Diniz's last finish for the team with a couple of spins and a hydraulics failure putting him out of the final three races. Salo managed to go one better with a placing in Luxembourg, even if he was bringing up the rear of the field in fourteenth place.

Finn Mika Salo was confirmed as driver for 1999 as the Arrows entered the pre-season amidst rumors of take-over bids which finally came to fruition when a consortium involving Nigerian businessman – prince Malik Ado Ibrahim – and an investman bank brought a 70% share in the team as part of a £77million deal.

Drivers and Results 1998

Driver	Races	Com	Ret	Dnq	HP	Pts	Psn	Comp%
Diniz, P.	16	5	11	0	4	3	13/22	31.25
Salo, M.	16	5	11	0	4	3	13/22	31.25
Aggregate	32	10	22	0	4	6	7/11	31.25

			Pedro Diniz			**Mika Salo**	
	Grand Prix	Gd	P	Details	Gd	P	Details
1	Australian	20	ret	Hydraulics	16	ret	Transmission
2	Brazilian	22	ret	Gearbox	20	ret	Engine
3	Argentinian	18	ret	Gearbox	17	ret	Gearbox
4	San Marino	18	ret	Engine	14	9	1:35:55.865
5	Spanish	15	ret	Engine	17	ret	Engine
6	Monaco	12	6	1:52:06.752	8	4	1:52:23.958
7	Canadian	19	9	1:43:19.361	17	ret	Steering/acc.
8	French	17	14	1:36:03.194	19	13	1:35:43.315
9	British	12	ret	Spin	13	ret	Spin
10	Austrian	13	ret	Accident dam.	6	ret	Accident dam.
11	German	18	ret	Throttle	17	14	1:21:13.440
12	Hungarian	12	11	1:45:27.272	13	ret	Gearbox
13	Belgian	16	5	1:44:39.089	18	dns	–
14	Italian	20	ret	Spin	16	ret	Throttle
15	Luxembourg	17	ret	Hydraulics	16	14	1:32:53.413
16	Japanese	18	ret	Spin	15	ret	Hydraulics

Arrows A20 Specifications

Engine

Type:	V10 (72 degree)
Capacity:	2996 cc
Fuel injection:	Zytek
Ignition:	Magneti Marelli

Car

Chassis:	Arrows manufactured Carbon Monocoque
Suspension:	Pushrod operated six damper system with dynamic dampers
Steering:	Arrows
Cooling system:	Secan oil and water radiators
Transmission:	Arrows 6-speed semi-automatic, in-line configuration
Clutch:	AP Racing (Carbon)
Brakes:	Brembo Al-Be composite callipers, Carbone Industrie discs and pads
Instruments:	Arrow data display

Engines 1978-99

1978-83: Ford. 1984-86: BMW Turbo. 1987-88: Megatron Turbo. 1989-90: Ford Turbo. 1991: Porsche. 1992-94: Mugen-Honda. 1995-96: Hart. 1997: Arrows 1998-99

Drivers 1989-99

1989: D.Warwick, E.Cheever & M.Donnelly. 1990: M.Alboreto & I.Capelli. 1991: M.Alboreto, A.Caffi & S.Johansson. 1992: M.Alboreto & A.Suzuki. 1993: D.Warwick & A.Suzuki. 1994: C.Fittipaldi & G.Morbidelli 1995: G.Morbidelli, T.Inoue & M.Papis. 1996: J.Verstappen & R.Rosset. 1997: D.Hill & P.Diniz. 1998: P.Diniz & M.Salo.

Grand Prix Best Performance

2nd position five times: 1978 Sweden (Patrese), 1980 USA (Patrese), 1981 San Marino (Patrese), 1985 San Marino (Boutsen), 1997 Hungary (Damon Hill).

BAR

British American Racing
Brackley, Northamptonshire, NN13 7BD
Tel: +44 (0)1280 844000   Fax: +44 (0)1280 844001

Chairman:	Martin Broughton
MD:	Craig Pollock
Tech. Director:	Dr Adrian Reynard
Com. Director:	Rick Gorne
Chief Designer:	Malcolm Oastler
Chief Engineer:	Steve Farrell
Team Manager:	Greg Field
Drivers/Engineers:	Jacques Villeneuve / Jock Clear
	Ricardo Zonta
Sponsors:	British American Tobacco, 555, Lucky Strike, Teleglobe

Brief History

1997: BAR team announced in December. 1998: Tyrrell acquired by BAR for £22 million.

Preview

British American Racing's entrance into Formula 1 was announced on December 2 1997 and was followed by the acquisition of Tyrrell for £22 million. Despite being controlled by BAR, the team continued under the Tyrrell name with the research and development for a brand new car and support structure being geared towards a start for the 1999 season.

  The pedigree of the new team has almost been established before it has started. A massive financial backing from the BAT group of companies, the acquisition of the 1997 F1 Drivers' Champion Jacques Villeneuve and the supply of the car chassis from the vastly experienced Adrian Reynard could, and perhaps should, ensure that the team provide one of the best debut seasons by a new team. All this is backed up by the support of what is arguably the best equipped R&D facility in the world. The facility, based in Brackley, includes an on-site wind-tunnel, which according to MD Craig Pollock allows the team to be virtually self-sufficient.

Joining Jacques Villeneuve (who is incidentally managed by BAR MD, Craig Pollock) in the BAR-Supertec 01 designated car will be Brazilian, Ricardo Zonta. The car has been designed by a team led by Malcolm Oastler and overseen by Technical Director Adrian Reynard, and is the result of some 1500 hours spent in wind tunnels at the Auto Research Centre in Indianapolis and at the University of Southampton.

British American Racing may be the new kids on the Formula 1 block, but a winning attitude seems to have been established before the team has raced its first Grand Prix. Keeping its drivers comfortable has been of prime importance, and in particular their number one. Villeneuve's race engineer Jock Clear has joined him at BAR, along with his physio Erwin Gollner. The Williams caterer has also been hired to provide his nourishment through the year!

Early testing looked encouraging and was aided by the appointment of another former Williams man, Jean-Christophe Bouillon, as test driver. Now it all has to be applied to qualifying and race situations.

BAR 001 Specifications

Engine:	**Supertec FB01 V10**
Capacity:	3000cc
Lubrication:	Elf
Ignition:	Magneti Marelli
Spark Plugs:	Champion
Car	
Chassis:	Moulded carbon fibre and honeycomb composite structure
Gearbox:	Triple-plate carbon
Transmission:	Gearbox Reynard/Xtrac longitudinal, six-speed unit Gear selection by sequential, semi-automatic, hydraulic activation. Reynard driveshafts
Steering:	Reynard-developed, rack and pinion
Suspension:	Front: Reynard pushrod-activated torsion springs and damper units, rockers, mechanical anti-roll bar Rear: Reynard pushrod-activated combined spring and damper units, rockers, mechanical anti-roll bar
Dampers	Koni (developed exclusively for BAR)
Brakes:	Brakes AP Racing. 2 x 6-piston calipers – front and rear
Wheels:	Wheels OZ forged magnesium Front: 305 mm/12.0 in wide. Rear: 348 mm/13.7 in wide
Fuel Tank:	ATL Kevlar-reinforced rubber bladder. 100 litres capacity.

Instrumentation:	Pi Research Intelligent Instrumentation set in steering wheel, integrated digital display with real-time/microwave telemetry
Dimensions :	Length: 4470 mm Wheelbase: 3020 mm Width: 1800 mm Height: 950 mm Front/Rear track 1800 mm

Benetton

Mild Seven Benetton Playlife
Benetton Formula Limited
Whiteways Technical Centre, Enstone,
Chipping Norton, Oxon, OX7 4EE
Tel: +44 (0)1608 678000   Fax: +44 (0)1608 678800

Chairman:	Luciano Benetton
CEO:	Rocco Benetton
Tech. Director:	Pat Symonds
Team Manager:	Joan Villadelprat
Chief Mechanic:	Mick Ainsley-Cowlishaw
Chief Designer:	Nick Wirth
Drivers:	Giancarlo Fisichella
	Alexander Wurz
Test Driver:	Laurent Redon
Sponsors:	Mild Seven, Benetton Sportsystem, FedEx, Agip,

Akai, Korean Air, Bridgestone, Hewlett Packard, A1, Minichamps.

Brief History

1986: Benetton Formula 1 established after taking over the old Toleman team. 1987: Gerhard Berger wins in Mexico to give Benetton their first victory. 1990: Nelson Piquet leads home fellow Brazilian Roberto Moreno for first one-two. 1992: Michael Schumacher wins his first Grand Prix in Belgium. 1994: Michael Schumacher wins the Drivers' World Championship. 1995: Michael Schumacher wins second Drivers' World Championship and Benetton win first Constructors' World Championship. 1997: Flavio Briatore resigns as CEO; David Richards appointed. 1998: Team switch to Bridgestone tyres; Richards resigns as CEO; Rocco Benetton takes over.

Contested:	267	(178 excluding Toleman)
Victories:	27	
Pole Positions:	16	
Fastest Laps:	36	
Constructors' World Titles:	1	(1995)
Drivers' World Championships:	2	(1994, 1995)
Most Points in a Season:	137	(1995)
Total Constructors' Cup Points:	805.5	
Average Points/Grand Prix:	3.02	

Review

New heads at the helm, new drivers in the cockpit, new engine suppliers and new tyre manufacturers. It was all change for Benetton in the lead-up to the start of the 1998 season. As such perhaps it wasn't a real surprise that the team finished in its lowest Constructors' Cup position since 1989.

The first three changes were planned in advance but the tyre switch from Goodyear to Bridgestone came very late in the pre-season and as such much of the lead-up to the opening race was designed to get the new rubber working in tandem with the B198. The Mecachrome-produced Renault was re-dubbed the Playlife V10 – a marketing decision the team indicated was to promote its marketing philosophy.

The new driver line-up for the 1998 season included former test driver Alexander Wurz, who had driven three races the previous season when the retiring Gerhard Berger had suffered with sinus problems. Wurz had performed exceptionally well and his third place at Silverstone at the end of the brief stint helped ensure that an Austrian was still in the Benetton line-up. He was joined by the Italian Giancarlo Fisichella.

All this was headed up by a new man-in-charge. David Richards took over the reigns after CEO Flavio Briatore had left at the end of the 1997 season. Richards, though, didn't see the season out and had resigned by the time of the final race after a reported disagreement with Rocco Benetton at the tail end of October.

In the driving seat, with two relative newcomers to the Benetton team, it was anticipated that mistakes would be made for the first year of their time together. In truth, there weren't that many and a few of their non-finishes of the season were down to driver error. In a few instances, positions and points were lost due to the race pressure. Inexperience rather than mistakes was probably the reason for occasional errors.

Both drivers were evenly matched throughout the season in terms of scoring points. However, whereas Fisichella's points came in the majority from a couple of second place finishes, it was the lanky Wurz who scored the most consistently, recording six finishes in the points out of the seven races he completed in the first half of the season. Both drivers fell away in this respect in the final third of the season.

A rear wing failure put Fisichella out in Australia while Wurz came home just outside the points. Both drivers scored in the next race in Brazil with the Austrian getting the better of his Italian team-mate. That was a trend that followed in Argentina and Spain where Wurz again came in fourth in both races.

Neither driver had been setting the world alight during qualifying but in Monaco Fisichella started fourth and drove a fine race to run home second having out-battled the senior Schumacher. It was a finish that was repeated instantly in Canada.

After the double top, the finishes fell away from Giancarlo. However, there was one outstanding highlight when he recorded his first ever pole position and what was to be Benetton's only front starting position of the year. It came in Austria and was to some degree helped by the changeable weather. Unfortunately a coming together with second placed Jean Alesi after 21 laps finished the race for Fisichella.

Eleventh and sixteenth place finishes in Germany and Hungary were followed by non-finishes in the next two races for Wurz and rather typified his ill luck in the final stretch of the season. A lengthened wheel base had been introduced in Hungary but the extra 3.5 cm in length failed to change fortunes. Both drivers made the chequered flag in Japan but were outside the points following disappointing qualifying performances.

Fisichella and Wurz will take additional experience with them into the 1999 season and a full year of development with new car and new tyres will have helped as the other Goodyear teams switch to the Bridgestone exclusives. Whether the B199 will be competitive in qualifying is perhaps a doubt but nevertheless both drivers are more than capable of recording their first Grand Prix victories in the 1999 season. That would help the new Benetton get back to its old ways.

Drivers and Results 1998

Driver	Races	Com	Ret	Dnq	HP	Pts	Psn	Comp%
Wurz, A.	16	12	4	0	4	17	7/22	75.00
Fisichella, G.	16	11	5	0	2	16	9/22	68.75
Aggregate	32	23	9	0	2	33	5/22	71.88

	Grand Prix	\multicolumn{3}{c}{**Giancarlo Fisichella**}	\multicolumn{3}{c}{**Alexander Wurz**}

	Grand Prix	Gd	P	Details	Gd	P	Details
1	Australian	7	ret	Rear wing	11	7	1:31:48.637
2	Brazilian	7	6	1:37:19.574	5	4	1:38:19.200
3	Argentinian	10	7	1:50:04.612	8	4	1:49:44.309
4	San Marino	10	ret	Accident	5	ret	Gearbox
5	Spanish	4	ret	Accident	5	4	1:34:40.159
6	Monaco	3	2	1:51:35.070	6	ret	Accident
7	Canadian	4	2	1:41:14.071	11	4	1:42:00.587
8	French	9	9	1:35:53.089	10	5	1:34:47.515
9	British	10	5	1:47:30.546	11	4	1:47:29.402
10	Austrian	1	ret	Accident	17	9	1:30:58.611
11	German	8	7	1:21:19.010	7	11	1:21:45.978
12	Hungarian	8	8	1:45:56.357	9	16	dnf/Gearbox
13	Belgian	7	ret	Accident	11	ret	Accident
14	Italian	11	8	1:17:11.752	7	ret	Gearbox
15	Luxembourg	4	6	1:33:16.148	8	7	1:33:19.578
16	Japanese	10	8	1:29:03.837	9	9	1:27:37.673

Benetton B199 Specifications

Engine: **Supertec**
Cylinders: 10 cylinders (71 degree angle)
Valves: 40
Dimensions: 623 mm (length), 542 mm (width), 395 mm (height)
Management: Magneti Marelli electronic engine management and static ignition.

Car
Chassis: Carbon fibre composite monocoque manufactured by Benetton Formula
Suspension: Carbon fibre top and bottom wishbones operating a titanium rocker(front)/spring damper (rear) via a push rod system. Coil spring and damper units mounted in recesses on top of monocoque. Titanium uprights and Benetton-designed axles.
Transmission: Benetton semi-automatic six-speed gearbox. Triple-plate clutch
Fuel System: ATL rubber fuel cell mounted within monocoque structure behind cockpit
Oil System: Oil tank within bell-housing providing two gallon/nine litres capacity
Cooling System: Separate water and oil cooling; water radiators in each sidepod

| Electrical: | Hardware and software developed jointly by Benetton and Magneti Marelli |
| Braking systems: | Carbon fibre discs and pads |

Engines 1981-99

(1981-85: Toleman.) 1981-85: Hart Turbo. 1986: BMW Turbo. 1987: Ford Turbo. 1988-94: Ford. 1995-97: Renault. 1998-99: Mecachrome (Renault).

Drivers 1989-99

1989: A.Nannini, J.Herbert & E.Pirro. 1990: A.Nannini, N.Piquet & R.Moreno. 1991: N.Piquet, R.Moreno & M.Schumacher. 1992: M.Schumacher & M.Brundle. 1993: M.Schumacher & R.Patrese. 1994: M.Schumacher, J.Verstappen, J.J. Lehto & J.Herbert. 1995: M.Schumacher & J.Herbert. 1996-97: J.Alesi & G.Berger. 1998-99: G.Fisichella & A.Wurz. *NB: Team name Toleman 81-85.*

Grand Prix Wins

1986 Mex (Berger); 1989 Jap (Nannini); 1990 Jap (Piquet), Aus (Piquet); 1991 Can (Piquet); 1992 Bel (M.Schumacher); 1993 Por (M.Schumacher); 1994 Bra (M.Schumacher), Pac (M.Schumacher), San (M.Schumacher), Mon (M.Schumacher), Can (M.Schumacher), Fra (M.Schumacher), Hun (M.Schumacher), Eur (M.Schumacher); 1995 Bra (M.Schumacher), Esp (M.Schumacher), Mon (M.Schumacher), Fra (M.Schumacher), GB (Herbert), Ger (M.Schumacher), Bel (M.Schumacher), Ita (Herbert), Eur (M.Schumacher), Pac (M.Schumacher), Jap (M.Schumacher); 1997 Ger (G.Berger).

Ferrari

Scuderia Ferrari Marlboro
Ferrari SpR
Via Ascari 55-57, 41053 Maranello, Modena, Italy
Tel: +39 0536 949 111   Fax: +39 0536 949 436
Chairman: Luca Di Montezemolo
Team Principle: Jean Todt
Tech. Director: Ross Brawn

Team Manager:	Stefano Domenicali
Designer:	Rory Byrne
Chief Mechanic:	Nigel Stepney
Engine TD:	Paolo Martinelli
Drivers/Engineers:	Michael Schumacher
	Eddie Irvine
Test Driver:	Luca Badoer
Sponsors:	Marlboro, Fiat, Shell, Asprey, Magneti Marelli,

Telecom Italia, Goodyear, Arexons, Brembo, SKF, TRW Sabelt, USAG, Veca.

Brief History

1929: Enzo Ferrari forms his company. 1947: Franco Cortese wins the Grand Prix of Rome to record Ferrari's first race win. 1951: Jose Gonzalez records Ferrari's first Formula 1 victory. 1952: Alberto Ascari wins the Drivers' World Championship in a Ferrari. 1953: Ascari wins back-to-back titles driving for the Modena-based team. 1956: Juan-Manuel Fangio wins World Championship with Ferrari. 1958: Mike Hawthorn becomes the third Ferrari driver to win the title. 1961: Phil Hill leads Ferrari to the 'double' of both Drivers' and Constructors' titles. 1964: John Surtees takes the World Championship in a Ferrari. 1969: Lowest ever Ferrari score of seven points achieved in Constructors' World Championship. 1975: Niki Lauda takes title in a Ferrari ahead of Emerson Fittipaldi. 1977: Lauda repeats his success of two years earlier. 1979: Jody Scheckter wins his only World Championship driving a Ferrari. 1983: Ferrari win the last of their eight World Constructors' Championships. 1996: Ferrari give double World Champion Michael Schumacher a record $25 million two-year contract. 1998: Ferrari finish second in Constructors' Cup.

Grand Prix Record

Contested:	603	
Victories:	119	
Pole Positions:	124	
Fastest Laps:	133	
Constructors' World Titles:	8	(61, 64, 75, 76, 77, 79, 82, 83)
Drivers' World Championships:	9	(52, 53, 56, 58, 61, 64, 75, 77, 79)
Most Points in a Season:	133	(1998)
Total Constructors' Cup Points:	2226.5	
Average Points/Grand Prix:	3.69	

After two years of developing and nurturing the Schumacher-Irvine tandem, the 1998 season started as the one in which most expected the prancing horse to reign supreme. In Schumacher Senior they had arguably the best driver of his time and in Eddie Irvine one of the most improved drivers. Despite being a clear and contractual number two to Schumacher some of his drives were quite exceptional.

The real thorn in the Ferrari side, though, was the car, whose handling characteristics seemed to change with every race – there was always an underlying problem somewhere. As such the team spent most of the season playing catch-up to McLaren, which they did to good effect. The cars were incredibly reliable and had a finish record second to none.

The Ferrari duo lost only one race each due to mechanical problems – three in total if you count Schumacher's clutch curiosity in Japan. The first of those came in the first race when Shuey's engine failed on the sixth lap in Melbourne but Irvine got the points board rolling with a fourth place.

For the Brazilian race Ferrari had an updated engine which featured a revised valve system – it seemed well suited to the track but this time it was the German driver who brought home the points with the team's first podium finish of the season – third. The new engine wasn't over suited to the tighter Argentine circuit and clutch problems beset both drivers. However, it didn't prevent Schumacher recording his first win of the season, while Irvine sailed home third.

Sidewings were introduced for Imola and again both drivers joined each other on the podium – this time as second and third. The additions were gone by the time the Spanish Grand Prix came around two weeks later but stability was improved by a new exhaust system for the cars. Schumi recorded his fourth successive podium by finishing third, while an accident put Eddie out midway through the race. Irvine returned to third place finishing at Monaco while Schumacher suffered from a collision and, after pit repairs, finished tenth.

In Canada new tyre developments by Goodyear, along with new brake cooling ducts, suited the Ferraris as the two came home for another one-three finish, despite both suffering accidents that required pit repairs. In qualifying Irvine was still finding problems but Schuey was starting to find those extra fractions of seconds by driving the car to its limits. Canada marked the first of three straight wins for Ferrari – all via Schumacher but matched by podium finishes by Irvine. Slowly Ferrari started to make in-roads into the Championship lead that had been established by McLaren – Schumacher two points behind Hakkinen in the Drivers' title and Ferrari three points behind McLaren in the Constructors' Cup.

In France it was a Ferrari one-two, their first since 1990, in a car that was sporting a new diffuser and front wing designs. After Schumacher's hat-trick of wins, third place in Austria would seem a let-down but it was in fact salvaged after he had pushed too hard and ended up having to replace the nose of his car after sliding off. Irvine scored points once again but failed to make any contribution to the team's cause in Germany when he finished eighth. Schumacher fared a little better with two points. Schumacher and Ferrari trailed the lead by 16 and 32 points in their respective Championships at this point

The bumpy circuit in Hungary upset Irvine who recorded the first of two non-finishes – the first after a failed gearbox. Schumacher rode the bumps well to come home victorious, but he joined Irvine with a non-finish in Spa, which was Ferrari's 600th Grand Prix. Leading the race in heavy rain, the German drove into the back of Coulthard's McLaren – something that led to a near ugly incident in the paddock after both drivers returned to their respective garages.

The Italian Grand Prix looked to turn the Championship on its head. At Ferrari's home race the former World Champion was at his pushing best and recorded his first double-first of the season: first on the grid and first in the race. With Hakkinen off the pace, Schumacher's win meant that both drivers left Monza equal on 80 points. Irvine was equally spectacular, coming home to record his second second place of the season and Ferrari's second one-two of the season. The Constructors' championship gap remained at ten points in favour of McLaren.

One-two was how it started for Ferrari at the Nurburgring for the Luxembourg Grand Prix. This time it was on the starting grid in a race where Schumacher had to score points. Ferrari drove a near perfect race, Irvine getting away quickest at the start to take it on before Schumacher passed him to take the lead. Tyre wear was the problem, though, Schumacher had to settle for second place with Irvine fourth. The Constructors' Cup margin was now 15 points.

It was double or nothing in the final race of the season, which needed Schumacher to win and Hakkinen to finish lower than third, for the German to take the Drivers' title, while the team needed a non-scoring McLaren team and maximum points in Suzuka to take the Constructors' title. Neither scenario materialised. Amazingly Schumacher stalled on the grid at the second start and had to begin the race from the back of the grid. Despite a charging performance, his eventual retirement with a blow-out meant that the Italian team finished double runner-up. In amongst this Eddie Irvine, who had qualified second, came home second in another fine drive.

While second place in the Constructors' Cup will have been a disappointment for the team, they achieved it with their biggest ever points haul and the team's completion average of 81.25% was the highest of the season. Both drivers remain for the 1999 season and the pressure on the team to deliver World Championships in 1999 will be immeasurable. What a shame Ferrari does not allow Eddie Irvine to race his team-mate – it would prove to be a fascinating battle. I wonder if Schumey could take the strain?

Drivers and Results 1998

Driver	Races	Com	Ret	Dnq	HP	Pts	Psn	Comp%
Schumacher, M.	16	13	3	0	1	86	2/22	81.25
Irvine, E.	16	13	3	0	2	47	4/22	81.25
Aggregate	32	26	6	0	1	133	2/11	81.25

	Michael Schumacher			Eddie Irvine		
Grand Prix	Gd	P	Details	Gd	P	Details
1 Australian	3	ret	Engine	8	4	1:31.47.075
2 Brazilian	4	3	1:38:12.297	6	8	1:37:28.184
3 Argentinian	2	1	1:48:36.175	4	3	1:49:33.920
4 San Marino	3	2	1:34:29.147	4	3	1:35:16.368
5 Spanish	3	3	1:34:24.715	6	ret	Accident
6 Monaco	4	10	1:52:16.789	7	3	1:52:04.973
7 Canadian	3	1	1:40:57.355	8	3	1:41:57.414
8 French	2	1	1:34:45.026	4	2	1:35:04.601
9 British	2	1	1:47:12.450	5	3	1:47:31.649
10 Austrian	4	3	1:31:23.178	8	4	1:31:28.062
11 German	9	5	1:21:00.597	6	8	1:21:19.633
12 Hungarian	3	1	1:45:25.550	5	ret	Gearbox
13 Belgian	4	ret	Accident	5	ret	Spin
14 Italian	1	1	1:17:09.672	5	2	1:17:47.649
15 Luxembourg	1	2	1:32:17.000	2	4	1:33:12.971
16 Japanese	1	ret	Puncture	4	2	1:27:29.026

Ferrari F301 Specifications

Engine:	**Ferrari**
Cylinders:	V10 – 40 valves
Power Output:	700hp
Injection:	Magneti Marelli
Electronics:	Magneti Marelli
Car	
Gearbox:	Ferrari longitudinal gearbox

Clutch: Manual command on steering wheel
Front Suspension: Push-Rod
Rear Suspension: Push-Rod
Dampers: Ferrari   Tyres: Goodyear
Brakes: Brembo Instruments: Magneti Marelli
* *Info based on 1996 specifications*

Engines 1950-99

1950-80: Ferrari. 1981-88: Ferrari Turbo. 1989-99: Ferrari.

Drivers 1989-99

1989: N.Mansell & G.Berger. 1990: A.Prost & N.Mansell. 1991:
A.Prost, J.Alesi & G.Morbidelli. 1992: J.Alesi, I.Capelli & N.Larini.
1993: J.Alesi & G.Berger. 1994: J.Alesi, G.Berger & N.Larini. 1995:
J.Alesi & G.Berger. 1996-99: M.Schumacher & E.Irvine.

Grand Prix Wins

1951 GB (Gonzalez), Ger (Ascari), Ita (Ascari); 1952 Swi (Taruffi), Bel
(Ascari), GB (Ascari), Ger (Ascari), Hol (Ascari), Ita (Ascari); 1953
Argentina (Ascari), Hol (Ascari), Bel (Ascari), Fra (Hawthorn), GB
(Ascari), Ger (Farina), Swi (Ascari); 1954 GB (Gonzalez), Esp
(Hawthorn); 1955 Mon (Trintignant); 1956 Arg (Musso/Fangio), Bel
(Collins), Fra (Collins), GB (Fangio), Ger (Fangio); 1958 Fra
(Hawthorn), GB (Collins); 1959 Fra (Brooks), Ger (Brooks); 1960 Ita
(Hill); 1961 Hol (von Trips), Bel (Hill), Fra (Baghetti), GB (von Trips),
Ita (Hill); 1963 Ger (Surtees); 1964 Ger (Surtees), Aut (Bandini), Ita
(Surtees); 1966 Bel (Surtees), Ita (Scarfiotti); 1968 Fra (Ickx); 1970 Aut
(Ickx), Ita (Regazzoni), Can (Ickx), Mex (Ickx); 1971 SA (Andretti),
Hol (Ickx); 1972 Ger (Ickx); 1974 Esp (Lauda), Hol (Lauda), Ger
(Regazzoni); 1975 Mon (Lauda), Bel (Lauda), Swe (Lauda), Fra
(Lauda), Ita (Regazzoni), USA (Lauda); 1976 Bra (Lauda), SA (Lauda),
Long Beach (Regazzoni), Bel (Lauda), Mon (Lauda), GB (Lauda); 1977
Bra (Reutemann), SA (Lauda), Ger (Lauda), Hol (Lauda); 1978 Bra
(Reutemann), Long Beach (Reutemann), GB TP (Reutemann), USA
(Reutemann), Can (G.Villeneuve); 1979 SA (G.Villeneuve), Long
Beach (G.Villeneuve), Bel (Scheckter), Mon (Scheckter), Ita
(Scheckter), USA (G.Villeneuve); 1981 Mon (Villeneuve), Esp
(G.Villeneuve); 1982 San (Pironi), Hol (Pironi), Ger (Tambay); 1983
San (Tambay), Can (Arnoux), Ger (Arnoux); 1984 Bel (Alboreto); 1985
Can (Alboreto), Ger (Alboreto); 1987 Jap (Berger), Aus (Berger); 1988

Ita (Berger); 1989 Bra (Mansell), Hun (Mansell), Por (Berger); 1990 Bra (Prost), Fra (Prost), GB (Prost), Por (Mansell), Esp (Prost); 1994 Ger (Berger); 1995 Can (Alesi); 1996 Esp, Bel, Ita (M.Schumacher); 1997 Mon, Can, Fra, Bel, Jap (M.Schumacher); 1998 Arg, Can, Fra, GB, Hun, Ita (M.Schumacher).

Jordan

Benson & Hedges Jordan Mugen Honda

Jordan Grand Prix Ltd
Buckingham Road, Silverstone, Towcester, Northants, NN12 8JT
Tel: +44 (0)1327 857153   Fax: +44 (0)1327 858120

Chairman:	Eddie Jordan
Team Manager:	Jim Vale
Designer:	Mike Gascoyne
Chief Mechanic:	Tim Edwards
Drivers/Engineers:	Damon Hill / Nick Burrows
	Heinz-Harald Frentzen / Andy Stevenson
Test Driver:	–
Sponsors:	Benson & Hedges, Imation, Esat Digifone,

Serengeti, Pearl Assurance, Mastercard International, OS Integration, Armor All, Hewlett-Packard, Bridgestone Corporation.

Brief History

1980: Eddie Jordan forms Jordan Motor Racing Team. 1987: Johnny Herbert wins British Formula 3 Championship driving a Jordan. 1988: Jean Alesi takes the International F3000 title for Jordan. 1990: Jordan F1 formed. 1991: Jordan score their first F1 points with Andrea de Cesaris fourth in Canada. 1993: Jordan signs a deal to use Hart engines until the end of the 1994 season. 1995: Exclusive deal with Peugeot engines. 1998: Switch to Mugen-Honda engines. Jordan win first Grand Prix with Damon Hill's victory at Spa – Jordan's 127th F1 race. Ralf Schumacher finishes in second place for first one-two finish.

Grand Prix Record

Contested:	130
Victories:	1
Pole Positions:	1
Fastest Laps:	1

Constructors' World Titles:	0	(Best: 4th 1998)
Drivers' World Championships:	0	(Best: 6th 1994, 1998)
Most Points in a Season:	34	(1998)
Total Constructors' Cup Points:	155	
Average Points/Grand Prix:	1.19	

Review

What Damon Hill so nearly achieved at Arrows he finally did for Eddie Jordan. The yellow of Eddie's team proved no banana skin for the former World Champion as he raced home to provide the team's first ever Grand Prix victory in their 127th race. Hill's win at Spa was a victory of delight for the team in that they also saw number two driver Ralf Schumacher follow Hill home in second place to record another remarkable first. It was the highlight of an amazing change in fortunes for the second half of the season which provided a stark contrast to a succession of early disappointments.

Jordan approached the new season not only having to cope, like all the other constructors, with new regulations but also with a new engine supplier – Peugeot having swapped to French-based Prost with Mugen Honda making the reverse journey. Giancarlo Fisichella had won his court battle that allowed him to move on to Benetton and thus paved the way for the arrival of Hill in a move that was long in coming and one many believed he should have made a year earlier.

With the experience of Hill and the burgeoning talent of Ralf Schumacher, optimism within the camp was high but soon knocked back as they had to wait until the ninth race of the season to claim their first Championship point while the first seven Grands Prix brought just five finishes and a disqualification from a possible fourteen. When the duck was broken, however, the points started to roll in and Jordan found itself mounting a very serious challenge to finish third in the Constructors' Cup behind McLaren and Ferrari.

The mid-season revolution that took place coincided perfectly with the redesign of the car that took place where chassis and aerodynamic improvements were massively beneficial and came together with the introduction of an improved engine. Masterminded by Gary Anderson, his close season move to join the Stewart team will have been a big blow to those in the Jordan factory.

Jordan tradition in recent years has shown that it has always been a slow starter. Nothing changed on the opening weekend of the 1998 season. While the car itself performed well the overall package wasn't quick enough. The two drivers qualified eighth and ninth and while Hill finished eighth, Schumacher had an accident on the second lap to end his race. The German failed to complete the first lap in Brazil and made it a hat-trick of non-finishes in Argentina when he damaged his suspension after a spin and was forced to retire. Hill was off the pace in Brazil and was subsequently disqualified from his tenth place when his car was found to be 7 kg underweight. On investigation it was found that this was due to the incorrect amount of ballast in the car before the race. This was compounded by a water leak and Hill losing 4 kg of weight since the first race of the year!

Double trouble was the result for Hill in San Marino and Spain where his engine expired twice in the later stages of the races while Schumacher almost got in the points at the former. Despite another eighth in Monaco, electrical and hydraulic problems brought premature ends to the Canadian and French races while a spin after an unlucky 13 laps terminated Hill's home Grand Prix at Silverstone.

Working with a revised clutch at Magny-Cours saw Schumacher make up on the first row again for the start but accident damage resulting in a long pit stop effectively ended his race. However, Silverstone proved to be the turning point for the German. Having been demoted to the back of the grid when he failed a scrutineering check he weaved some race magic and came home in sixth place to earn the first point of the season after 18 starts. The younger Schumi went one better in the next race in Austria while Hill, despite traffic problems following pit stops, managed to run home in seventh.

With three points in the bag the whole team took a positive lurch forward and in Hockenheim both Jordan drivers scored points, Hill his first of the season in fourth place and Schumacher in sixth. Much of this was down to the uprated Mugen Honda engine that was supplied for the race and offering an addition 10 bhp. Hill repeated the feat in Hungary a couple of weeks later and by the start of the Belgium race had qualified a season's best in third place. The attrition at the first start in Spa helped the Jordan cause and when the race restarted Hill stormed into a first corner lead. With Schumacher coming up the field from eighth place, the two Jordan drivers were pressing towards the front. Schumacher Senior's Ferrari took the lead after lap eight but then drove into the back of Coulthard's McLaren leaving the two Jordan drivers to race home for full points. It was close though – when the Jordan mechanics inspected Hill's car after the race they found that he had a deflating tyre that was probably only a whisker away from blowing out. Given the washer problems Hill had in his Arrows at the Hungaroring in 1997, perhaps the luck was due.

At the Italian race it was Schumacher who took the honours, getting back on to the podium in third place, with Hill scoring a single from sixth. Aerodynamic improvements made to the car helped its handling. After the string of good results the Luxembourg Grand Prix proved frustrating for the team with Hill coming home outside the points and Schumacher's brakes failing late in the race.

The Jordan team approached the final race of the season in fighting fashion knowing that it was possible for them to achieve their best ever placing in the Constructors' Cup. Despite having both drivers quickest in the first two sectors at Suzuka, they couldn't keep it together in the final segment of the track for what could well have been front row starts. With Ralf Schumacher retiring with a blown engine it was left to Damon Hill to skin Frentzen on the very last corner to claw a fourth place position out of the bag and give Jordan fourth place in the Constructors' Cup at the expense of Williams – their highest ever placing achieved with their biggest ever points tally.

During the tail end of the season Eddie Jordan found himself the subject of litigation from one of his drivers and with Schumacher getting away to Williams, Heinz-Harald Frentzen made the reverse journey. Frentzen will have an awful lot to prove in 1998 having not seemingly done himself justice during his two years at Williams.

Damon Hill will not be short of confidence having broken his duck with a GP win outside of Williams. The departure of Andersen aside, Jordan followers will be optimistic about 1999.

Drivers and Results 1998

Driver	Races	Com	Ret	Dnq	HP	Pts	Psn	Comp%
Hill, D.	16	11	5	0	1	20	6/22	68.75
Schumacher, R.	16	9	7	0	2	14	10/22	56.25
Aggregate	32	20	12	0	1	34	4/11	62.50

		Damon Hill			**Ralf Schumacher**		
	Grand Prix	*Gd*	*P*	*Details*	*Gd*	*P*	*Details*
1	Australian	10	8	1:31:47.279	9	ret	Accident
2	Brazilian	11	dq	1:37:29.652	8	ret	Spin
3	Argentinian	9	8	1:49:17.781	5	ret	Suspen./spin
4	San Marino	7	ret	Engine	9	7	1:34:34.790
5	Spanish	8	ret	Engine	11	11	1:33:49.657
6	Monaco	15	8	1:51:47.513	16	ret	Accident dam.
7	Canadian	10	ret	Electrics	5	ret	Loss of drive
8	French	7	ret	Hydraulics	6	16	1:35:42.686
9	British	7	ret	Spin	21	6	1:47:54.075
10	Austrian	15	7	1:31:57.710	9	5	1:31:34.740
11	German	5	4	1:20:55.169	4	6	1:21:17.722

12	Hungarian	4	4	1:46:20.626	10	9	1:46:15.311
13	Belgian	3	1	1:43:47.407	8	2	1:43:48.339
14	Italian	14	6	1:18:16.360	6	3	1:17:50.824
15	Luxembourg	10	9	1:32:22.990	6	ret	Brakes
16	Japanese	8	4	1:28:36.026	7	ret	Engine

Jordan Mugen-Honda 199 Specifications

Engine:	**Mugen-Honda MF301HD**
Cylinders:	V10 (72 degrees)
Valves:	40 – 4 per cylinder, with pneumatic return
Injection:	Honda PGM-F1
Ignition System:	Honda PGM-IG
Capacity:	3000 cc
Dimensions:	625 mm (length), 525 mm (width), 470 mm (height)
Brake Horsepower:	725ps
Car	
Chassis:	Full carbon fibre composite monocoque
Suspension:	Composite pushrods activating gearbox mounted Penske dampers, unequal length aerodynamic wishbones, composite top wishbone, titanium fabricated uprights and front/back anti-roll bar
Transmission:	In-house Jordan GP design. Six-speed and reverse longitudinal gearbox with electro-hydraulic sequential gear change
Clutch:	Triple plate Jordan/Sacks racing clutch
Brakes:	Brembo braking systems
Wheel Rims:	OZ Racing forged according to Jordan's specifications
Dimensions	Length 4550 mm Wheelbase: 3050 mm
	Front Track: 1500 mm Rear Track: 1418 mm
	Height: 950 mm

Engines 1991-99

1991: Ford. 1992: Yamaha. 1993-94: Hart. 1995-97: Peugeot. 1998-99: Mugen-Honda.

Drivers 1991-99

1991: A.de Cesaris, B.Gachot, R.Moreno, M.Schumacher & A.Zanardi. 1992: S.Modena & M.Gugelmin. 1993: R.Barrichello, I.Capelli, T.Boutsen, M.Apicella, E.Nespatti & E.Irvine. 1994: R.Barrichello,

E.Irvine, A.Suzuki & A.de Cesaris. 1995: R.Barrichello & E.Irvine.
1996: R.Barrichello & M.Brundle. 1997: R.Schumacher & G.Fisichella.
1998: D.Hill & R.Schumacher.1999: D.Hill & H-H Frentzen.

Grand Prix Wins

1998 Bel (D.Hill).

McLaren

West McLaren Mercedes

McLaren International Ltd
Unit 22, Woking Business Park, Albert Drive, Woking,
Surrey, GU21 5JY
Tel: +44 (0)1483 728211   Fax: +44 (0)1483 720157

Chairman:	Ron Dennis
TD:	Adrian Newey
Team Manager:	Dave Ryan
Chief Designer:	Neil Oatley
Chief Mechanic:	Mike Negline
Drivers/Engineers:	Mika Hakkinen / Mark Slade
	David Coulthard / Pat Fry
Test Driver:	Nick Heidfeld
Sponsors:	West, Mercedes-Benz, Technology Partners,

Mobil, Computer Associates, Boss, Schuco, Schweppes, Siemens,
Warsteiner, Tag Heuer, Loctite, Camozzi, British Aerospace,
Kenwood, Enkei, Samsung, Mazak, Targetti, GS Battery, Garnet
Dickinson.

Brief History

1959: Bruce McLaren makes his F1 debut driving for the Cooper works
team. 1963: Bruce McLaren Motor Racing Ltd founded. 1966: McLaren
make their Grand Prix debut at Monaco. 1968: Bruce McLaren wins in
Belgium for his own team's first F1 victory. McLaren finish second
behind Lotus in Constructors' World Championship. 1970: Bruce
McLaren killed at Goodwood whilst testing a CanAm sportscar. 1973:
Emerson Fittipaldi leads McLaren to the Drivers' & Constructors'
Championship double. 1976: James Hunt takes the Drivers' World
Championship by a point from Niki Lauda. 1984: Niki Lauda beats

team-mate Alain Prost by just half a point to take the Drivers' title. 1985: Alain Prost takes the title ahead of Michele Alboreto. 1986: Prost retains his title after Nigel Mansell goes out in the final race at Adelaide. 1988: Senna takes the title by three points from Prost. McLaren post a record Constructors' Championship score of 199 points. 1989: Prost takes the title from Senna by 16 points for another McLaren double. 1990: Senna regains the title from Prost by seven points. 1991: Senna wins his third World Drivers' Championship. 1997: McLaren win first and last Grands Prix of the season. 1998: McLaren win Constructors' Cup and driver Mika Hakkinen wins his first Drivers' Championship.

Grand Prix Record

Contested:	476	
Victories:	116	
Pole Positions:	92	
Fastest Laps:	80	
Constructors' World Titles:	8	(74, 84, 85, 88, 89, 90, 91, 98)
Drivers' World Championships:	10	(74, 76, 84, 85, 86, 88, 89, 90, 91, 98)
Most Points in a Season:	199	(1988)
Total Constructors' Cup Points:	2203.5	
Average Points/Grand Prix:	4.63	

Review

In the preamble to the 1998 season most commentators were expressing their views that McLaren should and probably would be competitive during the coming months and could well be amongst the frontrunners when the Championships were shared between driver and team. Pre-season testing seemed to indicate that the Woking-based team had got to grips with the new FIA regulations better than its competitors. Just how much was revealed during the opening weekend of the season where in a sunny Melbourne they dominated proceedings to such an extent they looked almost invincible. That air of superiority would be wafting around during the coming months and, apart from a noticeable dip in fortunes during the middle third of the season, they might have had the titles in the bag long before the final race ever arrived. As it was Mika Hakkinen finished all but four of his races and when he did finish he always scored at least a point. Equally he was only off the front row of the grid on four occasions. Apart from a couple of aberrations Coulthard's qualifying campaigns had much the same result and only once when he finished did he fail to advance his Drivers' Championship points tally.

The arrival of Adrian Newey from Williams as technical director had to have been a major factor in McLaren's season. Regarded by his peers as the best aerodynamicist around, his record of being involved with six Constructors' Cup victories in seven years is second to none and it could be argued that at a reported £2 million per year salary he is better value than most drivers.

When it was launched, the most noticeable thing about the MP4-13 was that it bucked the trend set by its rivals in that it maintained the low-nose front end from 1997 – all other teams opting for a raised-nose front end – and from there on it proved to be superior in all other aspects. From the start of qualifying for the Australian Grand Prix no-one got a look in as team-mates Hakkinen and Coulthard traded pole positions places. In the end the Finn won the lead-off honour for the first race with the Scot by his side. There was only 0.043 of a second in it though. The domination as both drivers came home in position was one talking point, the other was David Coulthard allowing his team-mate to overtake him a couple of laps out to secure victory. Hakkinen had led but made an error when he came into the pits for a stop that wasn't scheduled. As part of a pre-race agreement Coulthard allowed Hakkinen passage.

There was controversy, though, starting after the Australian GP when the team's domination seemed to lead to many of its rivals objecting to the rear-braking system. This continued in the lead-up to the race in Brazil at which point the team disabled the device before the weekend. It didn't make any difference as the McLarens again recorded a one-two finish, with the Finn producing his third successive win.

In Argentina it was a third successive pole position for the team, but this time Coulthard was the one in control. A spin on lap six reduced the Scot's race to one of chasing a point while Hakkinen improved on his grid position to come home second. Gearbox problems hindered both drivers over the weekend and continued to Imola where problems with the brakes led to Coulthard having his bled on the grid! The work was done at the front, though, with the Scot having flown to a second successive pole from where he would lead and win the race, despite rising gearbox temperatures causing concern in the final laps. The other McLaren was at his side on the grid, but unfortunately for Hakkinen his gearbox problems proved terminal.

The races in Spain and Monaco produced more great performances. Hakkinen got back on qualifying track with two poles and matched them with two victories. The win in Monaco celebrated his 100th

Formula 1 Grand Prix. Coulthard had to be content with second place on the grid in both races and, having come home second in Spain, experienced an engine blowout in Monaco to record his first non-finish of the season.

Mechanical problems besieged the team in Canada. At the restart Hakkinen's gearbox got stuck in first gear and forced him out and then Coulthard's throttle developed problems and forced him out on lap 19. It was McLaren's first and only double failure of the season.

The French Grand Prix was probably the first time in the season that either McLaren had been outraced and signified Ferrari's real entry into the two title races. Another pole for Hakkinen was converted into third place while Coulthard dropped from third to a final sixth. With Coulthard spinning out early on at Silverstone it was Hakkinen's second place which brought the team more Championship points. An accident in the qualifiers at the A1-Ring meant that the Austrian Grand Prix marked McLaren's worst grid position of the year – fourteenth by Coulthard – but a quite brilliant drive by the Scot saw him come home second behind team-mate Hakkinen for their fourth one-two of the year, which became the fifth when the two repeated the feat in Germany a couple of weeks later! The victory in Germany marked the first Mercedes-engined victory on home soil since 1954! Much the same result looked to be on the cards at the Hungaroring when the Hungary GP got underway and the McLarens occupied the front row for the eighth time of the season. Coulthard again brought the bacon home in second place but after his second stop, Hakkinen's car developed handling problems and he slid down the field to sixth place at the flag. This was achieved on new wider (25 mm) front tyres.

At Spa it was the front row of the grid once again with Hakkinen edging out Coulthard for his ninth pole of the season. That was where it ended, though, when he interacted with Herbert at the second start and was out of the race before it had really second-started. With Coulthard finishing seventh it was the first time that McLaren had come away from a race empty handed. Things improved at Monza but only marginally. Coulthard's engine failed early on and the brake problems from earlier in the season returned to restrict the Finn to fourth place.

Having dominated the Constructors' Championship throughout the season, McLaren entered the penultimate race at the Nurburgring having had their lead over Ferrari cut to ten points. With Schumacher level pegging with Hakkinen, the team were under pressure for the Luxembourg race. The pressure fell away though with a faultless race from the Finn who drove his best victory of the year. With Coulthard also securing a podium finish, McLaren ended the weekend all but guaranteed the Constructors' Cup.

McLaren claimed both crowns in the final race of the season. Although beaten for pole position in qualifying by Schumacher, Hakkinen found himself effectively starting from that point when the German stalled his engine on the grid. That all but secured the titles for McLaren and became fact when the former champion retired with a blown tyre.

Ironically the Championship victory brought McLaren level on Constructors' Cup wins with Ferrari and only one behind the record nine held by Williams. With the same two drivers and team set-up McLaren will undoubtedly be challenging Williams for their record.

Drivers and Results 1998

Driver	Races	Com	Ret	Dnq	HP	Pts	Psn	Comp%
Hakkinen, M.	16	13	3	0	1	100	1/22	81.25
Coulthard, D.	16	12	4	0	1	56	3/22	75.00
Aggregate	32	25	7	0	1	156	1/11	78.13

			Mika Hakkinen			**David Coulthard**	
	Grand Prix	*Gd*	*P*	*Details*	*Gd*	*P*	*Details*
1	Australian	1	1	1:31:45.996	2	2	1:31:46.698
2	Brazilian	1	1	1:37:11.747	2	2	1:37:12.849
3	Argentinian	3	2	1:48:69.173	1	6	1:49:55.826
4	San Marino	2	ret	Gearbox	1	1	1:34:24.593
5	Spanish	1	1	1:33:37.621	2	2	1:33:47.060
6	Monaco	1	1	1:51:23.595	2	ret	Engine
7	Canadian	2	ret	Gearbox	1	ret	Throttle link
8	French	1	3	1:35:04.773	3	6	1:34:52.416
9	British	1	2	1:47:24.915	4	ret	Spin
10	Austrian	3	1	1:30:44.086	14	2	1:30:49.375
11	German	1	1	1:20:47.984	2	2	1:20:48.410
12	Hungarian	1	6	1:45:29.932	2	2	1:45:34.983
13	Belgian	1	ret	Accident	2	7	1:43:51.512
14	Italian	3	4	1:18:05.343	4	ret	Engine
15	Luxembourg	3	1	1:32:14.789	5	3	1:32:48.952
16	Japanese	2	1	1:27:22.535	3	3	1:27:50.197

McLaren MP4-14 Specifications

Engine:	**Mercedes-Benz F0110H V10**
Cylinders:	10 – 4 valves per cylinder
Injection:	TAG 2000 electronic system
Capacity:	2998cc
Dimensions:	Length: 590mm. Width: 489mm (across water outlet). Height: 467mm to air filter

Car

Chassis:	McLaren moulded carbon fibre/honeycombed composite incorporating front, rear, side impact structures. Integral safety fuel cell
Transmission:	McLaren longitudinal six speed semi-automatic. Control by TAG electronic system. McLaren drive shafts and CV assemblies
Suspension:	Inboard torsion bar/damper system operated by pushrod and bellcrank with a double wishbone system
Lubricants:	Mobile 1 engine oil
Fuel:	Mobil unleaded
Springs:	Eibach
Dampers:	Penske
Brakes:	AP Racing callipers and master cylinders
Tyres:	Bridgestone
Race Wheels:	Enkei
Water Radiators:	McLaren/Calsonic/Secan
Oil Radiators:	McLaren/Calsonic
Electronics:	TAG Electronic Management System 2000 integrated engine and chassis control and data acquisition system. Electronic dashboard, ignition coils, alternator voltage control, sensors, data analysis and telemetry systems supplied by TAG Electronic Systems.

Engines 1966-99

1966-82: Ford. 1983-87: TAG-Porsche Turbo. 1988: Honda Turbo. 1989-92: Honda. 1993: Ford. 1994: Peugeot. 1995-99: Mercedes.

Drivers 1989-99

1989: A.Prost & A.Senna. 1990: A.Senna & G.Berger. 1991: A.Senna & G.Berger. 1992: A.Senna & G.Berger. 1993: A.Senna, M.Andretti & M.Hakkinen. 1994: M.Hakkinen, M.Brundle & P.Alliot. 1995: M.Hakkinen, N.Mansell, M.Blundell & J.Magnussen. 1996-99: M. Hakkinen & D. Coulthard.

Grand Prix Wins

1968 Bel (McLaren), Ita (Hulme), Can (Hulme); 1969 Mex (Hulme); 1972 SA (Hulme); 1973 Swe (Hulme), GB (Revson), Can (Revson);

1974 Arg (Hulme), Bra (Fittipaldi), Bel (Fittipaldi), Can (Fittipaldi);
1975 Arg (Fittipaldi), Esp (Mass), GB (Fittipaldi); 1976 Esp (Hunt), Fra
(Hunt), Ger (Hunt), Can (Hunt), USA (Hunt); 1977 GB (Hunt), USA
(Hunt), Jap (Hunt); 1981 GB (Watson); 1982 Long Beach (Lauda), Bel
(Watson), Detroit (Watson), GB (Lauda); 1983 Long Beach (Watson);
1984 Bra (Prost), SA (Lauda), San (Prost), Fra (Lauda), Mon (Prost),
GB (Lauda), Ger (Prost), Aut (Lauda), Hol (Prost), Ita (Lauda), Eur
(Prost), Por (Prost); 1985 Bra (Prost), Mon (Prost), GB (Prost), Aut
(Prost), Hol (Lauda), Ita (Prost); 1986 San (Prost), Mon (Prost), Aut
(Prost), Aus (Prost); 1987 Bra (Prost), Bel (Prost), Por (Prost); 1988 Bra
(Prost), San (Senna), Mon (Prost), Mex (Prost), Can (Senna), Detroit
(Senna), Fra (Prost), GB (Senna), Ger (Senna), Hun (Senna), Bel
(Senna), Por (Prost), Esp (Prost), Jap (Senna), Aus (Prost); 1989 San
(Senna), Mon (Senna), Mex (Senna), USA (Prost), Fra (Prost), GB
(Prost), Ger (Senna), Bel (Senna), Ita (Prost), Esp (Senna); 1990 USA
(Senna), Mon (Senna), Can (Senna), Ger (Senna), Bel (Senna), Ita
(Senna); 1991 USA (Senna), Bra (Senna), San (Senna), Mon (Senna),
Hun (Senna), Bel (Senna), Jap (Berger), Aus (Senna); 1992 Mon
(Senna), Can (Berger), Hun (Senna), Ita (Senna), Aus (Berger); 1993
Bra (Senna), Eur (Senna), Mon (Senna), Jap (Senna), Aus (Senna);
1997 Aus, Ita (Coulthard), Eur (Hakkinen); 1998 Aus, Bra, Esp, Mon,
Aut, Ger, Luxembourg, Jap (M.Hakkinen), San (Coulthard).

Minardi

Fondmetal Minardi Ford Team

Minardi Team SpA, Via Spallanzani 21, 48018 Faenza, Ravenna, Italy
Tel: +39 0546 696111   Fax: +39 0546 628140

Chariman/CEO:	Gabriele Rumi
Team Manager:	Gian Carlo Minardi
Chief Designer:	George Ryton
Tech. Director:	Gustav Brunner
Tech. Coord:	Gabriele Tredozi
Sporting Director:	Cesare Fiorio
Drivers:	Esterban Tuero
	tba
Test Driver:	–

Sponsors: Bossini, Brembo, Bridgestone, Carbone Industrie,
Cimatron, Diemme, Doimo, Donati, Fondmetal, Ircis, Magneti Marelli,
Microsystem, Milpass, RBM, Setrans, Sparco, TRW Sabelt.

Brief History

1979: Minardi formed by Gian Carlo Minardi. 1985: Minardi make their Formula 1 debut in Brazil. 1988: Pierluigi Martini picks up Minardi's first points with sixth in Detroit. 1990: Minardi record their only front row start with Martini behind Gerhard Berger in America. 1993: Christian Fittipaldi takes Minardi's highest placing thus far of fourth in South Africa. Minardi's best finish of seventh with seven points in the Constructors' World Championship.

Grand Prix Results

Contested:	221	
Victories:	0	(Best Finish: 4th – three times)
Pole Positions:	0	
Fastest Laps:	0	
Constructors' World Titles:	0	(Best: 7th 1993)
Drivers' World Championships:	0	(Best: 10th 1994)
Most Points in a Season:	7	(1993)
Total Constructors' Cup Points:	27	
Average Points/Grand Prix:	0.12	

Review

Minardi came into the 1998 season with an upgraded Ford V10 engine. The extra power provided by the engine certainly seemed to lift the spirits of the team and drivers in the early stages of the season. However, by the end of the tussles the Minardi team finished the season without a Championship point for a third successive season and, with a budget of less than a fifth of that of Ferrari's, perhaps wondering if they will ever turn the corner.

Despite that the enthusiasm remains as high as ever. They started the season with the most inexperienced team – Shinji Nakano having raced just 17 Grands Prix in the previous season for Prost, and with a real rookie in Esterban Tuero, making his debut at just 19 having brought an estimated £4 million in sponsorship monies to secure his drive.

The first two races of the season offered little encouragement for the team with both drivers not making the chequered flag as the M198 developed terminal problems in the early races. Nakano got the team's first chequered flag in Argentina, coming home thirteenth, while Tuero was involved in an accident at his home race. The rookie, though, delivered the goods at San Marino by driving a more mature race and finishing in eighth place – the highest of his four finishes. During the mid-portion of the season Nakano produced some more consistent performances and his seventh place in Canada was the team's best result of the season.

Engine and gearbox problems continued to hamper the team in practice, testing and race and just when these problems looked to be sorted, invariably a driver error provided the problems. The lack of reliability meant that the team only once managed to get both drivers home in a race – that coming in Spain.

Things are unlikely to improve drastically in the 1999 season and the hope for the team must be to at least get on the scoreboard.

Drivers and Results 1998

Driver	Races	Com	Ret	Dnq	HP	Pts	Psn	Comp%
Nakano, S.	16	10	6	0	8	0	–	62.50
Tuero, E.	16	5	11	0	8	0	–	31.25
Aggregate	32	15	17	0	8	0		46.88

		Esterban Tuero			**Shinji Nakano**		
	Grand Prix	*Gd*	*P*	*Details*	*Gd*	*P*	*Details*
1	Australian	17	ret	Engine	22	ret	Transmission
2	Brazilian	19	ret	Electrics	18	ret	Spin
3	Argentinian	20	ret	Accident	19	13	1:49:18.217
4	San Marino	19	8	1:35:48.285	21	ret	Engine
5	Spanish	19	15	1:34:42.163	20	14	1:34:11.328
6	Monaco	21	ret	Accident	19	9	1:51:48.485
7	Canadian	21	ret	Electrics	18	7	1:42:27:937
8	French	22	ret	Gearbox	21	17	Engine
9	British	18	ret	Spin	19	8	1:48:26.357
10	Austrian	19	ret	Spin	21	11	1:31:44.313
11	German	21	16	1:22:35.459	20	ret	Gearbox
12	Hungarian	21	ret	Engine	19	15	1:47:45.727
13	Belgian	22	ret	Electrics	21	8	1:46:01.069
14	Italian	22	11	1:17:59.838	21	ret	Engine
15	Luxembourg	21	ret	nc	20	15	1:32:56.589
16	Japanese	21	ret	Accident	20	ret	Electrics

Minardi M199 Specifications

Engine:

Injection:	Magneti Marelli electronic
Electronics:	Magneti Marelli
Fuel Tank:	ALT

Car

Chassis:	Carbon fibre monocoque
Suspension:	Inboard spring via rocker and pushrod to wishbone
Brake Pads:	Carbon Industrie
Brake Discs:	Brembo
Cooling System:	Water radiators (x2), oil radiator (x1)
Gearbox:	6 speed plus reverse. Longitudinal Minardi Xrtac gearbox with Minardi electrohydraulic system
Wheels:	Fondmetal: 11"x13" (front), 13.7"x13" (rear)
Tyres:	Bridgestone

Engines 1985-99

1985-87: Motori Moderni Turbo. 1988-90: Ford Cosworth. 1991: Ferrari. 1992: Lamborghini. 1993-96: Ford Cosworth. 1997: Hart. 1998-99: Ford.

Drivers 1989-99

1989: P.Martini, L.Perez Sala & P.Barilla. 1990: P.Martini, P.Barilla & G.Morbidelli. 1991: P.Martini, G.Morbidelli & R.Moreno. 1992: G.Morbidelli, C.Fittipaldi & A.Zanardi. 1993: C.Fittipaldi, F.Barbazza, P.Martini & J-M.Gounon. 1994: P.Martini & M.Alboreto. 1995: P.Lamy, L.Badoer & P.Martini. 1996: P. Lamy & T.Inoue. 1997: U.Katayama & J.Trulli. 1998: S.Nakano & E.Tuero. 1999: E.Tuero.

Grand Prix Best Performance

4th position three times: 1991 San (Martini), Por (Martini); 1993 SA (Martini).

Prost (+ John Barnard)

Equipe Prost Peugeot
Technopole de la Nievre, 58470 Magny-Cours, France
Tel: +33 3 86 60 62 00   Fax: +33 3 86 21 22 96

Owner:	Alain Prost
MD:	Bruno Michel
Chief Mechanic:	Robert Dassaud

Quartier des Sangliers
7 Avenue Eugene Freyssinet
78280 Guyancourt
France

Chief Designer:	Loic Bigois
Drivers/Engineers:	Olivier Panis
	Jarno Trulli
Test Driver:	–

(Stephan ?)
(Serrazin !)

Brief History

1976: Ligier enter F1 at the end of the 1976 season. Jacques Laffite takes pole and sets the fastest lap in Italy. 1979: Laffite wins the opening two Grands Prix in Argentina and Brazil. 1980: Ligier finish second in the Constructors' World Championship behind Williams. 1983: Ligier fail to score a point in the season for the first time in their history. 1996: Tom Walkinshaw leaves for Arrows. 1997: Alain Prost takes control of Ligier and renames team to Prost Grand Prix. 1998: Secure Peugeot engine for cars.

Grand Prix Record

Contested:	359	
Victories:	9	
Pole Positions:	9	
Fastest Laps:	11	
Constructors' World Titles:	0	(Best: 2nd 1980)
Drivers' World Championships:	0	(Best: 4th 1979, 1980, 1981)
Most Points in a Season:	66	(1980)
Total Constructors' Cup Points:	411	
Average Points/Grand Prix	1.14	

Review

A new works venue, a new engine supplier, new tyres and a new naming convention to reflect the Prost name on the car were how the French F1 team entered the 1998 season. In the end it all seemed to be a bit too much to bear as Alain Prost's team had by far the worst season since he took control, claiming just a single Championship point from its 32 race starts.

Getting the redesigned AP01 to function in perfect tandem with the Peugeot V10 and Bridgestone tyres became a real headache. Indeed, the car only just managed to be available for the opening race of the season after it passed its safety crash test days before the race, having failed the mandatory side-impact test three times! From there it was a succession of problems that hampered progress on the track with the rear suspension proving to be the worst of these.

The drive team was fairly settled. Having lost number one driver Olivier Panis for the second half of the 1997 season the team had uncovered a new protegé to partner Panis for 1998 – Italian Jarno Trulli taking the drive of Shinji Nakano who moved to Minardi.

In the first ten Grands Prix only five times did the AP01 reach the chequered flag. Gearbox and engine problems prevailed early on while relatively minor problems also accounted for early retirements along with spins attributed by the drivers to a lack of grip. The new gearbox design had the clutch situated at the rear instead of between the engine and the box itself. This concept was implemented to try to get better weight distribution but brought its own set of problems with it. The factory move to Versailles came late in the close-season and much of the testing had to be performed at Magny-Cours. Quotes attributed to Trulli indicated his dislike for the circuit as a basis for development.

The opening race in Melbourne came around too soon and with gearbox problems coming to the fore over the weekend of the Australian Grand Prix. Panis found himself demoted to the back row after abandoning his car in gear after a spin. He managed to work his way through the back end of the field and come home ninth. Trulli's gearbox failed in the first part of the race.

In Brazil neither driver made it to the end of the race due to mechanical problems. Argentina again showed positive signs with both drivers reporting better handling when the car was carrying a full load of fuel. As it would be throughout the season, grid position was a hindrance and only on a handful of occasions did either Prost car make it as high as even the fifth row. Panis's engine gave way late in the race but he was classified fifteenth. It was the first of five successive races in which Panis would not reach the chequered flag, with four of the retirements coming as a result of engine problems and another due to a loose wheel. Trulli's endeavours fared little better although he did match Panis's start of season ninth position at the Spanish GP achieved using a new version of the A16/EV0 engine.

The Prost team also had some pretty poor luck along the way and it was a perverse twist of fate that provided the one real highlight of the season. At Spa for the Belgium Grand Prix both Panis and Trulli were involved in the pile-up at the original start. Both cars were damaged and with only one T-car available it was given to Trulli because of his superior, albeit 'unlucky', thirteenth place on the grid. The Italian drove steadily throughout the race and for once, despite having gearbox problems, the maladies didn't prove terminal and he came home in sixth place to earn the team's only point of the season.

Not surprisingly that single point provided the team with a big boost and at the next race at Monza both drivers found themselves together on the fifth row of the grid. Vibration problems halted Panis but Trulli again came home, even if well outside the points.

Both drivers have been retained for the 1999 season and it would be difficult to believe that the new season can be anything as bad as the last. Insiders believe that Panis was only retained after much persuasion by the team's sponsors Gauloises. Hopefully a full close season's worth of development and testing will get the Prost team back into the upper half of the grid with finishes to match. Certainly a Constructors' Cup points tally in the low to mid twenties is a more realistic target for a talented team with two talented drivers.

Drivers and Results 1998

Driver	Races	Com	Ret	Dnq	HP	Pts	Psn	Comp%
Panis, O.	16	8	8	0	9	0	16/22	50.00
Trulli, J.	16	7	9	0	6	1	15/22	43.75
Aggregate	32	15	17	0	6	1	9/11	46.88

		Olivier Panis			**Jarno Trulli**	
	Grand Prix	*Gd*	*P*	*Details*	*Gd*	*P*	*Details*
1	Australian	21	9	1:32:03.548	15	ret	Gearbox
2	Brazilian	9	ret	Gearbox	12	ret	Fuel pressure
3	Argentinian	15	15	Engine	16	11	1:49:18.377
4	San Marino	13	ret	Engine	16	ret	Throttle
5	Spanish	12	16	Engine	16	9	1:33:46.888
6	Monaco	18	ret	Loose wheel	10	ret	Gearbox
7	Canadian	15	ret	Engine	14	ret	Accident
8	French	16	11	1:35:02.913	12	ret	Spin
9	British	22	ret	Spin	14	ret	Spin
10	Austrian	10	ret	Clutch	16	10	1:31:33.536
11	German	16	15	1:21:52.283	14	12	1:20:53.714
12	Hungarian	20	12	1:45:29.999	16	ret	Engine
13	Belgian	15	dns	ret	13	6	1:44:42.230
14	Italian	9	ret	Vibrations	10	13	1:17:27.397
15	Luxembourg	15	12	1:32:29.872	14	ret	Transmission
16	Japanese	13	11	1:28:20.327	14	12	dnf

Prost AP02 Specifications

Car

Chassis:	Carbon fibre composite monocoque manufactured by Prost Grand Prix
Suspension:	Double wishbone and push-rod

Brakes:	Brembo and/or AP one-piece callipers and master cylinders with Carbone Industries carbon fibre discs
Transmission:	Transverse semi-automatic six-speed gearbox. Multi-plate clutch
Fuel System:	ATL rubber fuel cell mounted within the monocoque structure behind the cockpit
Oil System:	Eight litre capacity oil tank
Cooling System:	Separate water radiators in each side pod plus oil radiator on right-hand side of engine

Based on 1998 information.

Engines 1976–99

1978-78: Matra. 1979-80: Ford. 1981-84: Matra. 1984-86: Renault Turbo. 1987: Megatron Turbo. 1988: Judd. 1989-90: Ford. 1991: Lamborghini. 1992-94: Renault. 1995-97: Mugen-Honda. 1998-99: Peugeot.

Drivers 1989–99

1989: R.Arnoux & O.Grouillard. 1990: P.Alliot & N.Larini. 1991: T.Boutsen & E.Comas. 1992: T.Boutsen & E.Comas. 1993: M.Brundle & M.Blundell. 1994: E.Bernard, O.Panis, J.Herbert & F.Lagorce. 1995: M.Brundle, A.Suzuki & O.Panis. 1996: P.Diniz & O.Panis. 1997: O.Panis & S.Nakano. 1998-99: O.Panis & J.Trulli.

Grand Prix Wins

1977 Swe (Laffite); 1979 Arg (Laffite), Bra (Laffite), Esp (Depailler); 1980 Bel (Pironi), Ger (Laffite); 1981 Aut (Laffite), Can (Laffite); 1996 Mon (Panis).

Sauber

Red Bull Sauber Petronas
Team Sauber Formel 1
Austrasse 9, FL-9490 Vaduz
Tel: +41 75 232 77 64   Fax: +41 75 232 77 47
Team Principal: Peter Sauber
Chief Designer: Leo Ress

Team Manager:	Beat Zehnder
Drivers:	Jean Alesi
	Pedro Diniz
Test Driver:	–
Sponsors:	Red Bull, Petronas, Parmalat.

Brief History

1993: Sauber record a scoring finish in their first Grand Prix with J.J. Lehto taking fifth in South Africa. The team end the season sixth in the Constructors' World Championship with twelve points. 1995: Achieve first podium finish when Frentzen finishes third at Monza. 1996: Herbert finishes third at Monaco. 1997: Herbert finishes third in Hungary.

Grand Prix Record

Contested:	98	
Victories:	0	(Best Finish: 3rd – four times)
Pole Positions:	0	
Fastest Laps:	0	
Constructors' World Titles:	0	(Best: 6th 1993, 1998)
Drivers' World Championships:	0	(Best: 8th 1994)
Most Points in a Season:	18	(1995)
Total Constructors' Cup Points:	79	
Average Points/Grand Prix:	0.81	

Review

In the simple terms of points earned Sauber failed to make progress on their outstanding 1997 season. Given that they had probably their best set of drivers since they entered the F1 arena, one assumes that it was the car that wasn't quite performing. Indeed the stats seem to bear this out. Only eight times were Alesi or Herbert able to break into the top ten of the qualifying grid and there was a total of 13 retirements throughout the season, although only on two occasions did they fail to get at least one driver to the chequered flag. It is also true to say that the team suffered some tough luck – Johnny Herbert seemed to suffer especially badly in this respect – not least in a number of third-party enforced retirements. There was also the odd occasion when the bad luck was self-inflicted or frustration caused the drivers to push just too hard.

Jean Alesi joined the team and his experience and performances effectively made him the number one driver alongside Johnny Herbert.

Alesi, although not matching the points totals he recorded under Ferrari and Benetton, settled in relatively quickly and before the season was out he had equalled the team 's best ever race finish and also secured their first ever position on the front row of the grid. Johnny Herbert, on the other hand, had a miserable season earning just a solitary point and was often the brunt of ill fortune. It was no surprise when he announced that he would be joining the Stewart Ford team for 1999, given what seemed to be an undercurrent of dissatisfaction between him and the team, much of which would seem to have been brought on by the arrival of Alesi.

It was Herbert who started the season better, securing a point at Melbourne in a race in which Alesi was forced to retire. The Frenchman recorded his first finish – ninth – in the next race where a sore neck, acquired in a practice crash, forced Herbert out. Alesi secured his first points with a fifth place in Argentina and followed it up with a sixth placing in the next race in San Marino. Herbert on the other hand completed a miserable hat-trick of three non-finishes. In Argentina Alesi had shunted into Herbert during practice and forced the Englishman to use the T-car in qualifying.

Herbert got the better of the finishing battles in Spain and Monaco where he came home seventh in both – but those were to be his highest finishes for the remainder of the season. Alesi started to get to grips with the car by the time of the British Grand Prix and at the Austrian race used the weather conditions to his advantage to fly home and secure second place on the grid, having briefly held pole position at one point. The race, though, ended early when he tangled with Fisichella who was returning to the circuit after a pit stop.

Herbert's luck was typified by the incident at Monza where, having started the race he found that a pair of pliers had been left in his cockpit. With this jamming in his footwell the distraction eventually proved too much and he spun out on the thirteenth lap. Alesi in the meantime had followed up his front row glory with a podium finish in third place at Spa, having managed to avoid the carnage at the first start and get away clear at the second.

Sauber will continue to use its Ferrari-sourced engines for a third successive season and these will be badged under their Petronas sponsor's name. The team is expected to have to pay over £15 million for the engines. This will be helped by the arrival of Pedro Diniz and his clutch of sponsors. Diniz – a much better driver than most cynical observers would let you believe – moves another step up the team ladder, but Sauber has a long way to go to move out of the middle rank of teams as it approaches its 100th Grand Prix.

Drivers and Results 1998

Driver	Races	Com	Ret	Dnq	HP	Pts	Psn	Comp%
Alesi, J.	16	12	4	0	3	9	11/22	75.00
Herbert, J.	16	7	9	0	6	1	15/22	43.75
Aggregate	32	19	13	0	3	10	6/11	59.38

			Jean Alesi			**Johnny Herbert**	
	Grand Prix	*Gd*	*P*	*Details*	*Gd*	*P*	*Details*
1	Australian	12	ret	Engine	5	6	1:31:46.420
2	Brazilian	15	9	1:37:42.228	14	ret	Neck injury
3	Argentinian	11	5	1:49:54.461	12	ret	Accident dam.
4	San Marino	12	6	1:34.30.693	11	ret	Puncture
5	Spanish	14	10	1:33:47.986	7	7	1:33:58.147
6	Monaco	11	12	Engine	9	7	1:52:36.186
7	Canadian	9	ret	Accident	12	ret	Spin
8	French	11	7	1:34:54.330	13	8	1:35:37.415
9	British	8	ret	Electrics	9	ret	Spin
10	Austrian	2	ret	Accident	18	8	1:30:56.888
11	German	11	10	1:21:36.355	12	ret	Gearbox
12	Hungarian	11	7	1:45:41.961	15	10	1:46:20.059
13	Belgian	10	3	1:43:54.647	12	ret	Accident
14	Italian	8	5	1:18:11.544	15	ret	Spin
15	Luxembourg	11	10	1:32:29.424	13	ret	Engine
16	Japanese	12	7	1:28:58.588	11	10	1:27:43.035

Sauber Petronas C18 Specifications

Engine:	**Sauber-Petronas SPE 03A**
Type:	V10
Valves:	40
Valve Mechanism:	Pneumatic
Management:	Magneti Marelli
Car	
Chassis:	Carbon fibre monocoque
Suspension:	Upper and lower wishbones, combined spring/damper units (Sachs), mounted inboard with pushrod actuation
Brakes:	Six-piston callipers (Brembo) front and rear; carbon pads and discs (Carbone Industrie/Hitco)
Transmission:	Semi-automatic, longitudinally mounted, seven-speed transmission (Sauber), carbon clutch (Sachs)
Dimensions:	Length: 4410 mm Width: 1800 mm

Height: 1000 mm   Wheelbase: 2980 mm
Front Track: 1470 mm   Rear Track: 1410 mm

Engines 1993-99

1993: Sauber. 1994: Mercedes. 1995-96: Ford. 1997-99: Petronas.

Drivers 1993-99

1993: K. Wendlinger & J. J.Lehto. 1994: K.Wendlinger, H-H.Frentzen, J.J.Lehto & A.de Cesaris. 1995: H-H.Frentzen, J-C.Boullion & K.Wendlinger. 1996: J. Herbert & H-H.Frentzen. 1997: J.Herbert & N.Larini. 1998: J.Herbert & Jean Alesi. 1999: J.Alesi & P.Diniz.

Grand Prix Best Performance

3rd position four times: 1995 Ita (Frentzen), 1996 Mon (Herbert), 1997 Hun (Herbert), 1998 Bel (Alesi).

Stewart

Stewart Ford
Stewart Grand Prix Ltd
The Stewart Building, Bradbourne Drive, Tilbrook, Milton Keynes, Bucks., MK7 8BJ
Tel: +44 (0)1908 279794   Fax: +44 (0)1908 279763

Chairman:	Jackie Stewart OBE
Managing Director:	Paul Stewart
Tech. Director:	Dave Stubbs
Chief Designer:	Gary Anderson
Chief Mechanic:	Dave Redding
Drivers/Engineers:	Rubens Barrichello
	Johnny Herbert
Test Driver:	–
Sponsors:	Ford, HSBC, Hewlett Packard, Lear, Technology Partners, Bridgestone, Visteon, Rolex, Espirit, Hertz, Highland.

Brief History

1996: Stewart Grand Prix formed. 1997: First season F1 racing. Finished 2nd in Monaco Grand Prix.

Grand Prix Record

Contested:	33	
Victories:	0	(Best Finish: 2nd)
Pole Positions:	0	
Fastest Laps:	0	
Constructors' World Titles:	0	(Best: 9th 1997)
Drivers' World Championships:	0	(Best: 12th 1998)
Most Points in a Season:	6	(1997)
Total Constructors' Cup Points:	11	
Average Points/Grand Prix	0.33	

Review

Despite a lot more hard work behind the scenes it is difficult to assess whether Team Stewart actually made any progress in their second full season of competitive racing. Never one to shy away from challenges the Stewart family took the new regulations for the 1998 season pretty much in their stride. It cannot have come as happy news to them that all their design efforts to create a car from scratch for their debut season in 1997 had to be ditched in favour of new scratch designs for the 1998 season. Added to this the team took on the development of a carbon-fibre gearbox – something other establishments have tried but then abandoned – and this in itself added to the design challenges for 1998. The announcement at the end of the 1998 season that Gary Anderson was joining them as chief designer from the Jordan camp will undoubtedly help but his efforts may take until mid season to filter their way into grid and race positions.

The season got underway with the driver combination of Barrichello and Magnussen in place although the Dane would be replaced by the more experienced Jos Verstappen before the season had reached the midway point. Despite being one of the first launches for the 1998 season, the Stewart SF-2 had done very few testing miles when the challengers gathered in Melbourne for the first race of the year.

By the time the final race at Suzuka had been completed the stats showed that a year of progression had been made with its three drivers having finished 12 of their 32 race starts – four more than 1997. The more consistent finish also translated into more points finishes with Barrichello recording two fifth places and Magnussen a single sixth – his first ever Championship point ironically coming in his last race for the team!

Inevitably the new gearbox was invariably the car's Achilles' heel at different points of the season. It couldn't have had a worse debut as far as Rubens Barrichello was concerned as he found himself unable to select gear at the start of the Australian Grand Prix and he was out of the race before it had even started. Magnussen fared little better when he spun off as early as his second lap. The Dane supplied the team's first finish of the season in Brazil while Barrichello had to wait until the next race in Argentina for his.

It was Spain before both drivers managed to complete a race together and by this time the rumours were again circulating about the future of Magnussen, heightened after he had careered into the back of Barrichello at the start of the San Marino race. Barrichello's point in Spain was the first scored by the team in dry weather and was achieved using a high-revving Phase Four version of the engine. The V10 engine itself continued to be developed with the C-Specification design being the one which seemed to respond best of all.

With both drivers coming home in the points for the Canadian race, it was announced thereafter that Jos Verstappen was joining the team to take the drive of Magnussen. The reason given for the Dane's dismissal was the lack of improvement in qualifying position. If that was the case the new boy responded well with a fifteenth place – the best for a number two at Stewart up until that point of the season – and he went on to better this with a twelfth at the A1-Ring. Neither driver managed to add to the team's points tally for the season, though additional finishes were achieved in amongst more gearbox and engine problems. The season finished as it had started with two retirements, these coming at Suzuka in the final race.

The arrival of Gary Anderson to work on the SF-3 will provide much-needed back-room experience, while Johnny Herbert will drive alongside Barrichello in 1998. More experience again which may help the Stewart cars get into double figures in the Constructors' Championship in 1999 – providing the gearbox maladies are sorted.

Drivers and Results 1998

Driver	Races	Com	Ret	Dnq	HP	Pts	Psn	Comp%
Barrichello, R.	16	6	10	0	5	4	12/22	37.50
Magnussen, J.	7	3	4	0	6	1	15/22	42.86
Verstappen, J.	9	3	6	0	12	0	–	33.33
Aggregate	32	12	20	0	5	5	6/11	37.90

	Grand Prix	Rubens Barrichello			Magnussen/Verstappen *		
		Gd	P	Details	Gd	P	Details
1	Australian	14	ret	Gearbox	18	ret	Accident
2	Brazilian	13	ret	Gearbox	16	10	1:37:41.719
3	Argentinian	14	10	1:49:03.354	22	ret	Transmission
4	San Marino	17	ret	Accident	20	ret	Gearbox
5	Spanish	9	5	1:33:54.435	18	12	1:34:01.002
6	Monaco	14	ret	Suspension	17	ret	Suspension
7	Canadian	13	5	1:42:18.868	20	6	1:42:26.707
8	French *	14	10	1:34:46.884	15	12	1:35:21.800
9	British *	16	ret	Spin	15	ret	Engine
10	Austrian *	5	ret	Brakes	12	ret	Engine
11	German *	13	ret	Gearbox	19	ret	Transmission
12	Hungarian *	14	ret	Gearbox	17	13	1:45:53.909
13	Belgian *	14	dns	ret	17	ret	Engine
14	Italian *	13	10	1:18:22.050	17	ret	Gearbox
15	Luxembourg *	12	11	1:32:28.610	18	13	1:32:52.806
16	Japanese *	16	ret	Hydraulics	19	ret	Gearbox

Stewart Ford SF3 Specifications

Engine: **Ford Cosworth V10 CR-1**
Cylinders: 10 (72 degree) – 40 valves
Capacity: 2998 cc
Management: Visteon
Lubrication: Dry sump
Ignition: Cosworth Racing
Spark Plugs: Champion
Weight: 100 kg
Dimensions: 569 mm (length), 506 mm (width), 485 mm (height)
Car
Chassis: Carbon fibre monocoque designed and built in-house, carrying engine as fully-stressed member
Transmission: Stewart magnesium-cased six speed gearbox, longitudinally mounted. High-pressure hydraulic system for power shift and clutch operation. Integrated centralised oil system
Clutch: AP Racing triple-plate pull-type clutch.
Suspension: Upper and lower carbon wishbones and pushrods. Stewart/Penske damper layout. Torsion bar springing (front)/coil springing (rear)
Brakes: AP Racing lithium alloy six-piston callipers (front). Twin AP Racing six-piston callipers (rear)

Brake Pads:	Carbone Industrie carbon fibre discs and pads
Wheels:	BBS forged magnesium
Electronics:	Visteon VCS single box. Integrated engine/chassis electronic control systems

Engines 1997-99

1997-99: Ford.

Drivers 1997-99

1997-98: R.Barrichello, J.Magnussen & J. Verstappen; 1999:
R.Barrichello & J.Herbert.

Grand Prix Best Performance

2nd position once: 1997 Mon (Barrichello).

Williams

Winfield Williams F1

Williams Grand Prix Engineering Ltd
Grove, Wantage, Oxfordshire, OX12 0QD
Tel: +44 (0)1235 777700   Fax: +44 (0)1235 764705

MD:	Sir Frank Williams
Tech. Director:	Patrick Head
Chief Designer:	Gavin Fisher
Aerodynamicist:	Geoff Willis
Race Team Mgr:	Dickie Stanford
Test Team Mgr:	Bryan Lambert
Senior Ops Eng:	James Robinson
Chief Mechanic:	Carl Gaden
Drivers/Engineers:	Alex Zanardi / Greg Wheeler
	Ralf Schumacher / Craig Wilson
Test Driver:	Juan Pablo Montoya
Sponsors:	Winfield, Castrol, Komatsu, Automotive

Products, Magneti Marelli, Bridgestone, Sparco, Petrobras, Andersen
Consulting, Auto Motor und Sport, Sonax, Universal Studios, Du Pont,
DSF, OZ Racing, Snap-on Tools, Champion, Brother International,
DF1, Fujistu Computers, Nortel Networks, Veltins, Entranet/Nat
Systems, S Oliver.

Brief History

1969: After building his business up, Frank Williams starts running cars. 1970: Piers Courage killed during the Dutch Grand Prix driving a private session. 1973: Entered Formula 1 under the name of ISO. 1976: Disappointing partnership with oil man Walter Wolf. 1978: Williams Grand Prix Engineering founded. Australian Alan Jones signed to drive. 1979: Clay Regazzoni wins in Britain for Williams' first Grand Prix victory. 1980: Alan Jones wins the Drivers' World Championship with Williams taking the Constructors' title for the first time. 1986: Frank Williams seriously injured in a car crash and confined to a wheelchair. 1992: Nigel Mansell becomes the first driver to win the opening five rounds of a season and achieves a record of nine victories in total as Williams take the Drivers' and Constructors' World Championships. 1993: Alain Prost wins his fourth world title and announces his retirement from the sport. 1994: Williams record their seventh Constructors' Championship victory to bring them level with Lotus in the all-time record. 1996: Williams win eighth Constructors' Championship, Damon Hill wins first Drivers' World Championship, Jacques Villeneuve runner-up in first season. 1997: Williams win ninth Constructors' Championship, Jacques Villeneuve wins first Drivers' World Championship in only his second season. 1999: Frank Williams knighted in New Year honours list.

Grand Prix Record

Contested:	332	
Victories:	103	
Pole Positions:	108	
Fastest Laps:	109	
Constructors' World Titles:	9	(80, 81, 86, 87, 92, 93, 94, 96, 97)
Drivers' World Championships:	7	(80, 82, 87, 92, 93, 96, 97)
Most Points in a Season:	175	(1996)
Total Constructors' Cup Points:	1948.5	
Average Points/Grand Prix:	5.87	

Review

With Williams having won the Constructors' Championship five times out of the previous six seasons and supplying four World Champion drivers in the same period, the more cynical-minded F1 followers may have had a sneaking suspicion that the specification changes made and implemented for the start of the 1998 season were in fact the FIA's way of trying to make the forthcoming season a more competitive event. If that was the case (and I don't for a moment really suggest it was!) then it worked and I mean really worked! Having scored a massive 298 points in the previous two seasons, the two Williams drivers – Villeneuve and Frentzen – managed just 38 between them and failed to contribute even a single win, pole position or fastest lap to the 1998 season statistics. The team finished third in the Constructors' Cup – its lowest placing since 1990.

How much the departure of designer Adrian Newey from Williams to McLaren and the loss of the Renault works engines had to do with the drastic change in fortunes is debatable – but must be borne in mind. Nevertheless, at the start of the 1998 season the Williams team were expected to be in the running for yet another Championship.

With Villeneuve in his third season and, as the early rumours proved, his last season, the time looked right for the Williams number two Heinz-Harald Frentzen to step up and take the mantle. The German looked like he might be in line to do just that when he outfinished the then reigning World Champion in the first three races of the season. In the end Frentzen also found himself out of the team and following Williams' previous World Champion Damon Hill to Jordan.

Both drivers suffered with their cars running high oil temperatures in Australian and as a consequence had to limit their revs and they came home third (Frentzen) and fifth (Villeneuve). A podium finish was achieved which got the season off to a better start then the dual Championship one of the previous year but that was as good as it got.

Moving to South America, Frentzen brought home the only two points from the two races where both drivers experienced handling problems late on in the race, not least with understeer.

Back in Europe problems with the fuel filler cap not opening and then staying open plagued Villeneuve, who still managed to finish fourth, while Frentzen came in one place behind. Four races gone and Williams were already trailing by 36 points in the Constructors' Cup!

The Spanish Grand Prix produced one of the worst qualifying performances by Williams in recent memory. Oversteer was now a problem and the team would have seen their tenth and thirteenth starting places as an embarrassment – Villeneuve at least salvaged a point by finishing sixth. The Canadian did little better in Monaco where his thirteenth place on the grid became his worst ever qualifying performance. From there, though, he climbed to fourth. For Frentzen it was the start of five races where he would fail to make the chequered flag although only the final one in the sequence – a blown engine at the

A1-Ring – could be attributed to the car mechanics. The others resulted from accidents or spins.

Villeneuve continued to pick up points here and there, but the major modifications to the FW20 that debuted at the Canadian GP failed to turn the tide and there were continued problems with tyre wear, despite the introduction of changes to the rear suspension and a longer wheel base.

As the Championship entered its final half dozen races both drivers started to get their cars home in the points in a more respectable position. Villeneuve managed two third place podium finishes and in Italy recorded a second place grid position – the only time a Williams car made the front row in 1998! In their final races for the team, both drivers got their FW20s home in the points to conclude a disappointing season for all concerned.

With two new drivers coming into the team, there must be a question mark over Williams' ability to challenge for the Championship. Ralf Schumacher started to prove his worth at Jordan in the final stages of the season but knows that he will have to start delivering the goods from race one unless he is to follow the path trod by his departing countryman.

Alex Zinardi follows in the wake of Villeneuve as reigning CART champion but, unlike the Canadian, the 31-year old Italian has had previous F1 experience, albeit without much success in short bursts with Jordan, Lotus and Minardi.

Both drivers have a lot to live up to. Since Williams' first Grand Prix win in 1979, 1998 was only the second season the team have failed to record a victory (the first being exactly ten years earlier in 1988) and they have never gone two seasons without success. 1999 got off to a good start when Frank Williams was knighted in the Queen's New Year honours list.

Drivers and Results 1998

Driver	Races	Com	Ret	Dnq	HP	Pts	Psn	Comp%
Villeneuve, J.	16	13	3	0	3	21	5/22	81.25
Frentzen, H-H.	16	12	4	0	3	17	7/22	75.00
Aggregate	32	25	7	0	3	38	3/11	78.13

			Jacques Villeneuve			**H-H. Frentzen**
	Grand Prix	Gd	P	Details	Gd	P	Details
1	Australian	4	5	1:32.20.799	6	3	1 lap
2	Brazilian	10	7	1:37:23.653	3	5	1:37:14.445
3	Argentinian	7	ret	Accident	6	9	1:49:43.772

4	San Marino	6	4	1:35:19.183	8	5	1:35:42.069
5	Spanish	10	6	1:33:55.147	13	8	1:33:42.553
6	Monaco	13	5	1:51:58.811	5	ret	Accident
7	Canadian	6	10	1:42:14.604	7	ret	Accident
8	French	5	4	1:35:51.991	8	15	Accident dam.
9	British	3	7	1:48:20.879	6	ret	Spin
10	Austrian	11	6	1:31:37.288	7	ret	Engine
11	German	3	3	1:20:50.561	10	9	1:21:20.768
12	Hungarian	6	3	1:46:09.994	7	5	1:46:22.060
13	Belgian	6	ret	Accident	9	4	1:44:19.650
14	Italian	2	ret	Spin	12	7	1:17:11.164
15	Luxembourg	9	8	1:32:20.762	7	5	1:33:15.036
16	Japanese	6	6	1:28:38.402	5	5	1:28:36.392

Williams FW21 Specifications

Engine: **Supertec V10**

Cylinders:	10 in V configuration 71 degrees
Valves:	Pneumatically controlled
Management:	Magneti Marelli electronic engine management and static ignition
Dimensions:	Length: 623 mm Width: 542 mm
	Height: 395 mm (to cylinder heads)
Weight:	120 kg (approximately depending on equipment)

Car

Chassis:	Carbon Aramid epoxy composite, manufactured by Williams
Transmission:	Six-speed Williams transverse semi-automatic
Clutch:	AP Racing
Suspension:	Williams with Williams-Penske dampers
Cooling system:	Two Secan water radiators either side of chassis; two IMI oil radiators
Brakes:	Carbone Industrie discs and pads operated by AP callipers
Lubricants:	Castrol
Fuel:	Petrobras
Instrumentation:	Williams digital data display
Dimensions:	Length: 4450 mm Wheelbase: 3050 mm
	Front Track: 1460 mm Rear Track: 1400 mm

Engines 1973-99

1973-83: Ford. 1984-87: Honda Turbo. 1988: Judd. 1989-97: Renault.
1998-99: Mecachrome.

Drivers 1989-99

1989: T.Boutsen & R.Patrese. 1990: T.Boutsen & R.Patrese. 1991:
N.Mansell & R.Patrese. 1992: N.Mansell & R.Patrese. 1993: A.Prost &
D.Hill. 1994: A.Senna, D.Hill, D.Coulthard & N.Mansell. 1995: D.Hill
& D.Coulthard. 1996: D.Hill & J. Villeneuve. 1997-98: J.Villeneuve &
H-H.Frentzen. 1999: A.Zinardi & R.Schumacher.

Grand Prix Wins

1979 GB (Regazzoni), Ger (Jones), Aut (Jones), Hol (Jones), Can
(Jones); 1980 Arg (Jones), Mon (Reutemann), Fra (Jones), GB (Jones),
Can (Jones), USA (Jones); 1981 Long Beach (Jones), Bra (Reutemann),
Bel (Reutemann), Las Vegas (Jones); 1982 Swi (Rosberg); 1983 Mon
(Rosberg), 1984 Dallas (Rosberg), 1985 Detroit (Rosberg), Eur
(Mansell), SA (Mansell), Aus (Rosberg); 1986 Bra (Piquet), Bel
(Mansell), Can (Mansell), Fra (Mansell), GB (Mansell), Ger (Piquet),
Hun (Piquet), Ita (Piquet), Por (Mansell); 1987 San (Mansell), Fra
(Mansell), GB (Mansell), Ger (Piquet), Hun (Piquet), Aut (Mansell), Ita
(Piquet), Esp (Mansell), Mex (Mansell); 1989 Can (Boutsen), Aus
(Boutsen); 1990 San (Patrese), Hun (Boutsen); 1991 Mex (Patrese), Fra
(Mansell), GB (Mansell), Ger (Mansell), Ita (Mansell), Por (Patrese),
Esp (Mansell); 1992 SA (Mansell), Mex (Mansell), Bra (Mansell), Esp
(Mansell), San (Mansell), Fra (Mansell), GB (Mansell), Ger (Mansell),
Por (Mansell), Jap (Riccardo Patrese); 1993 SA (Prost), San (Prost),
Esp (Prost), Can (Prost), Fra (Prost), GB (Prost), Ger (Prost), Hun
(Hill), Bel (D.Hill), Ita (D.Hill); 1994 Esp (D.Hill), GB (D.Hill), Bel
(D.Hill), Ita (D.Hill), Por (D.Hill), Jap (D.Hill), Aus (Mansell); 1995
Arg (D.Hill), San (D.Hill), Hun (D.Hill), Por (Coulthard), Aus (D.Hill);
1996: Aus (D.Hill), Bra (D.Hill), Arg (D.Hill), Eur (J.Villeneuve), San
(D.Hill), Can (D.Hill), Fra (D.Hill), GB (J.Villeneuve), Ger (D.Hill),
Hun (J.Villeneuve), Por (J.Villeneuve), Jap (D.Hill). 1997: Bra
(J.Villeneuve), Arg (J.Villeneuve), San (Frentzen), Esp (J.Villeneuve),
GB (J.Villeneuve), Hun (J.Villeneuve), Aut (J.Villeneuve),
Luxembourg (J.Villeneuve).

Retired Teams

Tyrrell Ford
Tyrrell Racing Organisation Ltd

Contested:	434	
Victories:	23	
Pole Positions:	14	
Fastest Laps:	20	
Constructors' World Titles:	1	(1971)
Drivers' World Championships:	2	(1971, 1973)
Most Points in a Season:	82	(1973)
Total Constructors' Cup Points:	617	
Average Points/Grand Prix:	1.42	

Review

Sunday 15 November 1998 and the doors at Tyrrell's Ockham factory close for the final time. Tyrrell Grand Prix Racing ceases to exist after 38 years in Formula 1. Having sold the team to Craig Pollock's British American Racing (BAR) set-up at the end of the 1997 season, 1998 was one where Tyrrell took part rather than competed and it was a sad goodbye for one of the great names in F1.

On the track for 1998 it was a disappointing departure with the team failing to score a point and in three Grands Prix having a driver failing to meet the qualifying time to start the race. The one bright point to come out of the season, though, was the debut of Japanese driver Takagi who impressed many informed people in the sport with his application and speed in his rookie year.

Australia and Brazil were double disappointments with neither car managing to last the distance. After qualifying an excellent thirteenth in his first ever race, Takagi perhaps let his inexperience show through when he spun out on the second lap. Gearbox problems forced Rosset out of his first two races and it wasn't until Argentina that Tyrrell drivers got to the finishing line with both drivers finishing well outside the points.

Rosset, who became the first driver (and so far only driver) to fall foul of the 107% rule for Lola in 1996, was ousted from the races in Spain, Monaco and Hungary because of it. He was excluded on medical grounds at Germany following a practice accident and was a victim of the multi-car pile-up at the start of the Belgium Grand Prix. Of the other 11 races he only managed to get home in four of them but did record the team's best finish with an eighth place in Canada – achieved from the back row of the grid.

Takagi finished eight of his races with his best results coming at Silverstone and Monza and he generally produced the better qualifying performances. The final race in Japan saw Rosset again failing to qualify and Takagi retiring following an accident.

Dr Harvey Postlethwaite, managing director of Tyrrell, departed from the Formula 1 arena by saying: "On behalf of myself and all the Tyrrell team, I would like to thank our drivers, sponsors and British American Racing for their effort and support this year. I would also like to thank all our team members for their loyalty, unflagging good humour and professionalism. Having to participate instead of compete has not been easy, and sometimes it causes a rage which is difficult to contain. The end of the Tyrrell Racing Organisation gives rise to just a moment of reflection. We are all looking forward to tomorrow."

Drivers and Results 1998

Driver	Races	Com	Ret	Dnq	HP	Pts	Psn	Comp%
Takagi, T.	16	8	8	0	9	0	–	50.00
Rosset, R.	12	4	8	4	12	0	–	33.33
Aggregate	28	12	16	4	9	0	10/11	41.67

			Ricardo Rosset				**T. Takagi**	
	Grand Prix	Gd	P	Details	Gd	P	Details	
1	Australian	19	ret	Gear selection	13	ret	Spin	
2	Brazilian	21	ret	Gearbox	17	ret	Engine	
3	Argentinian	21	14	1:48:49.538	13	12	1:50:15.941	
4	San Marino	22	ret	Engine	15	ret	Engine	
5	Spanish	dnq	–		21	13	1:34:37.820	
6	Monaco	dnq	–		20	11	1:52:31.704	
7	Canadian	22	8	1:43:17.371	16	ret	Loss of drive	
8	French	18	ret	Engine	20	ret	Engine	
9	British	20	ret	Spin	17	9	1:47:37.746	
10	Austrian	22	12	1:33:28.193	20	ret	Spin	
11	German	ret	ret	Practice accident	15	13	1:21:07.369	
12	Hungarian	dnq	–		18	14	1:46:08.141	
13	Belgian	20	dns		19	ret	Spin	
14	Italian	18	12	1:18:12.566	19	9	1:18:15.640	
15	Luxembourg	22	ret	Engine	17	16	1:32:57.269	
16	Japanese	dnq	–		17	ret	Accident	

Grand Prix Circuits 1999

Grand Prix Circuits – All-time List

Circuit	Active	No.
A1-Ring	1970-87	19
(Including 18 as Oesterreichring)		
Adelaide	1985-95	11
Ain-Diab	1958	1
Aintree	1955-62	5
Anderstorp	1973-78	6
Avus	1959	1
Brands Hatch	1964-86	14
Bremgarten	1950-54	5
Buenos Aires	1953-	21
Catalunya	1991-	8
Clermont-Ferrand	1965-72	4
Dallas	1984	1
Detroit	1982-88	7
Dinon-Prenois	1974-84	6
Donington Park	1993	1
East London, SA	1962-65	3
Estoril	1984-96	13
Fuji	1976-77	2
Hockenheim	1970-	21
Hungaroring	1986-	12
Imola	1980-	19
Indianapolis	1950-60	11
Interlagos	1973-	16
Jacarepagua	1978-89	10
Jarama	1967-81	10
Jerez	1986-97	7
Kyalami	1967-93	20
Las Vegas	1981-82	2
Le Mans Bugati	1967	1
Long Beach	1976-83	8
Magny Cours	1991	7
Melbourne	1996-	3
Mexico City	1963-92	15
Monaco	1950-	45
Monsanto	1959	1
Mont Tremblant	1968, 70	2
Montjuic Park	1969-75	4
Montreal	1978-	19
Monza	1950, 81-	47
Mosport Park	1967, 71-	8
Nivelles	1972, 74	2
Nurburgring	1951-	27
Oporto	1958, 60	2
Paul Ricard	1971, 85-90	14
Pedralbes	1951, 54	2
Pescara	1957	1
Phoenix	1989, 90, 91	3
Reims	1950-66	11
Riverside	1960	1
Rouen	1952-68	5
Sebring	1959	1
Silverstone	1950, 87-	31
Spa-Francorchamps	1950, 85-	32
Suzuka	1987-	11
TI Circuit	1994, 95	2
Watkins Glen	1961-80	20
Zandvoort	1952-85	30
Zeltweg	1964	1
Zolder	1973-84	10

A1-Ring

A1-Ring
Austrian Grand Prix – 25 July 1999
Lap Distance: 2.684 miles/4.321 km – Clockwise
Race Distance: 190.564 miles/306.808 km – 71 laps

The A1-Ring is an updated and redesigned version of the famous old Österreichring. It lies in a green, hilly area of Austria known as Styria, roughly central in a triangle formed by the cities of Vienna, Salzburg and Graz.

Originally built in 1968, a total of 18 Grands Prix were held there between 1970 and 1987, with the final event needing three starts to get it underway! It came back on to the calender in 1997 after £17 million had been spent on it to turn the circuit into one of the most modern in the world. The circuit has a square feel to it and combines a number of long straights with tight and sweeping corners that will test drivers and keep teams on their toes when it comes to car set-ups. Medium downforce is the normal choice as mechanical grip is very important here where heavy braking is required as cars go from fast straights into tight corners.

The Circuit

The starting line and grid are located in front of the medical centre and from here the cars power their way down past the garages in top gear at 180 mph. Changing down and braking hard, the bumpy Castrol Kurve is a sharp right-hand turn that is taken in 2nd gear at 45 mph. Once through the turn the cars come out on to the fastest part of the circuit and a near straight that is over half a mile in length. At a top speed of 180 mph, the stands of the Naturtribune West flash past on the left as the track curves slightly out to the left.

At the end of the straight the Remus Kurve looms – very tight, it takes the cars through 150 degrees. It is the hardest braking point in the circuit with drivers pulling -3.6 g as they decelerate hard to 40 mph at the apex of the corner. By getting the braking right, overtaking is a possibility at this point. Out of here is another long straight, only slightly shorter than the one leading into the Remus Kurve and just as

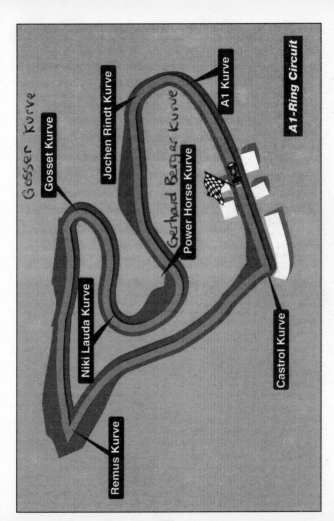

A1-Ring Circuit

A1 Kurve

Jochen Rindt Kurve

Gerhard Berger Kurve

Power Horse Kurve

Gosser Kurve

Gosset Kurve

Niki Lauda Kurve

Remus Kurve

Castrol Kurve

fast as it passes in front of the Naturtribune Nord stands at around 170 mph. The end of this straight marks the entry to the most curvaceous part of the circuit which swings inside and out.

The Gosset Kurve is a double right-hand turn, the 50 mph 2nd-gear entry being slower than the shallower exit which can be negotiated in 4th gear at 110 mph. The Niki Lauda Kurve is an open sweeping turn around to the left, taken at 95 mph in 4th gear, and leading into another similar turn called the Power Horse Kurve which is marginally faster at 100 mph.

Out on to a shorter straight, the cars run parallel to the Start-Finish line at 175 mph as they approach the Jochen Rindt Kurve. This is an open right-hand turn that is taken in 4th gear at 125 mph and leads into a short straight from where cars can re-enter the pit lane. The A1 Kurve slows the cars down through 3rd gear at 95 mph as they turn right before accelerating out along the straight across the Start-Finish line.

3-Year Record

Year	1st	2nd	3rd	4th	5th	6th
1987	Mansell	Piquet	Fabi	Boutsen	Senna	Prost
	(Williams)	(Williams)	(Benetton)	(Benetton)	(Lotus)	(McLaren)
1997	Villeneuve	Coulthard	Frentzen	Fisichella	R.Schum'r	M.Schum'r
	(Williams)	(McLaren)	(Williams)	(Jordan)	(Jordan)	(Ferrari)
1998	Hakkinen	Coulthard	M.Schum'r	Irvine	R.Schum'r	Villeneuve
	(McLaren)	(McLaren)	(Ferrari)	(Ferrari)	(Jordan)	(Williams)

Pole Positions

1987	1997	1998
Piquet (Williams)	Villeneuve (Williams)	Fisichella (Benetton)
	1:10.304	1:29.598

Notebook

Last year's race was run in hot and sunny conditions with David Coulthard setting the fastest lap at 1:12.878. In the last three races at the A1-Ring McLaren and Williams have dominated the top two places on the podium. Alain Prost holds the record for most wins on the circuit, his three victories coming in 1983, 1985 and 1986. The 1999 race will be the 21st at the circuit. Jarno Trulli led the field in his Prost for more than half the race in 1997 – his debut season. Austria has produced two World Champions – Jochen Rindt and Niki Lauda.

Buenos Aires

Autodromo de la Ciudad de Buenos Aires
Argentine Grand Prix – 12 April 1998
Lap Distance: 2.64 miles/4.259 km – Clockwise
Race Distance: 190.08 miles/306.654 km – 72 laps

The Autodromo is located in the park Almirante Brown on the southern outskirts of the city of Buenos Aires. The track was originally built with the support of President Peron, in the era of the legendary Juan Manuel Fangio. First used in 1952, the Grand Prix returned to Buenos Aires after an absence of 14 years. It was the site of the first F1 race to incur fatalities when Farina's Ferrari killed nine spectators in the first race to be held there in 1953.

Grip, grip, grip! The overriding factor at the Autodromo in three words. It is one of the smallest circuits but is technically difficult because of its low-speed corners, twisty nature and also the change in gradient – the track goes up and down and as such can be a little bumpy. Because of these factors, cars need to be set up for maximum grip so they tend to be set with a high degree of wing level to ensure maximum downforce. Passing is not impossible but very difficult and is often best attempted on the Start/Finish straight.

The Circuit

Off the starting straight and up to top gear and 180 mph as drivers approach the Curva Numero Uno. Braking hard and pulling -3g into this first corner, turning to the right at 60 mph in 2nd gear, cars accelerate out into a shallow right-hand bend which is taken at 140 mph. After a short straight the Curva de la Confiteria is an inner left-hand loop that is entered at 155 mph in 5th gear, quickly changing down to 2nd gear and 60 mph at its apex. A change to 3rd gear and the loop is exited at about 110 mph.

Curvón marks the end of the inner loop as the cars sweep tightly back round on themselves in 3rd gear at 80 mph. Coming out of the turn, the drivers find themselves on the second longest straight (0.25 miles) which is taken at 180 mph slowing to 165 mph as they enter the sweeping right-hander of the Curva de Ascari. As the curve straightens out the entry to the Esses approaches fast and cars are hard on the brakes (-3.1g).

The Entrata a Los Mixtos (Extrada a Esses) is a tight hairpin which is taken in 2nd gear at a sedate 55 mph before entering the Esses at Viborita which is a double sweep left and then right, both in 3rd gear, but slowing from 95 mph to about 75 mph as the Esses are completed.

Curva del Ombú is a bend taken in 2nd gear at about 75 mph. This used to signal the end of the lap before the circuit was redesigned. Now, though, the drivers continue down a shortened version of the old pit lane to the left-right wiggle that marks the Senna 'S'. What used to be called Tobogan is approached in 5th gear at 150 mph, after which a rapid change down reduces speed to 55 mph through the S bend. Hard on the accelerator out of Senna, up to 155 mph in 5th gear, and then comes Horquilla, braking hard back down to 2nd gear and 55 mph. The final 90-degree bend brings the cars out on to Tribunas, the longest straight (about 0.5 miles), and it's full speed ahead and across the finishing line in 6th gear at 180 mph.

3-Year Record

Year	1st	2nd	3rd	4th	5th	6th
1996	Hill (Williams)	Villeneuve (Williams)	Alesi (Benetton)	Barrichello (Jordan)	Irvine (Ferrari)	Verstappen (Arrows)
1997	Villeneuve (Williams)	Irvine (Ferrari)	R.Schum'r (Jordan)	Herbert (Sauber)	Hakkinen (McLaren)	Berger (Benetton)
1998	M.Schum'r (Ferrari)	Hakkinen (McLaren)	Irvine (Ferrari)	Wurz (Benetton)	Alesi (Sauber)	Coulthard (McLaren)

Pole Positions

1996	1997	1998
Hill (Williams)	Villeneuve (Williams)	Coulthard (McLaren)
1:30.346	1:24.473	1:25.852

Notebook

Austrian Alexander Wurz set his first ever fastest lap time here last year with 1:28.178 in cloudy conditions. Jean Alesi scored his first point for Sauber and has been in the points in three of the last four races. The legendary Juan Manuel Fangio's four victories at the track remains the record. Michael Schumacher's win last year broke a sequence of three successive Williams victories.

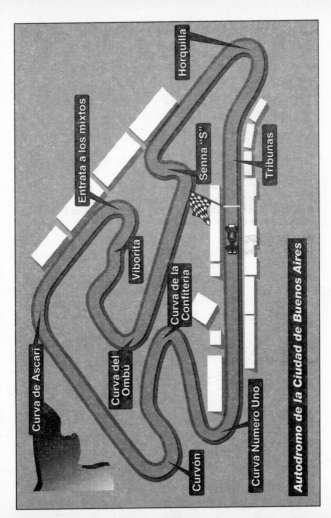

Autodromo de la Ciudad de Buenos Aires

Horquilla

Entrata a los mixtos

Senna "S"

Tribunas

Viborita

Curva de Ascari

Curva de la Confitería

Curva del Ombú

Curvón

Curva Numero Uno

195

Catalunya

Circuit de Catalunya
Spanish Grand Prix, Barcelona – 30 May 1999
Lap Distance: 2.937 miles/4.727 km – Clockwise
Race Distance: 191.69 miles/307.255 km – 65 laps

Located 12 miles north-east of Barcelona, Catalunya is one of five circuits to play host to the Spanish Grand Prix. Held here since 1991, the circuit continues to be improved and upgraded on an annual basis, making it one of the most advanced circuits in the world. Despite that, it remains bumpy and the track surface has ripples on it, complete with demanding fast corners and long high straights. In many respects the circuit is like Estoril, but it has many more run-off areas which make it popular with the drivers from a safety point of view.

Technically, the circuit is challenging with a good mixture of slow 2nd-gear and fast 4th-gear corners. Set-up is of paramount importance as teams try to trade the downforce they require for corners with reduction in drag for the fast straights. Generally, a neutral chassis setting is opted for which helps with understeer in the long corners. Tyre wear is high due to the abrasive nature of the track surface.

The Circuit

From the starting line cars accelerate downhill at 190 mph to Elf. The approach to Elf is downhill until almost the corner itself when it rises to the left. Braking hard at -3.8 g, this corner is taken in 3rd gear at 85 mph on the inside so that the car can drift out to the left for the next bend taken in 4th at around 100 mph. Curvone Renault is the first long, sweeping 180-degree right-hander, entered in 4th gear at 100 mph with 140 mph attained during its course.

Out of Renault and accelerating to about 180 mph before the circuit loops back on itself at Revolt Repsol. Entered in 2nd gear at 85 mph, cars catapult out up to 155 mph and in 5th gear along a short straight to Revolt Seat. Hard on the brakes, this tight left-hand hairpin drops the cars downhill at around 60 mph through a gentle left-handed sweep at 160 mph before braking again to enter Revolt Würth. Here, the track takes a sharp left-hand turn which is almost 90 degrees and is entered in

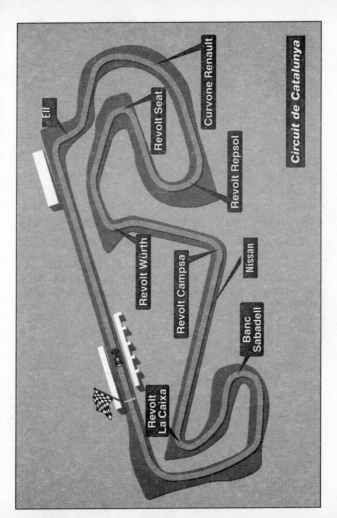

Circuit de Catalunya

Curvone Renault

Revolt Seat

Elf

Revolt Repsol

Revolt Würth

Revolt Campsa

Nissan

Banc Sabadell

Revolt La Caixa

197

2nd gear at 85 mph. On exit, the circuit turns slightly right as 5th gear and 155 mph is reached.

Revolt Campsa is a blind right-hander but can be navigated safely in 5th at 135 mph. Then it's down the short straight called Nissan in top gear at 185 mph, on the run into 180 degree hairpin Revolt La Caixa, which is taken in 2nd gear at 65 mph as it climbs to the right into the two 100-degree bends at Banc Sabadell. Entered in 3rd at 80 mph, it is exited in 5th gear as the car accelerates towards the penultimate corner, another right-hander that turns into a short straight leading to the final bend which is taken in 5th gear at about 140 mph. On to the Start-Finish straight where cars reach a maximum of 190 mph on the kilometre-long straight.

3-Year Record

Year	1st	2nd	3rd	4th	5th	6th
1996	M.Schum'r (Ferrari)	Alesi (Benetton)	Villeneuve (Williams)	Frentzen (Sauber)	Hakkinen (Jordan)	Diniz (Ligier)
1997	Villeneuve (Williams)	Panis (Prost)	Alesi (Benetton)	M.Schum'r (Ferrari)	Herbert (Sauber)	Coulthard (McLaren)
1998	Hakkinen (McLaren)	Coulthard (McLaren)	M.Schum'r (Ferrari)	Wurz (Benetton)	Barrichello (Stewart)	Villeneuve (Williams)

Pole Position

1996	1997	1998
Hill (Williams)	Villeneuve (Williams)	Hakkinen (McLaren)
1:20.650	1:16.525	1:20.262

Notebook

Mika Hakkinen set his third fastest lap of the season here last year recording a 1:24.275 in hot sunny conditions. McLaren occupied the front two positions but it was the first time a McLaren finished in the top six for this race since 1993! Rubens Barrichello scored his first points of the season with his fifth place finish. If Michael Schumacher wins here in 1999 he will set the record for most wins by one driver. He currently holds it jointly with Nigel Mansell with two victories.

Hockenheim

Hockenheimring
German Grand Prix – 15 August 1999
Lap Distance: 4.239 miles/6.829 km – Clockwise
Race Distance: 190.755 miles/309.305 km – 45 laps

Located some 50 miles south of Frankfurt and 15 miles west of Heidelberg, the circuit was originally built as a test circuit for Mercedes cars. The German Grand Prix has been staged here since 1986 and it is, for the majority, an open circuit that is very fast throughout. The exception to this is the stadium complex near the starting grid where the track twists back and forth through 360 degrees in front of the grandstands.

This makes it a very difficult circuit to set up for. Car settings are compromised for top speeds down the straights and downforce on the slow corners. At over four miles in length, it is one of the longest Grand Prix circuits, and it is often more infamously remembered as the circuit that took the life of Jim Clark in April 1968. Weather is often very changeable as the circuit winds its way through dense pine forests which can create dangerous patches of fog and mist.

The Circuit

From the Start-Finish line, cars approach Nord Kurve, a fast right-hander that is taken in 4th gear at 125 mph and exited in 5th ready to move up to top gear and accelerating to around 210 mph for the long run to the first chicane. The posthumously named Jim Clark Kurve slows cars to 2nd gear as they brake hard at -3.2g, decelerating to 60 mph before accelerating back up to 200 mph deep into the forest.

Before the Ostkurve, the drivers get busy. The previous straight turns into a sharp right-left turn taken in 2nd gear at 50 mph before it becomes a long right-hand bend about 350 metres before Ostkurve is entered – a chicane which is a right-left taken in 2nd gear leading into a long, fast right-hander and on to the next straight. The Ayrton Senna Kurve, which is also known as Bremskurve 3, is approached down the back straight at 205 mph. The left-right turn slows the cars drastically to 60 mph as it's taken in 2nd gear and then it's full-power as the cars accelerate back up to 195 mph before the stadium complex begins to come into view.

The Agip Kurve is a fast right-hander that is taken in 4th gear at 105 mph and leads quickly into the Sachs Kurve as drivers shift down to a 60 mph 2nd gear for the hairpin that has a well-earned reputation for being slippery. The final section in the stadium complex that leads back to the start line, the Süd or Opel Kurve, is a double-apex hairpin with both right-handers taken in 3rd gear at an average of 90 mph and leading into the finishing straight where cars can accelerate to 175 mph.

3-Year Record

Year	1st	2nd	3rd	4th	5th	6th
1996	Hill (Williams)	Alesi (Benetton)	Villeneuve (Williams)	M.Schum'r (Ferrari)	Coulthard (McLaren)	Barrichello (Jordan)
1997	Berger (Benetton)	M.Schum'r (Ferrari)	Hakkinen (Benetton)	Trulli (Mclaren)	R.Schum'r (Prost)	Alesi (Benetton)
1998	Hakkinen (McLaren)	Coulthard (McLaren)	Villeneuve (Williams)	Hill (Jordan)	M.Schum'r (Ferrari)	R.Schum'r (Jordan)

Pole Position

1996	1997	1998
Hill (Williams)	Berger (Benetton)	Hakkinen (McLaren)
1:43.912	1:41.873	1:41.838

Notebook

David Coulthard set the fastest lap time last year – 1:46.116 in overcast but dry conditions. Hakkinen and Coulthard's one-two finish was their fifth of the year. In the last three years the race winner has held pole position at the start. Damon Hill secured his first Jordan points here and it was the first race of the season where both Jordan drivers finished in the points. Ferrari have had at least one car finishing in the top six during the last eleven years. Nelson Piquet and Ayrton Senna have both had three victories apiece at Hockenheim – these remain the best individual career performances.

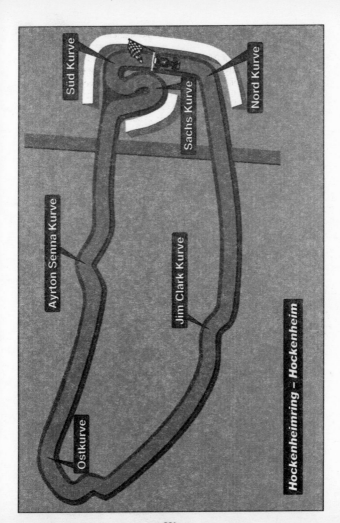

Süd Kurve

Nord Kurve

Sachs Kurve

Ayrton Senna Kurve

Jim Clark Kurve

Ostkurve

Hockenheimring – Hockenheim

Hungaroring

Hungaroring
Hungarian Grand Prix – 15 August 1999
Lap Distance   2.465 miles/3.968 km – Clockwise
Race Distance   189.805 miles/305.586 km – 77 laps

Just 12 miles to the north-east of Budapest, Hungaroring is a modern Grand Prix complex that has been created with F1 in mind. It has hosted the Hungarian Grand Prix since 1986 but is not the best liked of tracks amongst the drivers. Bumpy and slippery, there is limited scope for overtaking with no fast corners, which can make the race rather processional in nature. Grid position is therefore all important, as is a high downforce, and the circuit is second only to Monaco in this respect.

The Circuit

From the Start-Finish line it's full power to Turn 1 with speeds approaching 175 mph. Turn 1 is a long, right-hand downhill bend taking the drivers through 180 degrees, entered in 3rd gear at 75 mph, exited in 4th at 135 mph. The camber on this corner can also catch drivers out or, at the very least, see them slipping out of the drive line and into the dirty sections of the track, which does not benefit their tyres or subsequent grip. Entry and exit positions are also important as the corner is blind. A short straight brings the cars into Turn 2 and then Turn 3 and here there is a choice of two lines, but whether the car turns in early or late makes little difference to the amount of oversteer experienced as this long left-hander begins to sweep right. Turn 2 is entered at 135 mph, slowing to 70 mph before accelerating out of Turn 3 at 115 mph.

Cars approach Turn 4 leaving the straight at around 170 mph, changing down from top to 4th gear while braking to 110 mph before climbing uphill on the approach to Turn 5 – another long right-hander negotiated in 3rd gear at 80 mph and accelerated out of in 4th gear to 150 mph.

Turn 6 leads to the highest part of the circuit and is a right-left chicane that is entered in 2nd gear at 55 mph and exited in 5th at 115 mph. Turn 7 comes quickly and the approach to this left-hander is

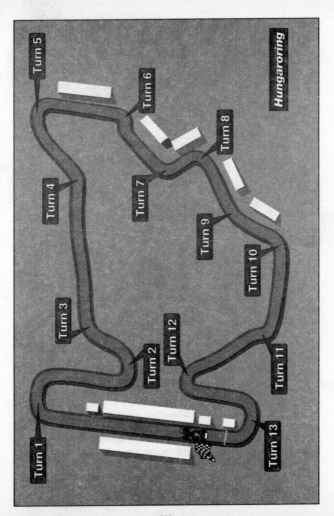

Hungaroring

Turn 1
Turn 2
Turn 3
Turn 4
Turn 5
Turn 6
Turn 7
Turn 8
Turn 9
Turn 10
Turn 11
Turn 12
Turn 13

bumpy. Third gear maintained throughout, 75 mph being the slowest point at the apex of the curve. Turn 8 is a right-hander and is taken in 3rd gear at 85 mph with the left-hander taken flat out. A curving straight forms Turn 9 and leads into Turn 10 which is not as fast as it looks as the corner suddenly tightens. It is taken in 4th at 110 mph.

Turn 11 is an off-camber and downhill right-left chicane which always seems to gather particles of grit, whilst a high kerb awaits the unsuspecting at the second apex. It is taken in 3rd gear at 90 mph. Turn 12 is almost a hairpin-like corner directly behind the pits and it's taken in 2nd at 60 mph. A long right-hander marks Turn 13, which mirrors Turn 1. Through it, the cars first oversteer, turning to understeer by the time they exit on to the straight via the kerb. Around 80 mph sees the cars through the apex of the curve from which they power towards 175 mph as they flash across the Start-Finish line.

3-Year Record

Year	1st	2nd	3rd	4th	5th	6th
1996	Villeneuve (Williams)	Hill (Williams)	Alesi (Benetton)	Hakkinen (McLaren)	Panis (Ligier)	Barrichello (Jordan)
1997	Villeneuve (Williams)	Hill (Arrows)	Herbert (Sauber)	M.Schum'r (Ferrari)	R.Schum'r (Jordan)	Nakano (Prost)
1998	M.Schum'r (Ferrari)	Coulthard (McLaren)	Villeneuve (Williams)	Hill (Jordan)	Frentzen (Jordan)	Hakkinen (McLaren)

Pole Position

1996	1997	1998
M.Schumacher (Ferrari)	M.Schumacher (Ferrari)	Hakkinen (McLaren)
1:17.129	1:14.672	1:16.973

Notebook

Michael Schumacher set the fastest lap time in last year's race with a 1:19.286 in hot and sunny conditions. He also held pole position but the owners of that spot in the last three races have not transformed it into victories. Williams have had good recent success at the Hungaroring with four wins in the past six years – Hill and Villeneuve recording two each. Michael Schumacher recorded the other two driving for Benetton and Ferrari. These three drivers can equal Ayrton Senna's record of three wins with another victory.

Imola

Autodromo Enzo and Dino Ferrari
San Marino Grand Prix – 2 May 1999
Lap Distance: 3.063 miles/4.931 km – Anti-clockwise
Race Distance: 189.906 miles/305.749 km – 62 laps

Located in north-central Italy in the principality of San Marino, Imola provides one of the most atmospheric race days anywhere in the world. Major modifications have been made to the very fast circuit in the wake of the 1994 event in which Ayrton Senna and Roland Ratzenberger lost their lives. This brought revision to Tamburello, Villeneuve and Variante Bassa which have now made the circuit a low-to-medium speed track which requires a lot of heavy braking. Medium downforce is required and teams usually have stiffer than normal settings for stability when braking; as such, this can hinder grip. The race's position in the 1999 calendar was under some threat at the time of going to press due to the legal fall-out still surrounding the death of Senna.

The Circuit

Tamburello is the first corner from the start and cars brake heavily at its entrance. The corner is a left-handed S-bend which is entered in 3rd gear at 75 mph and exited in 4th gear at 125 mph as cars power up the straight to Villeneuve. This is a second S-bend that slows the approach to the forthcoming hairpin and slows cars down from 130 mph to 105 mph in 4th gear. Accelerating quickly up to 150 mph, cars almost immediately brake for Tosa, a tight hairpin from right to left taken in 2nd gear at around 55 mph. On exit, cars accelerate to 175 mph and climb towards Piratella. This is a somewhat blind left-hander that pulls -3.5g as drivers brake at its entrance; it is taken in 4th gear at 100 mph and accelerated away from at 160 mph. Despite its nature it is a corner well liked by most drivers.

The approach to Acque Minerali is downhill at 165 mph. Slowing down to 4th gear at 125 mph the cars turn to the right and after a shot straight turn right again through 90 degrees at 65 mph. The track then turns slightly to the left as cars accelerate through 105 mph in 4th gear.

Variante Alta is next and, coming off a short straight, it is a fast chicane that can be tackled in 3rd gear – it certainly requires a 3rd-gear exit. It is entered in 6th gear at 170 mph and speeds of 75 mph are maintained through it. Drivers tend to take more chances at this chicane because it does have a safe run-off area.

Out of the chicane and the track plunges downhill through some stunning countryside, arriving at a sharpish double left-hander called Rivazza which swings the cars through 180 degrees. This requires very hard braking, down from 6th (180 mph) to 3rd gear (60 mph) at its entrance where a massive -3.8 g really tests the driver's strength. Shifting up briefly before changing down to tackle the final turn, which is taken at 80 mph, the cars arrive on a curving right-hand line and fly through the Variante Bassa, accelerating all the time up to 170 mph. The Tragurdo then looms up as a left-right chicane that feeds the pits and is taken in 2nd gear at around 55 mph. Cars then accelerate to 185 mph across the Start-Finish line.

3-Year Record

Year	1st	2nd	3rd	4th	5th	6th
1996	Hill (Williams)	M.Schum'r (Ferrari)	Berger (Benetton)	Irvine (Ferrari)	Barrichello (Jordan)	Alesi (Benetton)
1997	Frentzen (Williams)	M.Schum'r (Ferrari)	Irvine (Ferrari)	Fisichella (Jordan)	Alesi (Benetton)	Hakkinen (McLaren)
1998	Coulthard (McLaren)	M.Schum'r (Ferrari)	Irvine (Ferrari)	Villeneuve (Williams)	Frentzen (Williams)	Alesi (Sauber)

Pole Position

1996	1997	1998
M.Schumacher (Ferrari) 1:26.890	Villeneuve (Williams) 1:23.303	Coulthard (McLaren) 1:25.973

Notebook

Mika Hakkinen set the fastest lap time last season with 1:25.139 in sunny conditions. Michael Schumacher's second place was the fourth year in a row that Ferrari have finished as runner-up. Their second car has also finished third three times in the same period! The record for most wins at Monza belongs to Nelson Piquet with four.

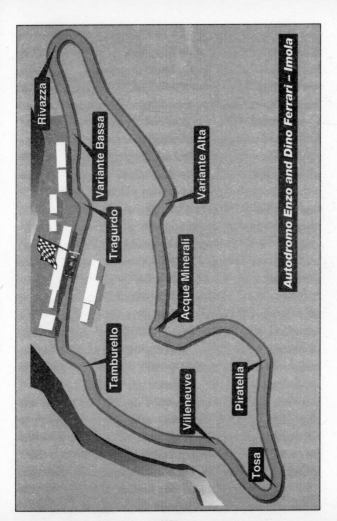

Rivazza

Variante Bassa

Tragurdo

Variante Alta

Acque Minerali

Tamburello

Villeneuve

Piratella

Tosa

Autodromo Enzo and Dino Ferrari – Imola

Interlagos

Autodromo Jose Carlos Pace
Brazilian Grand Prix – 28 April 1999
Lap Distance: 2.684 miles/4.325 km – Anticlockwise
Race Distance: 193.248 miles/311.400 km – 72 laps

Located ten miles south of central Sao Paulo, the track is named after Carlos Pace who won here in 1975. It has staged the Brazilian GP since 1991. The track was resurfaced for the 1995 season and reworked for the 1997 race, but the majority of drivers complain that it is still extremely bumpy. It remains one of the most tiring circuits that taxes even the fittest of drivers, not least because it undulates throughout its course. Cars will generally be set with a medium amount of wing, with downforce settings ranging from medium to high. The high humidity and track temperatures during March normally ensure that cars are set to maintain maximum grip on the track.

The Circuit

At the start, the cars race downhill to the left. It is approached in top gear at about 180 mph. Then braking very hard (-3.3 g), the cars approach the 'S' do Senna – a left-right-left section which begins with Curva 1, one of just two places were you might get to see overtaking manoeuvres as they try to out-brake one another. Cars take this corner in 2nd gear at 60 mph changing up to 3rd gear and accelerating through 100 mph towards the final turn in the sequence (Curva do Sol) and a 4th gear 140 mph. Hard on the throttle, cars accelerate to 180 mph along the Reta Oposta straight in top gear at 180 mph.

The Descida do Lago is a tight left-hand corner to which there is a bumpy entrance, which often throws rash drivers into a spin. Those who get through it take it in 3rd gear at 85 mph, having braked hard at its entrance. Drivers who get it right can often get past those who don't at this point. After a short straight, another left-hander (135 mph in 4th gear) swings the cars back on themselves as they accelerate to 170 mph before braking hard at the entrance to Ferradura.

The Ferradura is a sweeping, double apex right-hander with an extremely bumpy entrance. Probably the most difficult corner on the

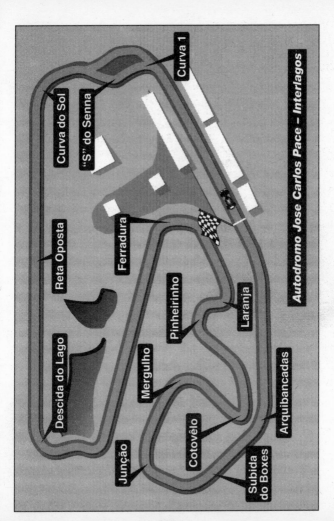

Autodromo Jose Carlos Pace – Interlagos

circuit as it is approached downhill and at speed – 5th gear at 165 mph. After going through the first apex in 3rd gear at around 100 mph, the car drifts out for the second apex and, on exiting at the top in 3rd, another right-hander is on top of you almost immediately as Pinheirinho approaches which is taken in 2nd gear at about 55 mph.

The Pinheirinho is a very tight left-hander that is only taken in 2nd gear at 60 mph, exited in 3rd gear, and then it's up to 4th for the approach to another tight corner, this time with a right-hand turn. The Cotovêlo is taken in 2nd at just over 45 mph and exited in 3rd gear, climbing to 5th as the car makes for a left-hander prior to turning for Mergulho. This sweeping corner is taken in 4th gear at 145 mph before accelerating along to the 3rd gear Junção.

Subida do Boxes marks the entrance to two left-handed curves, both banked and going uphill. The first is approached at 110 mph and is followed by Arquibancadas, which is taken in 5th gear at 160 mph. Acceleration continues as the Start-Finish line straight comes into view and is crossed at about 185 mph.

3-Year Record

Year	1st	2nd	3rd	4th	5th	6th
1996	Hill	Alesi	M.Schum'r	Hakkinen	Salo	Panis
	(Williams)	(Benetton)	(Ferrari)	(McLaren)	(Tyrrell)	(Ligier)
1997	Villeneuve	Berger	Panis	Hakkinen	M.Schum'r	Alesi
	(Williams)	(Benetton)	(Prost)	(McLaren)	(Ferrari)	(Benetton)
1998	Hakkinen	Coulthard	M.Schum'r	Wurz	Frentzen	Fisichella
	(McLaren)	(McLaren)	(Ferrari)	(Benetton)	(Williams)	(Benetton)

Pole Position

1996	1997	1998
Hill (Williams)	Villeneuve (Williams)	Hakkinen (McLaren)
1:18.111	1:16.004	1:17.092

Notebook

Mika Hakkinen set his second successive fastest lap of the season at Interlagos last year recording 1:19.337 in sunny and cloudy conditions. Hakkinen's win was his third successive Grand Prix victory. If Michael Schumacher wins in 1999 he will hold outright the record for most wins at the circuit. He is currently on two victories with Emerson Fittipaldi and Ayrton Senna.

Magny-Cours

Circuit de Nevers
French Grand Prix – 27 June 1999
Lap Distance   2.64 miles/4.25 km – Clockwise
Race Distance   190.08 miles/306.029 km – 72 laps

Located about halfway between Paris and Lyon, Circuit de Nevers was opened to Grand Prix racing in 1991 following a massive refurbishment. Its smooth surface makes it a favourite with the drivers but it is often difficult for teams to set the car up for, simply because there is no other circuit like it. Teams therefore normally opt for medium downforce with a lower than normal ride height, which helps to increase downforce whilst producing minimal drag. The circuit has a mix of high- and low-speed corners with relatively low grip.

The Circuit

From the starting grid, cars accelerate up to 170 mph before entering Grande Courbe, a long, left-hand bend which is driven in 5th gear at 165 mph. Drivers take great care to get the right line out of the curve into Estoril, which is a sweeping right-hand turn that goes through 180 degrees. Here, 4th gear is maintained at a speed of 110 mph. Understeer can be a real problem for drivers and time can be lost if the entry into Golf is not right. Golf itself is very nearly a straight but has a gentle curve to the right throughout its length. As such, it is taken full-out in top gear with speeds around 170 mph.

Adelaide is a 2nd-gear hairpin that brings the drivers back to earth. Braking hard at -3.2 g, and at 35 mph, it turns through 180 degrees and takes the vehicle back in the direction from which it has just come with the track immediately to the right. This leads straight into a fast right-left that is cleared in 4th and which leads to Nurburgring, a chicane that wriggles the cars left and right – not as tight as Adelaide but, nevertheless, tricky because it closes up in the middle. Hard on the throttle, cars approach 150 mph and brake hard at the entrance to 180 Degrees. This is another hairpin and again brings the cars through 180 degrees and back upon themselves – taken in 2nd gear at 50 mph.

From the 180 it's up quickly through the gears to 6th and 170 mph before changing down to meet the challenge of Imola at 110 mph, a right-left that protects the Chateau d'Eau, a virtual 90-degree turn entered in 4th and exited in 2nd at 55 mph on to a straight that allows the car to accelerate to 155 mph towards the 2nd-gear Chicane. This is a very tight right-left turn where drivers have to be very careful to avoid the kerbs, especially on the second part of the corner. Immediately following the Chicane is the sharp Lycée right-hander taken in 2nd gear as the cars slow to 40 mph. Positioning for exit out of Lycée is important as it affects the driver's ability to get on the throttle quickly to ensure maximum speed down the straight. The corner also provides the entry to the pit lane.

3-Year Record

Year	1st	2nd	3rd	4th	5th	6th
1996	Hill	Villeneuve	Alesi	Berger	Hakkinen	Coulthard
	(Williams)	(Williams)	(Benetton)	(Benetton)	(McLaren)	(McLaren)
1997	M.Schum'r	Frentzen	Irvine	Villeneuve	Alesi	R.Schum'r
	(Ferrari)	(Williams)	(Ferrari)	(Williams)	(Benetton)	(Jordan)
1998	M.Schum'r	Irvine	Hakkinen	Villeneuve	Wurz	Coulthard
	(Ferrari)	(Ferrari)	(McLaren)	(Williams)	(Benetton)	(McLaren)

Pole Position

1996	1997	1998
M.Schumacher (Ferrari)	M.Schumacher (Ferrari)	Hakkinen (McLaren)
1:15.989	1:14.548	1:14.929

Notebook

David Coulthard set last season's fastest lap with 1:17.523 in sunny conditions. The Ferrari one-two was the first the Italian team had achieved since 1990 when Prost and Mansell secured maximum points in Mexico City. Michael Schumacher won four out of the last five races here which is the record number of victories at this circuit. The barren year was in 1996 when neither Ferrari managed to finish. Schumacher's win here last season was the 30th of his career.

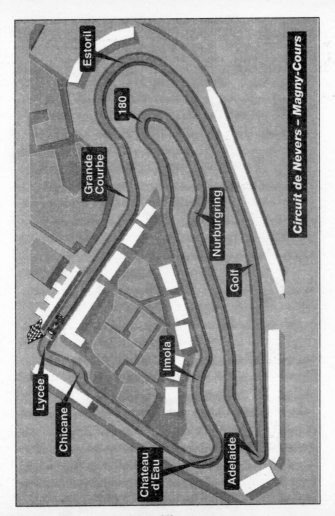

Circuit de Nevers – Magny-Cours

Estoril

180°

Grande Courbe

Nurburgring

Golf

Lycée

Chicane

Imola

Chateau d'Eau

Adelaïde

213

Melbourne

Albert Park Grand Prix Circuit
Australian Grand Prix – 7 March 1999
Lap Distance: 3.274 miles/5.269 km – Clockwise
Race Distance: 189.89 miles/305.6 km – 58 laps

Melbourne hosts its third Grand Prix in 1998. A street circuit situated in a park, the track is a combination of fast corners and tight hairpins along with sweeping curves. Not particularly challenging as a race circuit, but most drivers do consider it amongst their favourites. The approaches to some of the corners are a little bumpy and can create problems for the drivers. Expect to see cars with a high wing level to produce maximum downforce. The circuit can be heavy on tyres so teams often opt for soft set-ups that will prolong tyre life.

The Circuit

From the start, cars accelerate to 185 mph as they reach the Fangio Stand. Flanked by the Fangio and Brabham Stands are two 45-degree right- and left-handers – Turns 1 and 2. Turn 1 is the hardest braking point in the circuit pulling -3.5 g. A change down to 2nd gear sees the first turn taken at 70 mph before a short acceleration into Turn 2, which is taken at 100 mph. Turn 2 and Turn 3 mark the bumpiest parts of the circuit. From here the cars accelerate to 180 mph before braking hard again (-3.4 g) towards a sharp right-left S-bend, taking Turn 3 in 2nd gear at around 55 mph. Accelerating again the cars catapult out through Turn 4 at 80 mph, accelerating past the Whitford Stand in 5th gear at 170 mph.

A short, sharp right-hander marks Turn 6 with cars again braking hard (-3.0 g) and slowing to 70 mph. The circuit then loops round to the right, negotiating Turn 8 at 155 mph, and then past the Clark Stand at 175 mph. The Fittipaldi Stand is at Turn 9 where cars brake hard again (-3.3 g) before setting off to a long, inner-loop curve turning the cars left at a speed of 160 mph. They slow to 90 mph and swing right, past the Waite Stand and changing up to 5th and 140 mph before passing the Hill Stand at 160 mph. Braking hard again (-3.5 g) the cars change down to 3rd gear and enter the right-hand Turn 13 at 80 mph.

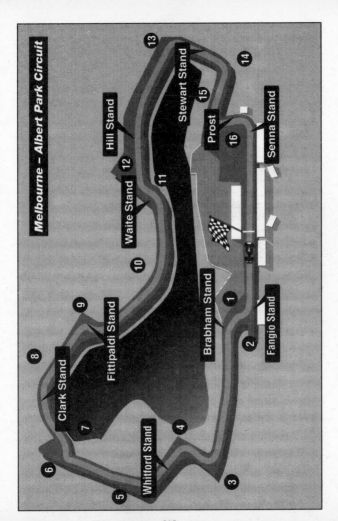

Melbourne – Albert Park Circuit

Accelerating to 100 mph in front of the Stewart Stand, Turn 14, another right-hander, is taken in 3rd gear at 100 mph.

The Prost Stand marks the entrance to the most difficult section of the circuit with the cars turning through two sharp 90-degree turns, going first left (Turn 15) and then right (Turn 16). Cars approach Turn 15 at 130 mph, braking hard and changing down from 4th to 2nd to negotiate the near hairpin turn at 50 mph. Turn 16 is less demanding but still requires 2nd gear with cars accelerating in front of the Senna Stand from 80 mph on to the finishing straight. The longest section of straight on the circuit, cars can go flat out in 6th gear at 180 mph as they flash across the Start-Finish line.

3-Year Record

Year	1st	2nd	3rd	4th	5th	6th
1996	Hill	Villeneuve	Irvine	Berger	Hakkinen	Salo
	(Williams)	(Williams)	(Ferrari)	(Benetton)	(McLaren)	(Tyrrell)
1997	Coulthard	M.Schum'r	Hakkinen	Berger	Panis	Larini
	(McLaren)	(Ferrari)	(McLaren)	(Benetton)	(Prost)	(Sauber)
1998	Hakkinen	Coulthard	Frentzen	Irvine	Villeneuve	Herbert
	(McLaren)	(McLaren)	(Williams)	(Ferrari)	(Williams)	(Sauber)

Pole Position

1996	1997	1998
Villeneuve (Williams)	Villeneuve (Williams)	Hakkinen (McLaren)
1:32.371	1:29.369	1:30.010

Notebook

Mika Hakkinen swept the board last year. In addition to a win and a pole position he recorded the fastest lap – 1:31.649 in sunny conditions. McLaren will be looking for their third successive win in Australia in 1999. Since the track was only opened in 1996 Hill, Coulthard and Hakkinen hold the record for the most wins in Victoria. Johnny Herbert scored his only point of the season here.

Monaco

Circuit de Monaco
Monaco Grand Prix Monte Carlo – 16 May 1999
Lap Distance: 2.082 miles/3.352 km – Clockwise
Race Distance: 162.24 miles/261.478 km – 78 laps

Probably the most famous Grand Prix circuit in the world, taking its macadam from the busy city streets and harbour front of Monte Carlo in the south of France. A tight, demanding circuit, there is little room on the track with overtaking a near impossibility – as such, pole position can be decisive. The circuit is not hard on the engines as they are never operating at full power; it is demanding on the drivers, however – a typical lap of the circuit requires 36 gear changes, and that's over 2800 per race! Teams look for maximum downforce as mechanical grip is vital because the roads that comprise the circuit have very low grip. Suspension settings are soft with increased ride height to avoid the bumps. When wet weather prevails, look out for cars sliding into the Armco barriers that surround most of the circuit.

The Circuit

The start of the Monaco Grand Prix is all about getting to, and through, the very first corner safely. Do that and you have a chance! The Virage de Sainte Devote is a near 90-degree right-hander that is approached from the Start-Finish line at 170 mph. Then, it's a hard brake at -3.6 g and down to a 2nd gear 55 mph for cornering. The Montée du Beau Rivage is a short straight that takes the cars past the world-famous Rosie's Bar in 6th gear at 165 mph and then it's over the crest of the hill and down to 4th gear as Virage Massenet beckons. A long left-hander, the car must be kept close to the inside kerb in 3rd gear at 80 mph. The cars then come to Virage Casino which is a quick right-hander that is taken in 2nd gear at 70 mph.

Coming out of Casino the cars get a chance to accelerate briefly along a short straight before they enter one of the most complex sections of the course. The Virage Mirabeau is approached downhill in 4th at 130 mph, requiring fast gear changes to get into 2nd gear for this bumpy right-hander, taken slowly at 30 mph. Out of this comes the short approach to the Virage Loews, a left-hand hairpin negotiated in 2nd gear at about 20 mph with the steering turned full lock, then right – this is one of the most famous TV and photographic views in F1. The turns are ended by the Virage du Portier, another sharp right-hander cleared in 2nd gear at 50 mph. Coming out of the turns, the cars start on a long sweep through the Tunnel. Noise and sparks fly as the cars change up to 5th gear and 145 mph. Once out of the tunnel, left-right Nouvelle Chicane is approached at 175 mph before drivers change down to 2nd gear and a sedate 30 mph.

The most spectacular and glamorous part of the course is Tabac, lying, as it does, alongside the harbour, which is driven through at 95 mph in 4th gear. Piscine or the Swimming Pool Complex provides a short kink in the circuit which pushes the drivers through a succession of gear changes and speeds ranging from 50 mph to 100 mph. This section of the circuit underwent major revision prior to the 1997 Grand Prix to make it safer.

Virage de la Rascasse is the slowest part of the circuit with a very tight hairpin that is taken in 1st gear at a crawling 20 mph. Along a very short straight and a faster right-hander, Virage Anthony Noghes, is taken in 2nd at 45 mph before accelerating and climbing upward into the Start-Finish straight.

3-Year Record

Year	1st	2nd	3rd	4th	5th	6th
1996	Panis	Coulthard	Herbert	Frentzen	Salo	Hakkinen
	(Ligier)	(McLaren)	(Sauber)	(Sauber)	(Tyrrell)	(McLaren)
1997	M.Schum'r	Barrichello	Irvine	Panis	Salo	Fisichella
	(Ferrari)	(Stewart)	(Ferrari)	(Prost)	(Tyrrell)	(Jordan)
1998	Hakkinen	Fisichella	Irvine	Salo	Villeneuve	Diniz
	(McLaren)	(Benetton)	(Ferrari)	(Arrows)	(Williams)	(Arrows)

Pole Position

1996	1997	1998
M.Schumacher (Ferrari)	Frentzen (Williams)	Hakkinen (McLaren)
1:20.356	1:18.216	1:19.798

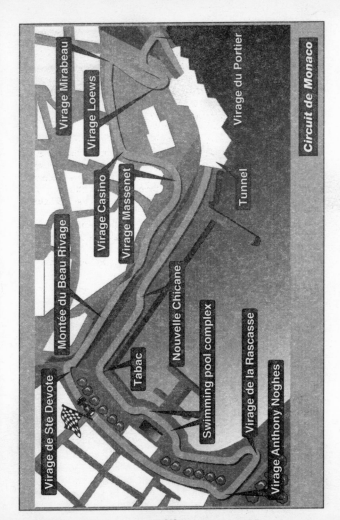

Circuit de Monaco

Virage du Portier

Tunnel

Virage Mirabeau

Virage Loews

Virage Casino

Virage Massenet

Montée du Beau Rivage

Nouvelle Chicane

Tabac

Swimming pool complex

Virage de Ste Devote

Virage de la Rascasse

Virage Anthony Noghes

Montreal

Gilles Villeneuve Circuit
Canadian Grand Prix – 13 June 1999
Lap Distance: 2.747 miles/4.421 km – Clockwise
Race Distance: 189.543 miles/305.049 km – 69 laps

Located on the Ile Notre Dame, the circuit is within easy reach of the Montreal city centre. It has a picturesque backdrop which includes views of the Lawrence River and the old Olympic Rowing Basin. The Canadian Grand Prix has been staged here since 1978 and the track is part permanent and part street circuit. This is the only race to take place on the course each year, so the roads collect a great amount of grit which the wind shifts about causing severe grip problems. It is a high-speed circuit with equally fast chicanes, but it also has slow corners which are fed by straights; as such, braking is paramount and brake performance often proves critical.

The Circuit

From the starting grid, the cars accelerate to 170 mph and swing quickly through Turn 1 as the track waves right and left. Once through they brake heavily, pulling -3.8 g at the entrance to Virage Senna. This hairpin is marked by a tight 90-degree turn to the left before the hairpin itself turns the cars through 180 degrees and it is negotiated at 45 mph in 2nd gear. Cars quickly accelerate to 150 mph and 5th gear as the track curves gently to the right. A series of bends (Turns 2-6) see the cars down to 3rd gear and speeds averaging 60 mph as the circuit turns to the right.

Turn 7 marks the Pont de la Concorde which occupies about a third of the track length. This is a long straight, broken up by a quick right-left turn – Turn 8 and Turn 9 – that can be negotiated in 3rd gear. Decelerating from 170 mph, the right bend is entered at 50 mph and then exited at 65 mph.

The lead-up to Turn 10, which marks the Virage du Casino, is done at full throttle with a top speed of around 170 mph. This hairpin comes at a point where the entrance and exit run side by side, and so it gives the drivers a chance to see who is behind them. It is a relatively wide

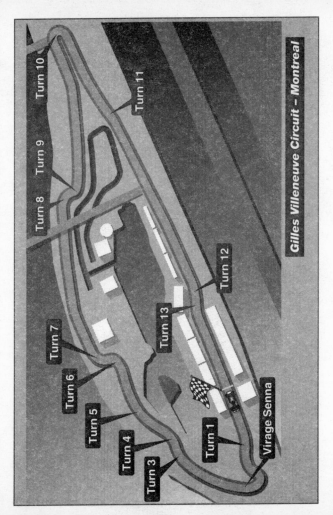

Gilles Villeneuve Circuit – Montreal

portion of the track and it is common to see overtaking manoeuvres here as cars try to out-brake one another. It is also the slowest part of the track, with cars braking down from 180 mph to around 40 mph.

Patients in the nearby hospital get a good view of the cars accelerating up through the gears along the Casino Straight. This is the fastest section of track with cars hitting speeds of 190 mph in top gear. Turn 11 marks the hardest braking point on the circuit with drivers experiencing -3.8 g. This was modified for the 1996 Grand Prix, from the Casino Bend (Turn 12 and Turn 13) which used to be a chicane, slowing the cars down into the final straight. Now it is much shallower, with cars swinging through it at around 60 mph before accelerating again as they cross the Start-Finish line.

3-Year Record

Year	1st	2nd	3rd	4th	5th	6th
1996	Hill (Williams)	Villeneuve (Williams)	Alesi (Benetton)	Coulthard (McLaren)	Hakkinen (McLaren)	Brundle (Jordan)
1997	M.Schum'r (Ferrari)	Alesi (Benetton)	Fisichella (Jordan)	Frentzen (Williams)	Herbert (Sauber)	Nakano (Prost)
1998	M.Schum'r (Ferrari)	Fisichella (Benetton)	Irvine (Ferrari)	Wurz (Williams)	Barrichello (Stewart)	Magnussen (Stewart)

Pole Position

1996	1997	1998
Hill (Williams)	M.Schumacher (Ferrari)	Coulthard (McLaren)
1:21.059	1:18.095	1:18.213

Notebook

Race winner Michael Schumacher set the fastest lap time last season, with his 1:19.379 coming in cool conditions. The German will be looking for his third successive win in 1999 while Ferraris have won three of the last four races (Alesi won in 1995). If Schumacher succeeds he will join Nelson Piquet as having the most wins at the circuit. Stewart got both drivers in the points for the first time ever last year. Magnussen scored his first ever Championship point in what proved to be his last race!

Monza

Autodromo Nationale di Monza
Italian Grand Prix – 12 September 1999
Lap Distance: 3.585 miles/5.772 km – Clockwise
Race Distance: 191.005 miles/305.908 km – 53 laps

Fifteen miles north-east of Milan, Monza was built in 1922. The modern-day autodromo combines fast, sweeping corners and long straights, with Parabolica and Lesmo two of the more famous. The Italian Grand Prix has been staged here for all but one year since the World Championship was introduced in 1950. Downforce requirements are normally low with stiff settings on the car to help ride some of the big bumps that the circuit is notorious for. The low wing levels make grip poor in the low-speed turns, which can create problems for drivers who brake too late into them. This is countered somewhat by cars having stiff set front ends.

The Circuit

The Rettifilio Tribune is the long start straight and leads to the Variante Goodyear (also known as Variante del Rettifilio). This is approached in top gear at around 205 mph and it is marked by the wide pit straight that precedes it. It is a very fast but bumpy left-right-left-right 2nd gear chicane that's entered in 2nd at 60 mph and exited at 80 mph. Almost immediately after is Curva Grande, which is a very bumpy, longish right-hander that is hard work on the steering. Entered in 4th gear at 160 mph, drivers invariably use the kerb at its exit at 185 mph and then it's along the back straight where 200 mph is touched.

The Variante della Roggia is also known as 2A Variante. The braking area prior to entering this left-right chicane is both bumpy and slippy. Approached in top gear, it is negotiated in 2nd at 60 mph and exited in 3rd at 85 mph. Curva di Lesmo is a contentious sharp right-hander – invariably taken fast, shifting between 4th and 3rd gears, with speeds ranging between 150 mph and 95 mph. Coming out of the turn, the cars rocket down Curve del Serraglio, a long straight that means the driver approaches the next chicane at speeds approaching, and often exceeding, 200 mph.

Drivers hope their brakes are in good order as they approach Curva del Vialone, a left-hander, braking from 200 mph in 6th gear to 4th gear at the 100-metre board. Then, on to Variante Ascari, the second part of the chicane, quickly flicking right, then left and changing down into 2nd gear at 85 mph. Exited in 4th gear at 135 mph, cars accelerate on to the Rettifilio Centro straight and attain 205 mph on the approach to the final curve.

The Curva Parabolica is a long, looping right-hander that is important to lap times as the entry and exit to it determine how quickly drivers can get on the gas as they come out on to the longest straight on the circuit. Braking hard at 3.2 g, cars decelerate to 100 mph and 3rd gear at its apex. As the curve opens out it is exited in 5th gear at 175 mph as the cars arrive in the long Rettifilio Tribune straight, before applying full throttle and crossing the Start-Finish line.

3-Year Record

Year	1st	2nd	3rd	4th	5th	6th
1996	M.Schum'r (Ferrari)	Alesi (Benetton)	Hakkinen (McLaren)	Brundle (Jordan)	Barrichello (Jordan)	Diniz (Ligier)
1997	Coulthard (McLaren)	Alesi (Benetton)	Frentzen (Williams)	Fisichella (Jordan)	Villeneuve (Williams)	M.Schum'r (Ferrari)
1998	M.Schum'r (Ferrari)	Irvine (Ferrari)	R.Schum'r (Jordan)	Hakkinen (McLaren)	Alesi (Sauber)	Hill (Jordan)

Pole Position

1996	1997	1998
Hill (Williams)	Alesi (Benetton)	M.Schumacher (Ferrari)
1:24.204	1:22.990	1:25.298

Notebook

Mika Hakkinen recorded the fastest lap here last year – 1:25.139 in sunny conditions. Jordan has a good record at Monza in the past three years with five of their six starters finishing in the points. Nelson Piquet's four wins at this track remains a record. The Italian Grand Prix, along with the British Grand Prix, are the only two races that have formed part of the World Championship every year since it was started.

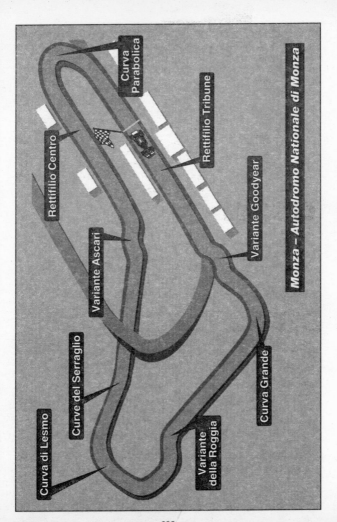

Monza – Autodromo Nationale di Monza

Curva Parabolica

Rettifilio Tribune

Rettifilio Centro

Variante Goodyear

Variante Ascari

Curve del Serraglio

Curva di Lesmo

Variante della Roggia

Curva Grande

Nurburgring

Nurburgring (Germany)
Luxembourg Grand Prix – 26 September 1999
Lap Distance   2.831 miles/4.568 km – Clockwise
Race Distance   190.079 miles/306.027 km – 67 laps

Despite being situated in Germany, about 55 miles south-west of Cologne, the Nurburgring is staging the Luxembourg Grand Prix. The circuit was opened for Grand Prix action in 1984, when Alain Prost won the European event. This was followed by the German Grand Prix, which was the last for some time. Then, after ten years of Grand Prix inactivity, the circuit was used for the European Grand Prix in 1996.

Situated in beautiful countryside, the Nurburgring is both fast and forgiving with wide run-off areas and large gravel traps. Its 12 corners and curves make for an exciting race, especially as cars generally suffer with understeer problems which can make handling problematic. Medium downforce settings are normally employed.

The Circuit

Out of the blocks and into top gear at 180 mph towards the Castrol 'S' bend and hard on the brakes at the entry to the right-left at 80 mph in 3rd gear. The curve is exited at 100 mph as drivers change up. Quickly up to 6th gear and accelerating to 170 mph for the approach to Ford Kurve which is taken at 110 mph in 3rd gear and leads directly into the Ford Kurve at 65 mph in 2nd gear. Then, hard on the throttle, the cars approach the Dunlop Kurve at 175 mph in 6th gear.

The Dunlop Kurve is a right-hand 190-degree loop, making it the second slowest part of the circuit taken at 50 mph in 2nd gear. Provided cars have managed a good line through the loop, they can get on to the gas quickly and through 155 mph as the track swings gently left and right. Out of here the approach to the RTL Kurve sees the cars in top gear at 170 mph, which is almost halved to 3rd gear at 95 mph through the near 90-degree left-hand turn. Having swept left, the Bit Kurve sweeps another 90 degrees through a right-hand turn, again in 3rd gear at around 105 mph.

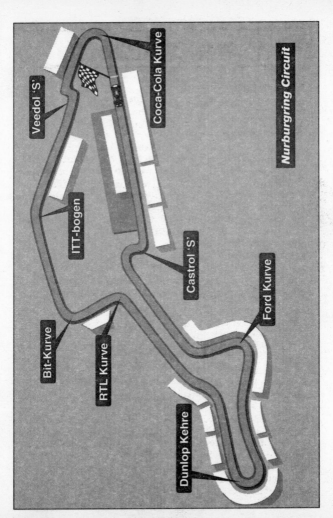

Nurburgring Circuit

Veedol 'S'

Coca-Cola Kurve

ITT-bogen

Castrol 'S'

Bit-Kurve

Ford Kurve

RTL Kurve

Dunlop Kehre

227

On to the straight, taken full-out in top gear at 180 mph, slowing to 165 mph as they sweep right through ITT-bogen – up to 180 mph – before braking hard to the Veedol-S which is negotiated at 60 mph. Sweep left and then right in 2nd gear, before accelerating to 135 mph in 4th gear. Out of here comes the sharp left-hand turn through 160 degrees which marks the Coca-Cola Kurve. This is taken in 2nd gear at 70 mph before accelerating out into the finishing straight at top speed.

3-Year Record

Year	1st	2nd	3rd	4th	5th	6th
1996*	Villeneuve	M.Schum'r	Coulthard	Hill	Barrichello	Brundle
	(Williams)	(Ferrari)	(McLaren)	(Williams)	(Jordan)	(Jordan)
1997	Villeneuve	Alesi	Frentzen	Berger	Diniz	Panis
	(Williams)	(Benetton)	(Williams)	(Benetton)	(Arrows)	(Prost)
1998	Hakkinen	M.Schum'r	Coulthard	Irvine	Frentzen	Fisichella
	(McLaren)	(Ferrari)	(McLaren)	(Ferrari)	(Williams)	(Benetton)

* *European Grand Prix.*

Pole Position

1996	1997	1998
Hill (Williams)	Hakkinen (McLaren)	M.Schumacher (Ferrari)
1:18.941	1:16.602	1:18.561

Notebook

Mika Hakkinen recorded the fastest lap last year with 1:20.450 in cool conditions. The circuit provided Jacques Villeneuve with his first win in the Formula 1 European Grand Prix in 1996. If he wins in 1999 he will equal the total of three wins achieved by Jackie Stewart and Juan Manuel Fangio.

Sepang

56 laps

Malaysian Grand Prix – 17 October 1999
Lap Distance: 3.367 miles/5.421 km

The Sepang Circuit opened for business in December 1998 just one month after being completed at a cost of $120 million. The F1 track is 5.542km in length and consists of eight straights and 15 turns (five left-hand and ten right-hand). The longest 'home' straight is located between the first and last turns (Turn 1 and Turn 15) and at almost 1 km in length, it should allow cars to reach speeds of some 210mph. This section of track also includes the world's first double frontage grandstand. With an especially wide track there should be plenty of overtaking opportunities, especially as the average track speed is anticipated at being 140mph.

The Sepang Circuit is located about 40 miles from the capital city of Kuala Lumpur and about 10 miles from the Kuala Lumpur International Airport (KLIA). The main grandstand has a capacity of 30,000 with another 80,000 capable of cramming into the rest of the circuit.

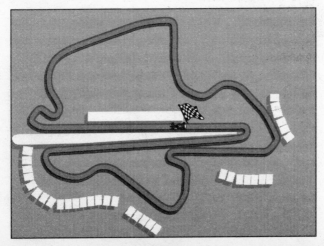

Silverstone

Silverstone Circuit
British Grand Prix – 11 July 1999
Lap Distance: 3.194 miles/5.142 km – Clockwise
Race Distance: 191,634 miles/308.52 km – 60 laps

Silverstone is Britain's longest continually used race circuit and staged the first ever British Grand Prix in 1926. Although not used for all British Grands Prix, it has held the event since 1987. The circuit is located in the Northamptonshire countryside near the village of the same name.

Operated and owned by the British Racing Drivers' Club, Silverstone held the first ever round of the World Championship in 1950. It has undergone design revisions in recent years, with changes made to a number of corners. The surface is smooth and teams generally opt for a mid-range set-up to take advantage of good grip.

The Circuit

From the grid, cars pull away and the straight allows speeds of 175 mph to be reached on the approach to Copse. This right-hand corner is blind but, at 145 mph, very fast; so fast in fact that drivers don't normally brake – just change down a gear. Switching back up, cars thunder on towards Maggotts at 180 mph and shift down twice as they wave their way first through Maggotts and then Becketts – as the track wiggles left-right, left-right, slowing down to 100 mph before Chapel ends the series of left-right bends and is accelerated through, coming out at 145 mph in 5th gear.

The Hanger Straight is the fastest part of the circuit, at 190 mph in top gear, before braking hard into Stowe, a right-hand turn that can be taken in 4th gear and speeds of 105 mph maintained. Vale is a quick straight in which the cars go through at something like 160 mph with a 2nd-gear, sharp left into Club, a right-hand corner taken at 50 mph and then accelerated through and the cars swing back on themselves at 130 mph. Both Vale and Club present good overtaking opportunities, not least because they are tricky to negotiate and understeer comes into play. Up through two gears into 6th and 170 mph towards Abbey, a 3rd

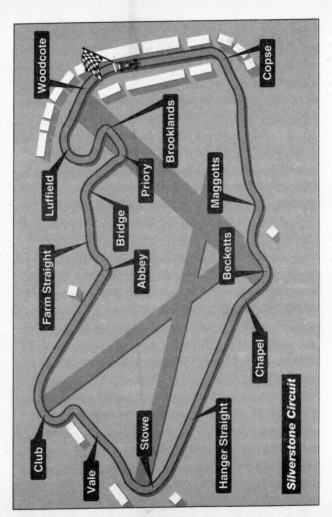

Silverstone Circuit

Woodcote
Copse
Luffield
Brooklands
Priory
Maggotts
Bridge
Abbey
Becketts
Farm Straight
Chapel
Club
Vale
Stowe
Hanger Straight

231

gear, 75 mph corner which flips into Farm at 100 mph and up to 160 mph along this straight.

Bridge marks the entrance to the 'Complex', a section of the track containing bends at Priory, Brooklands and Luffield. The corners at Bridge and Priory are fast, entering the first at 150 mph and exiting the second at 100 mph. Priory, along with Brooklands, steer the car through 180 degrees. Brooklands, along with Luffield, again turn the car around and are both negotiated in 2nd gear at between 50-80 mph. Luffield used to be two corners called Luffield 1 and Luffield 2 prior to 1996. On exit, it's a quick dash through Woodcote at 165 mph and a smooth turn to the right before hitting the Start-Finish straight at 175 mph. At the start of 1998 Silverstone renamed the sequence of corners from Priory to Luffield as 'The Grandstand' but the individual corners are still referred to by name.

3-Year Record

Year	1st	2nd	3rd	4th	5th	6th
1996	Villeneuve (Williams)	Alesi (Benetton)	Hakkinen (McLaren)	Barrichello (Jordan)	Coulthard (McLaren)	Brundle (Jordan)
1997	Villeneuve (Williams)	Alesi (Benetton)	Wurz (Benetton)	Coulthard (McLaren)	R.Schum'r (Jordan)	Hill (Arrows)
1998	M.Schum'r (Ferrari)	Hakkinen (McLaren)	Irvine (Ferrari)	Wurz (Benetton)	Fisichella (Benetton)	R.Schum'r (Jordan)

Pole Position

1996	1997	1998
Hill (Williams)	Villeneuve (Williams)	Hakkinen (McLaren)
1:26.875	1:21.598	1:23.271

Notebook

Michael Schumacher's 1:35.704 time was the fastest lap time in last year's race which was run in wet conditions. It brought his tally of fastest laps to 31 – the same number of career victories his win also gave him! Alain Prost's five wins at Silverstone remains a record.

Spa

Circuit de Spa-Francorchamps
Belgian Grand Prix – 29 August 1999
Lap Distance: 4.33 miles/6.971 km – Clockwise
Race Distance: 190.527 miles/306.7375 km – 44 laps

Lying 30 miles south-east of Liege, Spa-Francorchamps is located in central Belgium. It was first used in 1985 and, at 4.33 miles in length, it is the longest circuit in use in the World Championship. A temporary circuit that makes use of public roads, it remains a firm favourite with most drivers, not least because of its picturesque setting, and because it is demanding enough to present a difficult challenge to those racing. Low to medium downforce settings are used to enable drivers to cope with varied high- and low-speed sections and a number of corners which are all the faster for being downhill.

The Circuit

From the start, the corner at La Source comes very quickly and is a hairpin that is taken in 2nd gear at around 40 mph after which drivers have two long straights that are separated by Eau Rouge – which amounts to a small kink in the circuit. Accelerating to 180 mph along the first section, Eau Rouge can be taken in 6th gear with only a slight loss of speed (165 mph) as it goes downhill and then uphill left, right, and left. Cars exit at Raidillon and then encounter the fastest part of the course along the Kemmell straight at 190 mph.

As the track bears round slowly to the right, there exists good overtaking possibilities at Les Combes due to the wide run-off areas. The right-left combination chicane is taken in 3rd gear and 85 mph and is exited at Malmedy, which is a right-hander taken at 100 mph.

Rivage is a virtual hairpin which, due to being off camber and downhill, causes cars all sorts of steering problems. It is approached in 4th gear at 155 mph, taken in 2nd at 60 mph and exited in 3rd at 110 mph. Out of Rivage the cars sweep along a short straight at 155 mph before the track veers left at 90 mph and on to Pouhon at 100 mph, a double left-hander. Also off camber, it is entered and exited in 4th gear at an average of 140 mph. On exit, cars power through the gears to 180 mph before slowing at Fagnes – a right-left chicane which is taken in 3rd gear at 100 mph.

Stavelot is a double right-hand loop, turning the cars through 180 degrees as they go downhill. Entered in 3rd with 4th (135 mph) being engaged in the middle, but it is bumpy and cars tend to skip about a bit as cars speed up to 150 mph on exit. Blanchimont is a long, sweeping left-hander taken full-out in 6th gear at 185 mph. With the Start-Finish line almost in sight, Bus Stop Chicane appears, a sharp right-left-right chicane that slows the cars right down to a 2nd gear 45 mph before they emerge on to the pit straight at 170 mph.

3-Year Record

Year	1st	2nd	3rd	4th	5th	6th
1996	M.Schum'r (Ferrari)	Villeneuve (Williams)	Hakkinen (McLaren)	Alesi (Benetton)	Hill (Williams)	Berger (Benetton)
1997	M.Schum'r (Ferrari)	Fisichella (Jordan)	Frentzen (Williams)	Herbert (Sauber)	Villeneuve (Williams)	Berger (Benetton)
1998	Hill (Jordan)	R.Schum'r (Jordan)	Alesi (Sauber)	Frentzen (Williams)	Diniz (Arrows)	Trulli (Prost)

Pole Position

1996	1997	1998
Villeneuve (Williams)	Villeneuve (Williams)	Hakkinen (McLaren)
1:50.574	1:49.450	1:48.682

Notebook

Wet conditions meant that Michael Schumacher's fastest lap time of 2:03.766 was one of the slowest of recent times. Last year's race had to be restarted after a massive pile-up at the start. Damon Hill recorded his first win in two years and in doing so gave Jordan their first ever Grand Prix victory. It was complemented by Ralf Schumacher finishing second – his best result and Jordan's first one-two. Prior to that, in 1997 Giancarlo Fisichella had equalled Jordan's best ever finish when he came second. Michael Schumacher had won the previous three races while Ayrton Senna's five victories is the record for the circuit.

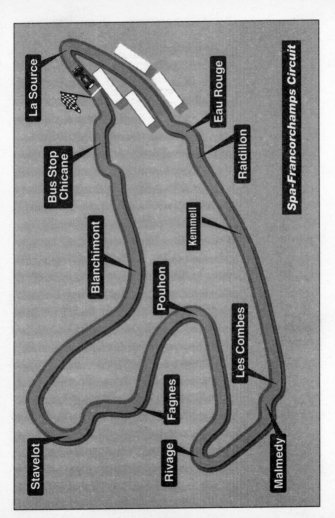

Spa-Francorchamps Circuit

La Source

Bus Stop
Chicane

Eau Rouge

Raidillon

Blanchimont

Kemmell

Pouhon

Stavelot

Fagnes

Les Combes

Rivage

Malmedy

Suzuka

Suzuka International Racing Course
Japanese Grand Prix – 31 October 1999
Lap Distance: 3.642 miles/5.864 km – Figure of Eight
Race Distance: 193.026 miles/310.772 km – 53 laps

Located between Osaka and Nagoya, south-west of Tokyo, Suzuka has been a regular date on the Grand Prix calendar since 1987. The circuit is unique to the Championship in that it follows a figure of eight pattern with numerous turns and straights, thus providing both clockwise and anti-clockwise movement for the cars. Setting up the cars is difficult as drivers have to balance between aerodynamic downforce and mechanical grip. The track requires low grip but has some bad bumps in it. Thus drivers normally opt for medium to soft settings for the smooth surface with stiff suspension to take in the various bumps.

The Circuit

The start is downhill and this can help cars get away. Indeed, in 1988, it helped Ayrton Senna get away after he stalled just before the go signal. Once away, the cars approach First Curve flat out in top gear at speeds of up to 190 mph with a change down to 5th and 150 mph into the bend and into a second curve that is much tighter than the first and can only be negotiated in 3rd with speed dropping to 95 mph.

The S Curve is a left-right-left-right combination that severely taxes any car that is not well balanced. It can usually be taken all the way through in 4th. The sequence is entered at 135 mph, dropping to 85 mph on exit of the final curve. On exiting, the S Curve's 4th gear is maintained for the approach to the Dunlop Curve. This long left-hander is extremely bumpy with plenty of understeer at 135 mph.

Accelerating to 160 mph, the Degner Curve is a tight right-hander that is taken in 4th gear at 120 mph, down to 3rd as the second part of the corner becomes tighter still, and then generally exited with the use of the kerb. Then it is up to top gear at 170 mph to go under the bridge where the course crosses itself to the Hairpin Curve. This is guarded by a short right-hander which slows the cars, but then they have to get down very quickly to 2nd gear for the 45 mph hairpin. Out of the

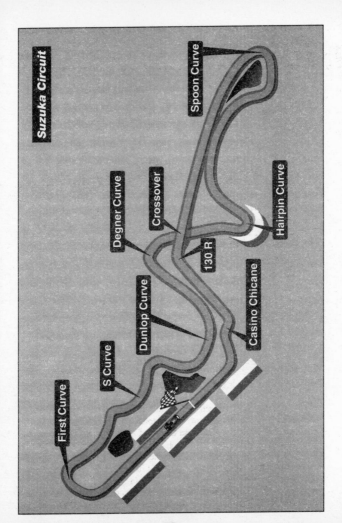

Suzuka Circuit

Spoon Curve

Degner Curve

Crossover

130 R

Hairpin Curve

Dunlop Curve

Casino Chicane

S Curve

First Curve

hairpin the circuit curves to the right and on completion of the curve the majority of cars will be in top gear at 170 mph.

Spoon Curve awaits at the end of the looping right-hander. It is negotiated in 3rd gear, with speeds dropping from 105 mph on entry to 85 mph on exit. Then it's full on the throttle and it's a 185 mph straight-screamer over the Crossover to 130 R, a very fast left-hander which forces a slight deceleration to 155 mph. The Casino Chicane (also known as Triangle Chicane or Casino Triangle) guards the entrance to the finishing straight. The right-left combination is taken in 2nd gear at 40 mph, with the cars having to brake hard from 175 mph as they approach it. Once through, the cars swing right at 120 mph and on to the Start-Finish straight for the next lap.

3-Year Record

Year	1st	2nd	3rd	4th	5th	6th
1996	Hill (Williams)	M.Schum'r (Ferrari)	Hakkinen (McLaren)	Berger (Benetton)	Brundle (Jordan)	Frentzen (Sauber)
1997	M.Schum'r (Ferrari)	Frentzen (Williams)	Irvine (Ferrari)	Hakkinen (McLaren)	Villeneuve (Williams)	Alesi (Benetton)
1998	Hakkinen (McLaren)	Irvine (Ferrari)	Coulthard (McLaren)	Hill (Jordan)	Frentzen (Williams)	Villeneuve (Williams)

Pole Position

1996	1997	1998
Villeneuve (Williams)	Villeneuve (Williams)	M.Schumacher (Ferrari)
1:38.909	1:36.071	1:36.293

Notebook

Michael Schumacher recorded the fastest lap last year with 1:40.190 coming in warm conditions. Schumacher, who needed a win to have a chance of the Championship, stalled the car on the grid and had to start from the back row. He ultimately retired after 31 laps. Hakkinen's win gave him the Drivers' World Championship and McLaren the Constructors' Cup. It was the first McLaren win at Suzuka since Senna won in 1993. Schumacher ties Senna and Gerhard Berger with two wins at the circuit.

Zhuhai

Zhuhai International Circuit
Chinese Grand Prix – Reserve Grand Prix
Lap Distance: 2.683 miles/4.32 km

The Zhuhai International Circuit is located some ten km from the centre of Zhuhai City, 60 km west of Hong Kong and 15 km north-east of Macau. Constructed on a 1,000 acre site, it includes an 11,000-seat grandstand and 36-hole golf course.

The site was constructed after a street circuit race in Zhuhai City in 1993 had attracted over 100,000 spectators and a national TV audience. With the support of the FIA, the Grand Prix circuit was built and opened in 1996. Being named as a reserve circuit in 1998, it seems certain that F1 races at Zhuhai will soon be a regular occurrence.

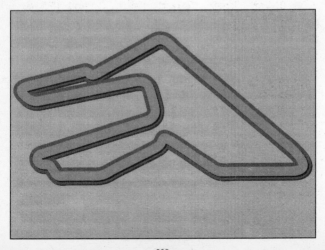

Race Diary '99

Listed below are provisional dates and venues for the 1999 Formula 1 season. They were awaiting final FIA confirmation at the time of going to press. As such they are subject to change and alteration.

Date	Grand Prix	Circuit	Laps	Start GMT	
7 March	Australian	Melbourne	58	04.00 hours	
29 March	Argentinian	Buenos Aires	72	16.00 hours	cancelled
11 April	Brazilian	Interlagos	71	16.00 hours	
2 May	San Marino	Imola	62	12.00 hours	
16 May	Monaco	Monte Carlo	78	13.30 hours	
30 May	Spanish	Catalunya	65	12.00 hours	
13 June	Canadian	Montreal	69	18.00 hours	
27 June	French	Magny-Cours	72	12.00 hours	
11 July	British	Silverstone	60	13.00 hours	
25 July	Austrian	A1-Ring	71	12.00 hours	
1 August	German	Hockenheim	45	12.00 hours	
15 August	Hungarian	Hungaroring	77	12.00 hours	
29 August	Belgian	Spa	44	12.00 hours	
12 September	Italian	Monza	53	12.00 hours	
26 September	Luxembourg	Nurburgring	67	12.00 hours	
17 October	Malaysian	Kuala Lumpur	tba		
31 October	Japanese	Suzuka	53	04.00 hours	